APPLYING AA EXPERIENCE TO ACIM

A Proposal

Steve H.

CONTENTS

Title Page	
Foreword:	4
Introduction:	5
Chapter I - Twelve Steps to Spiritual Enlightenment and Miracles	15
Step 1: We (humbly) admitted that we were powerless over "EGO" - We (humbly) admitted that our lives	18
Step 2: We (humbly) came to believe that HOLY SPIRIT could restore us to sanity. (AA)	22
Step 3: We (humbly) made a decision to turn our will and our lives over to the care of HOLY SPIRIT (	24
Step 4 : We (humbly) made a searching and fearless moral inventory of ourselves. (AA)	26
Step 5 : We (humbly) admitted to HOLY SPIRIT, to ourselves, and to another human being the exact nat	31
Step 6: We were entirely ready to have HOLY SPIRIT remove all these defects of character. (AA)	35
Step 7: We humbly asked HOLY SPIRIT to remove our shortcomings. (AA)	38
Step 8: We (humbly) made a list of all persons we had harmed and became willing to mak amends to the	40
Step 9: Made direct amends to such people wherever possible, except when to do so would injure yours	42
Step 10: We (humbly) continued to take personal inventory and when we were wrong (and in EGO) we pro	46
Step 11: We (humbly) sought through prayer and meditation to improve our conscious contact with God	50
Step 12: Having had a spiritual awakening (a miracle) as the result of working these steps, we conti	65
Chapter 2 - The Twelve Traditions to Protect the Individual and Common Welfare of ACIM (AA)	73
Tradition 1 :	78
Tradition 2:	79
Tradition 3:	80

Tradition 4:	82
Tradition 5:	83
Tradition 6 :	84
Tradition 7:	85
Tradition 8:	86
Tradition 9:	88
Tradition 10:	89
Tradition 11:	90
Tradition12:	92
Chapter 3 – Meetings to Teach and Carry the ACIM Message	94
Chapter 4 - AA Ideas on Sponsorship for ACIM Teachers & Students	100
WHAT ARE THE CHARACTERISTICS OF GOD'S (HOLY SPIRIT'S) TEACHERS? It says "...the advanced teachers of	110
Chapter 5 – The 12 Concepts and 12 Warranties of a Venerable Democratic Corporate Fellowship	114
Concept I:	116
Concept II:	118
Concept III:	120
Concept IV:	122
Concept V:	125
Concept VI:	129
Concept VII:	130
Concept VIII:	131
Concept IX:	132
Concept X:	134
Concept XI:	135
12 warranties recommended to ACIM:	138
EPILOG:	140
what love is not:	142
Appendix A - THE A.A. SERVICE MANUAL combined with TWELVE CONCEPTS FOR WORLD SERVICE by Bill W.	146
Appendix B	147
Appendix C -	151
Appendix D	152
Appendix E	153
Appendix F	154

Appendix G	155
Appendix H	158
Appendix I -	162
Appendix J	167
Appendix K	175
Appendix L	177
Bibliography:	182
AA References:	183

STEVEH.

The information provided in this document represents only the ideas and opinions of the author/editor and does not represent the fellowships of Alcoholics Anonymous (AA) or A Course In Miracles (ACIM) or any other fellowship or affiliation as a whole. It is requested that the anonymity of the author/editor be respected and maintained at the levels of press, radio, television, telephone, internet and any other form of public information media.

Applying AA Experience to ACIM - A Proposal

The Meaning of the Last Judgment: (Jesus Course In Miracles, page 18.)The Last Judgment is one of the greatest threat concepts in man's perception. This is only because he does not understand it. Judgment is not an essential attribute of God. Man brought judgment into being only because of the separation. After the separation, however, there was a place for judgment as one of the many learning devices which had to be built into the overall plan. Just as the separation occurred over many millions of years, the Last Judgment will extend over a similarly long period and perhaps an even longer one. Its length depends, however, on the effectiveness of the present speed-up.

We have frequently noted that the miracle is a device for shortening but not abolishing time. If a sufficient number of people become truly miracle-minded quickly, the shortening process can be almost immeasurable. It is essential, however, that these individuals free themselves from fear sooner than would ordinarily be the case, because they must emerge from the conflict if they are to bring peace to other minds.

The Last Judgment is generally thought of as a procedure undertaken by God. Actually it will be undertaken by man.... It is a Final Healing, rather than a meting out of punishment, however many men may think that punishment is deserved. Punishment is a concept in total opposition to right-mindedness. The aim of the Last Judgment is to restore right-mindedness to man.

What is Ego? (excerpt from ACIM Workbook)The Ego is insane. In fear it stands beyond the Everywhere, apart from All, in separation from the Infinite. In its insanity it thinks it has become a victor over God Himself, ...The Ego is idolatry - the sign of limited and separated self, born in a body, doomed to suffer and to end its life in death. It is the will that see the Will of God as enemy and takes a form in which It is denied. The ego is the "proof" that strength is weak and love is fearful, life is really death, and what opposes God alone is true.

What am I? (excerpt from ACIM Workbook)I am God's Son, complete and healed and whole, shining in the reflection of His Love. In me is His creation, sanctified and guaranteed eternal life. In me is love perfected, fear impossible, and joy established without opposite. I am the holy home of God Himself. I am the Heaven where His Love resides. I am His holy Sinlessness Itself, for in my purity abides His Own.

Seek and Ye shall find: (excerpt from ACIM text) does not mean that you should seek blindly and desparately for something you would not recognize. Meaningful seeking is consciously undertaken, consciously organized and consciously directed. The goal must be formulated and kept in mind.

Into Action: (excerpt from Alcoholics Anonymous, p. 87) We are careful never to pray for our own selfish ends. Many of us have wasted a lot of time doing that and it doesn't work. You can easily see why.

Step Twelve: (excerpt from Twelve Steps and Twelve Traditions, p. 125)… we are problem people who have found a way up and out, and who wish to share our knowledge of that way with all who can use it. For it is only by accepting and solving our problems that we begin to get right with ourselves and with the world about us, and with Him who presides over us all. Understanding is the key to right principles and attitudes, and right action is the key to good living; therefore the joy of good living is the theme of AA's Twelfth Step.

Preface: Applying AA Experience to ACIM – A PROPOSAL is a public domain document. Material in this document has been extracted from other documents almost verbatim. Acknowledgments have been provided in the text at the quoted material and at the end of the book in the section entitled References. Reproduction of any material from other works should comply with all US Laws. The intent of this document is for altruistic purposes and it is requested that the information be passed on for non-profit motives only. In order to respect the Traditions of Alcoholics Anonymous, the author/editor must remain anonymous and requests that all comply. Please take what you need and leave the rest.

This work is a proposal to review the past seventy years of organizational experience accumulated by Alcoholics Anonymous (AA) in order to set up guidelines for A Course In Miracles (ACIM) posterity. Egoless principles such as anonymity, equality, non-judgment, unconditional love, humility, etc., already set up, tried, and proven effective in keeping AA together as an altruistic organization can be applied to the future of ACIM.

ACIM is at a point in its evolution where in order for its message to be passed on throughout the U.S. and the world, decisions as to methods of disseminating such information are to be made either by the EGO or the HOLY SPIRIT. (And just to let you know if you haven't been checking the score, EGO is winning many of the games on this playing field. We might have a long wait in order to gain enough critical mass to get all of us back to reality). Some existing methods of disseminating and practicing ACIM such as building churches, creating ministers, lecturers, authors, etc. are predominately ego based (and those whom are not will not be offended by this comment). Reading groups are often haphazard and go awry turning into EGO contests. What often starts out as altruism becomes influenced by EGO and turns into dogma. Humility becomes egomania, etc. EGO will always participate in the degeneration of all things good including ACIM, but a sound set of guidelines based on the above established and tested spiritual principles of AA will greatly assist and expedite the HOLY SPIRIT with its mission to bring us home..

AA is a spiritual organization. In 1935, Bill Wilson discovered that a Jesuit method of spiritual enlightenment used with the Oxford Group of that day of "moral inventory, confession of personality defects, restitution to those harmed, helpfulness to others and the necessity of belief in and dependence upon "HOLY SPIRIT", proved to be an effective treatment for alcoholism (in combination with an in-depth medical knowledge of the disease of alcoholism and in order to save himself, his going about telling anyone, especially other alcoholics, his life experience with alcohol and his success in not drinking using these spiritual methods).

Although the disease of alcoholism had brought him to the very depths of hell, despair and depravity, Bill had originally come from a background with a formal education, a military officer career, a stock broker and early in his sobriety a frustrated corporate director. This life experience enabled Bill to author a book documenting his success and describing precisely how to put his spiritual method of recovery from alcoholism into effect. The phenomenon of AA meetings began within a relatively short period of time. The recoveries and subsequent lifelong memberships to Alcoholic Anonymous meetings grew rapidly. Although Bill's EGO had aimed high in the corporate world, HOLY SPIRIT was able to successfully use Bill's skills for a much greater divine purpose. Bill humbly established traditions and concepts for the continuation of AA that can be considered as great a work as the Bill of Rights or Magna Charta, etc. and has successfully kept AA intact for the last seventy years.

The AA meetings, steps, traditions, concepts can readily be adapted to ACIM. This document is organized as a proposal to specify how. AA respects autonomy, and therefore this writing is only to be used as a guideline and never as scripture. As best as I can do, this book will be a joint effort of EGO & HOLY SPIRIT (if such a thing is possible) and as usual I will not have much of idea which I am representing at the time as I write this document. Because AA values anonymity and humility, this work will remain anonymous and altruistic. I actually did not author anything; most of the material is extracted as originally written with maybe the person or tense altered or some words were omitted. There is no new or original thought with the exception of the idea for ACIM to take a look at AA experience. Sufficient information was provided from the listed references
so that this information may be valuable to all audiences that might read this document. I refer to myself as the editor, because I just organized the existing material from the books referenced (after the appendices at the end of this document) to present the proposal and add some transitional words or personal experience. It is my hope that this information can benefit AA members and ACIM students, as well as the general public.

Many present spiritual students have their spiritual heads stuck in the clouds, sand (or elsewhere) and will never be able to get past the preface of this book because they are too sensitive and closed-minded. They only imagine that they have left EGO behind. They have never achieved the first principle of a Teacher of God, yet they profess to be one. They are easy to spot, their language is often scripture mumbo-jumbo and they teach the most difficult to grasp concepts first in order to help you seek, but do not find. They would never be able to identify the hypocrisy inside themselves, let alone EGO. These words scare and anger them because they dare not look at the dark side of themselves. Many just want to lead but do not have the humility necessary to join as equals. However, if you managed to get past that barrage, then just maybe you are ready for what the rest of this proposal may be able to provide you. To transpose an AA saying: "this is where we separate the adults from the children".

ACIM text states, "Let us today be neither arrogant nor falsely humble. We have gone beyond such foolishness. We cannot judge ourselves, nor need we do so. These are but attempts to hold decision off, and to delay commitment to our function. It is not our part to judge our worth, nor can we know what role is best for us; what we can do within a larger plan we cannot see in its entirety. Our part is cast in Heaven, not in hell. And what we think is weakness can be strength; what we believe to be strength is often arrogance."

FOREWORD:

As the editor I have a little over 25 years of AA experience. I began AA at the age of 29. At the age of around 40, I found it necessary to seek outside of AA for some answers to questions that AA could not sufficiently answer to my satisfaction. I wanted to know more about prayer and meditation. AA has no restrictions and in fact encourages seeking outside help. In the AA text where it discusses physicians and clergy it suggests "to see where they may be right". AA uses a slogan that to the effect says "Contempt prior to investigation will keep a man in everlasting ignorance". AA had also provided me many other philosophical clichés, such as: "Take what you need and leave the rest"; "When you ask for a drink of water, be careful they don't get out the fire hose"; "AA doesn't need my defense, it stands on its own merits"; etc., which greatly assisted me in my investigation of other spiritual organizations and dealing with other personalities. "Keep it simple" was the AA slogan, so I kept it simple and I was able to grasp one simple concept at a time and over a period of time build a better spiritual house to live in.

AA also uses the statement: "EGO has to be smashed" but once some of my youthful arrogance passed, I realized that I didn't know what EGO was. I had taken a college psychology course and I read some books about Id, Ego, and Superego (e.g. I'm OK, You're OK; Adolescence & Discipline), but the term Ego was used in a Freudian sense, where Ego was the balancing force between the extremes and Ego had to be built up, not smashed. (With that information I determined that I had a fractured EGO that needed love and healing.)

Instead of seeking outside psychological help, which wasn't too successful with an arrogant know-it-all like me (and therapy is very expensive), I decided to seek outside spiritual help (the love donations are much less expensive). With my AA experience I was able to investigate, check my pride at the door and try out many new spiritual concepts. I did not stop going to AA meetings daily and much of the information that I learned in other spiritual courses and teachings, I found to already exist in the AA literature (but I wasn't listening or paying attention when I was first exposed to it in AA). I also read a lot and I changed most of my reading from psychological self help to spiritual and mystical Self-help. During an AA meeting once, a former priest mentioned the book "A Course In Miracles". I got the book and began using it for enlightenment (and as a substitute for the sensation I sought with alcohol). I didn't really understand it, so I asked the priest if he could help me, but he didn't remember ever mentioning the book and was unfamiliar with it. I did find a study group and within a year I learned a great deal about the EGO that has to be smashed. I also received some good information about prayer and meditation. I would highly recommend the ACIM books to any AA member who would like to find out more information about EGO and Step 11. I recommend reviewing the Appendices of this proposal for more information on EGO and ACIM basic concepts and terminology. I hope that words such as God, Holy Spirit, and Jesus Christ do not frighten off the novice spiritual reader and prevent them from gaining the knowledge provided in this document.

Please feel free to change such words to more comfortable ones of your own comprehension.

"...and though perhaps he came to scoff, he may remain to pray." William D. Silkworth, M.D.

INTRODUCTION:

First of all, to those not familiar with ACIM (A Course In Miracles) or AA (Alcoholics Anonymous), if you are presently content with your life, satisfied and in joy, this book may not be for you. (Put the book down and walk away from the book.) But remember, contempt prior to investigation can keep a person in everlasting ignorance. Some of the information presented in this book is for those who are presently dissatisfied with their lives, jobs and relationships. The steps (found in Chapter 1) will teach you a concept of EGO and then ask you to ignore and forget all about EGO and with the help of HOLY SPIRIT it will teach you to create holy relationships instead of hostile relationships. Also these steps may lead you to become a Teacher of God and may require that you teach others what you have learned through your experience with the steps and ACIM literature. It's only fair to give you the heads up from the start, so that later you won't feel deceived or tricked into something you don't have a desire to do. It is the hope of the editor of this proposal that not only will this information benefit the present social order of ACIM students, teachers and leaders, but will greatly benefit anyone who reads and follows the information taken from the Fellowship of AA in order to achieve a spiritual awakening in their life.

This book is entitled "Applying AA Experience to ACIM – A PROPOSL" because it is just as the title says: a proposal to those involved with organizing ACIM study groups and service operations to consider and possibly use some of AA experience. AA is a spiritual and altruistic fellowship set up using democratic as well as corporate principles, and chapters 2 through 5 will discuss the details of those spiritual principles used to run a spiritual organization. This proposal will present the following chapters on AA methods and ideas that might be adapted to ACIM.

1. The Twelve Steps to Spiritual Enlightenment
2. The Twelve Traditions to Protect the Individual and Common Welfare of ACIM
3. Meetings to Teach and Carry the ACIM Message
4. AA Ideas on Sponsorship for ACIM Teachers and Students
5. The Twelve Concepts and Twelve Warranties of a Venerable Democratic Corporate Altruistic Fellowship

The editor recommends contacting and consultation with the AA General Service Office, AA World Services INC. Box 459, Grand Central Station, NY NY 10163 (www.aa.org) for more information and a better understanding of the AA Charter and their instituted organizational concepts.

Chapter 1 is entitled "The Twelve Steps to Spiritual Enlightenment" but it is just rewording the AA steps to ACIM terminology with the addition of certain information from other theologies about prayer and meditation and editorial comments guiding one through the process. This proposal will suggest that the twelve steps be used to introduce our population to EGO and HOLY SPIRIT. There are many who are at a level of spirituality that may not be ready for ACIM conceptions of EGO, HOLY SPIRIT, miracles, forgiveness, atonement, etc. and the 12 steps are a system that could be used for anyone ready to do a self evaluation of how extensive EGO is still operating and degenerating their thinking, actions and life. The steps are a lifeline for those who are lost spiritually and in the grips of EGO. The process eventually leads them to a place (Step 11) where they should seek through prayer and meditation for conscious contact with HOLY SPIRIT, which would be a perfect place to start ACIM. The steps not only benefit the newcomers but could also point out the insidious nature of EGO operating in our lives even after we may have studied and practiced spiritual concepts and ACIM for quite awhile. They are an excellent method of maintaining our humility and spiritual condition especially at times when we get lost in the verbiage of ACIM instead of its purpose. Also people who are in fellowships such as AA who are familiar with the steps might readily accept this view on "powerless over EGO" and be willing to study and accept some of the tenets of the ACIM text, workbook and teachers manual.

Chapter 2 is entitled "The Twelve Traditions to Protect the Individual and Common Welfare of ACIM"

which are the 12 Traditions of AA that have successfully protected AA from its egotistical, immature, grandiose, anarchist EGO. Egoism surfaces frequently in AA mostly in groups who believe that they carry the pure message and others must succumb to their beliefs for the benefit of all. Such controversy happened with the 1st, 2nd, 3rd (and so on) Century Christians and it will continue ad infinitum in the world of EGO in which we all are presently experiencing. The traditions will be especially useful if ACIM is to attempt to reach the general population with this information. Certain ground rules will be necessary for the diversity involved with the general population and the AA traditions have proven themselves very effective in such situations. The traditions are based on a spiritual principle of treating all people, no matter what their walk in life may be, with dignity and respect and in turn they will develop dignity and respect for the fellowship that provided it to them.

Chapter 3 is entitled "Meetings to Teach and Carry the ACIM Message" which is the way the AA word of mouth program has reached millions. The traditions create a safe house for many agnostics to receive and digest spiritual principles through meetings. It does so in a readily acceptable manner of democratic spirit and with less preaching from the same dogmatic pitch of a few individuals. The meetings expand the truth so that it can reach many different perspectives and life experiences. The meetings also allow for continual joining and support in practicing ACIM and spiritual principles. The AA meetings propagated the spiritual fellowship and their ideas through out this country and many others to the point that every population center in the U.S. (Canada and Mexico) has an extensive opportunity to attend meetings in close proximity to where they live and at very convenient times. It is proposed that the idea and success of meetings might prove to be a very beneficial method of getting Jesus' message provided in the ACIM text to the world. The system of traditions and meetings provide a way for outsiders to review the information in their own language without feeling obligated or forced into anything.

Chapter 4 is entitled "AA Ideas on Sponsorship for ACIM Teachers and Students" which would change the present teacher - student relationship of one or two scholars (or not so scholarly) attempting to teach the masses, to a one on one, "Each one teach one" teaching (and holy) relationship of two equals meeting to share their experience, strength and hope found in the steps and ACIM literature. The benefit is in the process of the new student teaching a newer one, he learns the lessons better than just by reading or listening. The process of teaching another, forces the teacher to learn the lessons better. First we talk the talk, but eventually we must also walk the talk. Teaching facilitates this process. AA has an established method of teaching that is called sponsorship. Sponsorship occurs with the literature, in the meetings and then individually one on one before and after the meetings. It might be wise to incorporate these AA methods of training newcomers, if meetings were to become an acceptable method of joining ACIM students and teachers and disseminating Jesus' ideas presented in ACIM. Certainly AA sponsors could greatly benefit by reviewing and learning the qualities of teachers provided in the ACIM Manual for Teachers.

Chapter 5 is entitled "The Twelve Concepts and Twelve Warranties of a Venerable Democratic Corporate Altruistic Fellowship" and is quite a remarkable social system (and venerable because it is based on spiritual principles of equality, non judgment, unconditional love, etc.) developed to handle altruistic service to the world through the democratic voice of the membership (fellowship) in a corporate business fashion. The ideas are complex but have been very successful and effective with AA that they might be worthy of review by ACIM leaders for the benefit of consolidating their efforts and joining in a unified undertaking to provide Jesus' ACIM knowledge and wisdom to the world.

Appendices A & B provides the AA Service Manual Table of Contents and the AA Charter for anyone interested in greater detail than what is provided in Chapter 5 about the AA organizational procedures for providing altruistic service in a democratic – corporate format. Appendices C through F are excerpts of ACIM definitions and explanations of certain ambiguous words and terms in order to assist the reader in understanding what direction the editor of this proposal is pointing toward and to eliminate any confusion
with the use of these same terms as they may be used in other spiritual and religious organizations. Appendices G through I are excerpts of speeches taken verbatim from the Book "Alcoholics Anonymous Comes of Age" presented by representatives from medicine, clergy and law depicting a theme similar to ACIM of using a spiritual approach to eliminate EGO from our activities and our society in hope that the reader may see how the AA experience along with ACIM may be applied to assist people that do not have the disease of alcoholism but still suffer from a spiritual malady. Appendix J is an excerpt from Eckhart Tolle's book "A New Earth" which contains many descriptions of the EGO that this proposal defines.

The following literary works were quoted and paraphrased extensively to create this document:
    AA Questions and Answers on Sponsorship, Anonymous. New York
    A Course in Miracles, Anonymous. New York
    Alcoholics Anonymous, Anonymous. New York
    Alcoholics Anonymous Comes of Age: A Brief History, Anonymous. New York
    A New Earth : Awakening to Your Life's Purpose, Eckhart Tolle. New York
    Ask and It Is Given, Esther and Jerry Hicks, Hayhouse.
    Being A Christ, Ann & Peter Meyer. CA
    The AA Service Manual combined with Twelve Concepts for World Service, Bill W. New York
    The Bhagavad Gita, Paramahansa Yogananda. CA
    The Disappearance of the Universe, Gary Renard. Hayhouse
    The Language of the Heart, Bill W., The Grapevine Inc., New York
    The Science of Mind, Enerst Holmes, New York
    The Twelve Concepts for World Service, illustrated, Anonymous. New York
    To Love Or To Be Loved, Tom Johnson. Redondo Beach, CA
    Twelve Steps and Twelve Traditions, Anonymous. New York
    Power vs. Force, Dr. David R. Hawkins, Ph.D., Hayhouse

What Love Is Not (Article), Robert Perry. Sedona, Az

This proposal is not designed to usurp any existing group or method of disseminating ACIM information to others. It is designed to offer yet but another path to God for those who seek Him. At one time, the AA book was going to be called "A Way Out" and indeed its information has been a way out from King Alcohol (and EGO) for many. Allow your intuitive connection with all that is good to decide and direct you in the application of this proposal, if it is for you.

In this proposal, the words taken from AA literature will be rephrased to more adequately encompass ACIM ideas. As with AA, "this book is meant to be suggestive only"... HOLY SPIRIT "will constantly disclose more to you and us. Ask Him in your morning meditation what you can do for the man who is still sick (with EGO). The answers will come, if your own house is in order. But obviously you cannot transmit something you haven't got. See to it that your relationship with Him is right and great events (miracles) will come to pass for you and countless others. This is the Great Fact for us. Abandon yourself to "HOLY SPIRIT" as you understand Him. Admit your faults (errors) to Him and to your fellows. Clear away the wreckage of your past. Give freely of what you find and join us. We shall be with you in the Fellowship of the Spirit"... (AA)

Beware that in AA, we often have had a tough time with the word "GOD" and ACIM will discuss "HOLY SPIRIT" in the same light. [Also caution to the ladies, because our English language does not have a gender for both sexes, masculine terminology (as in AA) and use of the word father may be a turn off for some]. One other foreboding is that the word Jesus is not used in the ACIM text except in the end in the Manual for Teachers and Clarification of Terms, but a lot of charismatic Christians are attracted to "The Course" and use the word freely. There is a lot of ambiguity with the word and it can be used by EGO to create much contention, whereas my recommendation would be to check the word "Jesus"
as well as EGO (titles, degrees, positions, heroics, etc.) at the door with your hat and coat. Also, this proposal will not use the word Christian very often because it is not used in the ACIM text and the word encompasses far too many definitions and ideologies that are not pertinent to the study of the ACIM text. However let it be very clear from the very start, especially for those readers not familiar with the AA Steps or A Course In Miracles that first, the Twelve Steps are said to be 1st Century Christianity and second A Course In Miracles is a channeled work authored by Jesus Christ. (If this makes you squeamish, its best to put this information right up front and not to milk you along and surprise you with this information later on after have digested too much of this material) Although I attempt to leave out the word Jesus from most of this book (and use the word HOLY SPIRIT) I wish to provide you some text of how ACIM defines Jesus Christ: **"The name of Jesus Christ as such is but a symbol, but it stands for love that is not of this world. It is a symbol that is safely used as a replacement for the many names of all the gods to which you pray. It becomes the shining symbol for the Word of God, so close to what it stands for that the little space between the two is lost, the moment that the Name is called to mind. Remembering the Name of Jesus Christ is to give thanks for all the gifts that God has given you. And gratitude to God becomes the way in which He is remembered, for love cannot be far behind a grateful heart and thankful mind. God enters easily, for these are the true conditions for your homecoming."..."In his complete identification with Christ--the perfect Son of God, His one creation and His happiness, forever like Himself and one with Him--Jesus became what all of you must be. He led the way for you to follow him. He leads you back to God because he saw the road before him, and he followed it. He made clear distinction, still obscure to you, between the false and the true. He offered you a final demonstration that it is impossible to kill God's Son; nor can his life in any way be changed by sin and evil, malice, fear, or death. "Is he God's only Helper? No, indeed, for Christ takes many forms**

with different names until their oneness can be recognized." (ACIM)

ACIM is a channeled work that came through Helen Schucman from September 1965 to September 1972 and was scribed by Bill Thetford. (For more information, I recommend reading JOURNEY WITHOUT DISTANCE by Robert Skutch.) When I was first exposed to channeling, I was extremely skeptical, however after years of reading on the subject of persons such as Edgar Cayce and Robert Monroe and channeled works such as THE AQUARIAN GOSPEL OF JESUS CHRIST, I am very comfortable with channeled works and believe them to be very credible, genuine and reputable. Also let it be known to the reader, in the event it might raise any prejudice later, the editor of this proposal does not identify himself as a Christian nor does he acknowledge Jesus Christ as the only path to GOD. The editor is open-minded to all spiritual principles and concepts regardless of their origin and looks for the similarities rather than the differences. The editor does concur that spiritual principles found in AA and ACIM are true and they will lead anyone desiring a holy relationship with God and holy relationships with their fellows to that Truth.

Throughout this book, the AA text (and other pertinent literature) will be quoted. For the most part, I will not put the reference and page number, and the writing will be continual without break for paragraphs, etc. The editor believes that AA text (as well as many other spiritual books) is divinely written, and to refer someone to the pages of the paragraphs taken out of context with the original way it was presented may be misleading. The editor may very well be using the information to present a completely different meaning than the one the original author intended. I will also mostly substitute the word HOLY SPIRIT for any reference to God (Higher Power, etc.); I will often use the word EGO to replace alcohol (disease, etc.); and I will omit parts of the paragraph that directly talk about alcoholism or do not follow with the point the editor of this book is trying to make. This is not intended to offend anyone. Please choose words of your own understanding that brings comfort to your mind.

For those agnostic or atheist, the term HOLY SPIRIT used in this book might raise some hairs. The following explanation from the AA Text, Chapter entitled BILL'S STORY (with the word HOLY SPIRIT
substituted for the word God) may be of some help: "...there remained in me the vestiges of my old prejudice. The word "HOLY SPIRIT" still aroused a certain antipathy. When the thought was expressed that there might be a "HOLY SPIRIT" personal to me this feeling intensified. I didn't like the idea. I could go for conceptions as Creative Intelligence, Universal Mind, or Spirit of Nature but I resisted the thought Czar of the Heavens, however loving His sway might be. I have since talked with scores of men who have felt the same way. My friend suggested what then seemed a novel idea. He said, "Why don't you choose you own conception of" HOLY SPIRIT. "That statement hit me hard. It melted the icy intellectual mountain in whose shadow I had lived and shivered many years. I stood in the sunlight at last. It was only a matter of being willing to believe"... "Nothing more was required. I saw that growth could start from that point. Upon a foundation of complete willingness I might build what I saw in my friend. Would I have it? Of course I would! Thus was I convinced that" HOLY SPIRIT "is concerned with us humans when we want Him enough. At long last I saw, I felt, I believed. Scales of pride and prejudice fell from my eyes. A new world came into view." (AA) This is a part of AA literature that allows newcomers the right to discern for themselves; the editor has used it to introduce the ideas to someone being exposed to the concepts of HOLY SPIRIT, JESUS, and GOD that may have unfavorable past experiences with such terminology and concepts. The editor recommends that anyone in this category be able to work out these issues with themselves

(and possibly by using the steps) before jumping into the ACIM literature.

For another angle, in the book THE DISAPPEARANCE OF THE UNIVERSE, Gary Renard says "I realized that if I was to continue on this path then I'd need a lot of help in forgiving the very realistic images that were being shown to me, and were designed by EGO to get the better of me on any given day. J was the one I would ask for that help. I could have asked Arten or Pursah, to whom I was deeply grateful, or I could have prayed to them as Thaddeus and Thomas. Or, as most" ACIM "students did, I could have emphasized my relationship with" HOLY SPIRIT "who was wisely referred to in the" ACIM text "not as the Voice of God, but the Voice for God. But I had already established a relationship with J, and I was more than happy to continue to develop it. From what I had learned and experienced, I knew the instant I took J's hand the separation was over. Of course this would also be true if I took the hand of the HOLY SPIRIT. In fact, any symbol of God would do; this was a personal decision. What mattered was that a person had such a symbol and could join with God through this symbol with no sense of distance or separation. With" ACIM, HOLY SPIRIT "was no longer a removed concept, but right here and right now." (Renard) This quote is another example of the very liberal approach to spirituality that this proposal is recommending to the reader.

Gary further explains "As far as observing the world was concerned," ACIM "explained everything in it without exception. I could look at my entire life, as well as the present, and understand the cause of all human behavior. For example, in school the bullies who had made other students' lives miserable might as well have been saying, "We're cool, you're not. You're the guilty and wrong one, not us." The "good" students who could see the injustice in this, as well as the ludicrous nature of many other things in the world, were simply playing their own part in the victim-victimization cycle by seeing guilt in the perpetrators of the injustice instead of in themselves. And what were most members of various extreme religious sects really saying while proselytizing? Perhaps something like, "You're the guilty ones, not us. We've got God! Not you. We're going to Heaven and you're going in the fire". What were the insane terrorists of the world really saying when they took away the lives of innocent men, women and children? How about, "You're responsible for our problems. You're the guilty party, certainly not us." Human beings tend to blame each other for their lot in life, but what we all do is blame each other for our seeming separation from God, resulting in the loss of peace that feels like a permanent fixture in our existence. The variations are endless. Whether in a close personal relationship or a distant one, someone or something else can always be found to be the cause of the problem -- excepting those tortured souls who project all guilt within, consciously blaming themselves for their own unfavorable circumstances. Yet is this really different than blaming another body?"(Renard) "One of the necessary changes in my thinking along the road to the ultimate experience was the acceptance of the idea that the mind projects everything, observes its own projection from a different and seemingly separate point of view, and then interprets that perception as an external fact. The body, being itself an idea of separation, existed only in the mind as a way to experience separation! All my life I had assumed that my eyes saw the world, my body felt it and my brain interpreted it. The" ACIM "Workbook was helping me comprehend that it was silly to think the body's eyes could really see, or that the brain could think or interpret anything. The mind told my body what to see and feel, and how to interpret what I was seeing and feeling. The body was simply a trick, a device within the EGO mind that was designed to convince me my worldly life was the truth. The" ACIM "Workbook not only taught the opposite of Newtonian science, but also gave me experience at accepting the HOLY SPIRIT's interpretation of everything, thus facilitating the beginning of the end for my EGO. I was quite annoyed by the first sentence of the" ACIM "Workbook Epilogue, but not the second one. "This course is a beginning, not an end. Your Friend goes with you. I knew by now that my Friend, the" HOLY SPIRIT "was really my own higher Self. Yet it was very helpful for me to use the" ACIM "soothing and artistic metaphors, and think of myself as being helped by another. In fact, this was very necessary. I still had the world in my face, and the Course was always practical, "This Course remains in the EGO framework, where it is needed". (Renard) ACIM Lesson 134 ends with "In everything you do remember this: No one is crucified alone, and yet no one can enter Heaven by himself." (ACIM) With Gary's presentation, it is apparent that this document's presentation of the steps (Chapter 1) may not be appropriate for all (but it certainly won't harm anyone either). Many may be able to go directly to ACIM and receive all the guidance they will ever need. The above information from Gary's book was provided for that purpose. His book has led many to ACIM literature and practices of forgiveness. Hopefully, the steps might reach and lead another fraction of our society to ACIM. **The more the merrier.**

The remaining chapters are directed to all interested in gathering a sufficient number of individuals that wish to free themselves from fear (EGO) sooner than what would be the ordinary case (millions of years) and become miracle minded, quickly, in order to speed up mankind's return to rightmindedness. We must emerge from the conflict if we are to bring peace to other minds. Remember, no one goes to heaven by themselves; we either all go or no one goes.

In the AA text from the Chapter Doctor Bob's Nightmare, I used his words to solicit the reader to get help from others in order to look at EGO: "If you think you are an atheist, an agnostic, a skeptic, or have any other form of intellectual pride which keeps you from accepting what is in this book, I feel sorry for you. If you still think you are strong enough to beat the game alone, that is your affair. But if you really and truly want to quit" EGO "and sincerely think you must have some help, we know that we have an answer for you". HOLY SPIRIT "will never let you down." (AA) It is with the editor's deepest sincerity that you can accept a God that will assist you with spiritual progress in your life. To regress spiritually can cause great distress in your life and in others that you love.

Also to motivate the novice to spirituality that they might continue reading at least the 1st chapter in this proposal about the steps, the following is how ACIM describes our destiny in this world of EGO: "You feel threatened by this changing world, its twists of fortune and its bitter jests, its brief relationships and all the "gifts" it merely lends to take away again; attend this lesson well (ACIM Workbook lesson 153). The world gives rise but to defensiveness. For threat brings anger, anger makes attack seem reasonable, honestly provoked, and righteous in the name of self-defense. Yet is defensiveness a double threat. For it attests to weakness and sets up a system of defense that cannot work. Now are the weak still further undermined, for there is treachery without and still a greater treachery within. The mind is now confused, and knows not where to turn to find escape
from its imaginings. It is as if a circle held it fast, wherein another circle bound it and another one in that, until escape no longer can be hoped for nor obtained. Attack, defense; defense, attack, become the circles of the hours and the days that bind the mind in heavy bands of steel with iron overlaid, which are turning but to start again. There seems to be no break nor ending

in the ever-tightening grip of the imprisonment upon the mind. Defenses are the costliest of all prices which the EGO would exact. In them lies madness in a form so grim that hope of sanity seems but to be an idle dream, beyond the possible. The sense of threat the world encourages is so much deeper, and so far beyond the frenzy and intensity of that which you can conceive, that you have no idea of all the devastation it has wrought. You are its slave. You know not what you do, in fear of it. You do not understand how much you have been made to sacrifice, who feels its iron grip upon your heart. You do not realize what you have done to sabotage the holy peace of God by your defensiveness. For you behold the Son of God as but a victim to attack by fantasies, by dreams, and by illusions he has made; yet helpless in their presence, needful only of defense by still more fantasies, and dreams by which illusions of his safety comfort him." (ACIM)

Pretty grim poetry! This was obviously extracted to motivate the reader to go further with the self help part in the next chapter. Many self help books are done in this manner; creating a morbid picture of the problem to motivate the reader. It is much like reading your horoscope (or a book on diseases), you begin to relate and identify the symptoms. Unfortunately many such books go into extensive detail of the disease or the problem and do not provide an effective solution. They leave the reader high and dry. Fortunately both ACIM and AA provide effective solutions that have worked successfully for many. Much of this document extracts large sections from other books in order to motivate the reader. They are ideas that are extremely well written and can be read over and over, each time getting a greater depth to the meaning. It is like peeling the layers of an onion. Often during the rereading it will appear as if the words have been changed. Sometimes the same information is repeated until one day in a certain situation the idea comes as a new revelation about life. Different meanings can come from one or two sentences, but the editor chose to take larger sections so more of the ideology of the original author is portrayed. Also this document uses various authors to provide a wider spectrum of thought to the reader. If you were to read Lee Stroebel "A Case for Christ" you would undoubtedly come up with similar conclusions as he did, however if you read Elaine Pagels "Beyond Belief" your conclusions may be altered and somewhat expanded. Naturally just as these authors lead to certain conclusions, all the material that has been extracted for this proposal has been done in the same light, to persuade the reader toward certain conclusions. There is nothing new about this methodology in this world, but please note that it is the work of my EGO and not necessarily HOLY SPIRIT. And EGO doesn't really know what is best for you. The steps are designed for you to contact a loving and merciful power that can assist you in doing things that you cannot do by yourself. Use the steps to make contact and find a guardian that can lead and guide you through the valley of death. Each section of writing in ACIM text is done in a similar fashion; the first part identifies with EGO and brings you to those feelings and the finale always brings you back up again to HOLY SPIRIT. Don't get distracted, lost or veer off the path. ACIM lesson 153 goes on to say: "You who have played that you are lost to hope, abandoned by your Father, left alone in terror in a fearful world made mad by sin and guilt; be happy now that the game is over. Now a quiet time has come, in which we put away the toys of guilt, and lock our quaint and childish thoughts of sin forever from the pure and holy minds of Heaven's children and the Son of God. We pause but for a moment more, to play our final, happy game upon the earth. And then we go to take our rightful place where truth abides and games are meaningless. So is the story ended. Let this day bring the last chapter closer to the world, defeat of all his hopes, his pitiful defense against vengeance he can not escape, is but his own deluded fantasy. God's ministers evoked in his confused, bewildered memory of this distorted tale. God's Son can smile at last, on learning that this is not true." (ACIM) Isn't this much more comforting. After numerous repetitions of this script, we develop the ability to lift ourselves out of despair and hopelessness with our new ability to think and envision joy and happiness. The steps also follow that sequence of having to go down before you can go up. In order to solve the problem, we must first spend some time identifying it, so that we can repair it or let it go with the help of our new found power, HOLY SPIRIT. Otherwise we remain blind to it and don't see the "Elephant in our living room".

I have also taken material from other ideologies to convey the similarities and often to show the sequence much further down the road of spiritual progress. Going from first grade to second grade can be a pretty frightening process, but after a while we become comfortable in our surroundings and often confident until we have to move on to 3rd grade. And often the third graders get so big and sure of themselves that they pick on the 2nd and 1st graders, just like they were and it makes them feel big and important. This process goes on in adult life too and sometimes for much longer periods than a school year. We like the security and we don't want to move on. In that light EGO does serve a purpose because EGO will cause enough pain if we stand still too long that sooner or later we cry out for help from a loving and merciful entity and we are forced to grow in spirit. EGO will drive us back to HOLY SPIRIT. Also 8th grade chemistry for some was revelational information; but the ideas must be discarded later in order to grasp the deeper concepts of chemistry and physics. And the process goes on. What we learned in Bible school or high school catechism must be later discarded for deeper spiritual concepts. We can't remain in third grade. AA asks for spiritual progress not spiritual perfection, but spiritual progress is an ongoing responsibility to learn and do more.

As a finale to the Introduction, words from the great Yogi Paramhansa Yogananda are provided to you to give you an idea of what spiritual progress down the road looks like: "The ordinary man selfishly perceives pleasure and pain only in connection with his own body. But the yogi who is identified with God perceives Him everywhere--in both animate and inanimate worlds. His mind is expanded in Cosmic Consciousness. As not a sparrow falls outside the sight of God, so the yogi who is one with the Father is conscious simultaneously of the smallest and the greatest happenings in the universe. A devotee who perceives God in all beings feels naturally as his own the pleasures and pains of other beings. He wishes evil to none and tries to do good to all. The accomplished yogi is conscious of God alone. When he appears like an ordinary mortal, but within himself he always retains the consciousness of the Ever Blessed Lord." "The ordinary individual looks upon the world as made of matter, but the yogi who by ecstasy has united his soul with the Spirit perceives the Absolute Cosmic Consciousness and also its manifestation as the Cosmic Dream to be made of one Substance. When a dreamer partially wakes up in the middle of his dream, he realizes that his consciousness and the objects in the dream are made of the same substance--his own mind. The yogi awakened in God can similarly perceive all the earthly dream-objects in the so-called material world to be woven of the consciousness of God. It is in this state that the yogi realizes Unity everywhere: he perceives not only that God dwells in all beings, but that all beings are His manifestations. The yogi dissolves all dual perceptions of matter and mind into the sole perception of Cosmic-consciousness. A yogi who is awake in God is ever united with Him, whether in life or death, whether in this world of activity or in any other mode of existence." "The thirst for affection can never be quenched by the imperfect love of mortals. When the devotee, by practice of loving mortals truly, learns to love all beings, and by meditation learns to love God supremely, then and then only is his longing for love satisfied." (SRF)

CHAPTER I - TWELVE STEPS TO SPIRITUAL ENLIGHTENMENT AND MIRACLES

In 1935, a former drinking buddy of Bill Wilson came to see him. Bill was still drinking alcoholically at the time. His friend who was also alcoholic came to see Bill to tell him that he was able to quit by using some spiritual principles provided to him by some religious folk that rescued him in court from going to jail. The man did not stay sober for long and Bill shortly afterward ended up in an alcoholic hospital, where he had a "Flash of Light" spiritual experience. The doctor who had attended him over the years was amazed at the immediate change and recommended that Bill better hold on to what he got. Bill tried to carry this discovery to other alcoholics with no success; however his wife reminded him that by doing so he was able to stay sober for six months. Bill also tried to get back on his feet financially and left New York to compete for a corporate directorship with a firm in Akron, Ohio. Bill put in a great deal of effort and failed to get the position. With the lure of the barroom to console his dejection, Bill decided to call several ministers listed in the Hotel lobby to see if they knew of an alcoholic to whom he could present his spiritual ideas. Fortunately, his persistence paid off and he eventually was able to talk with an Akron physician who also had the affliction of alcoholism. The doctor was not receptive at first, until Bill presented that the doctor would be helping him stay sober. The two hit it off, but the doctor did not stay sober right away. When the doctor did finally stop drinking, he worked the spiritual ideas in one day and continued to do so successfully for the rest of his life. The two began trying to deliver the concept to other alcoholics in Akron and (although not right away, which the AA book leads you to believe, but) eventually found a third that succeeded in staying sober with their ideas. (This event snowballed into over 2 million members, 100,000 groups in 150 countries existing today).

The point of this rendition of the AA story is that the Steps are not magical or fool proof. There is no magic in the words or a special secret recipe for performing the steps. There are directions for working the Steps in AA literature and countless other versions and interpretations from members of the fellowship. Although Bill initially claimed that the Steps could rocket you into a forth dimension, that has not always been the result for him through the rest of his life or of those who have followed Bill. It is strictly a one day (or one minute) at a time deal. The Steps can be worked in a day, even in a couple of hours (and with practice much shorter periods than that). What they can do is take you from the mind of EGO to the mind of HOLY SPIRIT. When ever you recognize the warning bells (anger, pride, greed, envy, lust, gluttony, self pity, etc.) and the emotions that are the signs that you are in grip of EGO, you can apply the Steps to reach HOLY SPIRIT. And that is a miracle (what AA calls is a Spiritual Experience or a Spiritual Awakening.).

AA claims that "Faith without works is dead". Pages 86 & 87 of the AA Big Book provide specific directions for the application of the Steps when we retire at night, upon awakening and throughout the day. Also, the ACIM Workbook provides us a variety of activities to accomplish this, without allowing EGO to defeat us with boredom or redundancy. The Steps written by Bill Wilson come from other spiritual leaders and orders which at that time may include St. Ignatius of Loyola, founder of the Jesuit order of priests and the twelve step process to spiritual enlightenment. And although alcoholics are an extremely undisciplined and often anarchists, with as little application of the steps as they were able to incorporate into their lives, they have been able to effect dramatic initial improvements in their lives and spiritual well being which often results in long term sobriety. Alcohol and drugs can smash the EGO (to the point where we are willing to surrender and ask for help), but unfortunately the EGO recovers too (and rather rapidly sometimes), and the initial improvements from drunkenness to sobriety are usually as far as we get for quite a while. We are saved from a sinking ship and we get back to the surface of the water, but then we spend a great deal of time treading water and trying to keep our head out. We don't recognize that the steps are the life raft that will bring us back to shore. The AA text puts it like this: "The "EGO" is like a tornado roaring its way through the lives of others. Hearts are broken. Sweet relationships are dead. Affections have been uprooted. Selfish and inconsiderate habits have kept the home in turmoil. We think a "person" is unthinking when he says "HOLY SPIRIT' is enough. He is like the farmer who came up out of his cyclone cellar to find his home ruined. To his wife, he remarked, "Don't see anything the matter here, Ma. Ain't it grand the wind stop blowing, Yes, there is a long period of reconstruction ahead. We must take the lead. A remorseful mumbling that we are sorry won't fit the bill at all. (With the help of the HOLY SPIRIT), we ought to sit down with the family (friends and co-workers) and frankly analyze the past as we now see it, being very careful not to criticize them. Their defects (EGO) may be glaring, but chances are that our own actions are partly responsible. So, we clean house with the family (friends and co-workers), asking each morning in meditation that" HOLY SPIRIT "show us the way of patience, tolerance, kindliness and love." (AA).

The Steps in this proposal will be worded as follows:
1 We (humbly) admitted that we were powerless over EGO -- We (humbly) admitted that our lives had become unmanageable.
2 We (humbly) came to believe that HOLY SPIRIT could restore us to sanity.
3 We (humbly) made a decision to turn our will and our lives over to the care of HOLY SPIRIT (as we understood HIM).
4 We (humbly) made a searching and fearless moral inventory of our EGO.
5 We (humbly) admitted to HOLY SPIRIT, to ourselves, and to another human being the exact nature of our wrongs
6 We were entirely ready to have HOLY SPIRIT remove all these defects of character.
7 We humbly asked HOLY SPIRIT to remove our shortcomings.
8 We (humbly) made a list of all persons we had harmed, and we (humbly) became willing to make amends to them all.
9 We (humbly) made direct amends to such people wherever possible, except when to do so would injure them or others.
10 We (humbly) continued to take personal inventory and when we were wrong (in EGO) promptly admitted it (to our self, HOLY SPIRIT, and another human being [and not necessarily to the one supposedly wronged]).
11 We (humbly) sought through prayer and meditation to improve our conscious contact with God (through HOLY SPIRIT) praying only for knowledge of His will for us and the power to carry that out.
12 Having had a spiritual awakening (a miracle) as the result of working these steps, we continue to study and practice spiritual principles; and we help to teach others spiritual principles and forgiveness (with the guidance from the ACIM Text, Workbook and Manual for Teachers and other similar information). (AA)

Please accept the suggestion to memorize these at some point, so in the event when all else fails, and there is nothing standing between you and EGO, you can use these steps to contact HOLY SPIRIT. Also at this point, just read them and do them. Keep it simple. Ask for internal guidance.

STEVEH.

Consult with others. Trust your ability to comprehend and discern. Beware not to do anything foolish or heroic. See what happens and share it with others. The steps have a built in loop (step 10) and each time you go back through them your sphere of knowledge will expand. The rest of this information is superfluous and mixes and matches various concepts and methods of doing the steps that might be useful as the years go by when boredom and complacency rear their ugly heads. Often the information is contradictory. One day we say the sky is blue and the next we say it is gray. Each of us has our own perspective which changes with our moods or the point we are trying to make. The truth is larger than EGO, so EGO's interpretation is very limited. For example, where I live there is a mountain, elevation around 11,000 feet. In the winter it is snow capped and in the summer above the forest line, it is barren usually covered with majestic white capped storm clouds. The people who live in my neighborhood might have some variations about what they see, but basically we could come up with a consensus about how the mountain appears. However our opinion may vary significantly from those who live in other parts of the valley and quite substantially from those who live on the other side. Also those who live on the mountain would describe it much differently than those who can see it from 100 miles away. If we all got together and shared our concepts, we might draw closer to the truth about the mountain but still from our limited perspective we may not be able to comprehend the entirety of the mountain, but each time we discussed it, visited it, viewed it from a different angle, our sphere of knowledge of the mountain would expand (at least until it was no longer accessible to our conscious memory).

Prior to starting the Steps, self-honesty should be discussed a little. Usually all AA meetings start their meetings and discussions by reading the first few paragraphs from the Chapter from their Big Book entitled How It Works. The Chapter starts with an observation and a promise "Rarely have we seen a person fail who has thoroughly followed our path", but continues with the observation and an admonition that those who fail are "usually men and women who are constitutionally incapable of being honest with themselves"… "They are naturally incapable of grasping and developing a manner of living which demands rigorous (self) honesty". (AA) So, if you are Egocentric (self-righteous, arrogant, hypocritical, egomaniacal, etc.) like the rest of the human race and cannot admit it to yourself or anyone else, then the AA literature predicts that your chances for success in achieving the goal of the Steps are "less than average". Those who suffer from grave emotional and mental disorders but have the capacity to be (self) honest, stand a better chance of succeeding with the program of working the Steps and achieving its goal (a Spiritual Awakening) than the dishonest. You are just not at the point of hopelessness, despair, and defeat in which the insidious EGO will inevitably lead you. AA suggests "To Thy Own Self Be True" and "The Truth Shall Set You Free". As the editor of this proposal, I hope that any self-righteous, arrogant, hypocritical, egomaniacal (and may I add aloof) attitudes do not keep the reader from gaining the knowledge and wisdom provided in this document.

STEP 1: WE (HUMBLY) ADMITTED THAT WE WERE POWERLESS OVER "EGO" - WE (HUMBLY) ADMITTED THAT OUR LIVES HAD BECOME UNMANAGEABLE. (AA)

We fall in love with our thinking (EGO). Our education and experience justifies that we are more correct than you and even in the midst of every day calamity and turmoil, we will not ever admit that we may be in error (even if we weren't straight A students and didn't read every book or have unlimited retention skills for the rest of our lives). "My thinking system is superior to yours", says the EGO "and we are not equal". The EGO guided us through out our life, through the tough times and the good times. It brought us success, experience and knowledge and we use those past experiences to make decisions and judgments in the present, expecting more success. When we fail, we lick our wounds, pick ourselves back up and double our effort. Unfortunately the wages of EGO are ultimately despair, bewilderment, hopelessness and death. "Seek, but do not find." Only HOLY SPIRIT will provide the joy, peace and happiness that we are looking for, yet we lack the discipline to resist the temptation and false promises of EGO. EGO is cunning and baffling and a powerful foe. How then can we possibly do this step, admitting defeat, we can't trust our own thinking, and that our head may be filled with lies. Not only will you need the help of the HOLY SPIRIT, but you will also need the help from another human being, preferably someone who has worked the steps and has studied the text.

In AA there is a "Speaker Meeting". In about one hour, a member stands before other members and honestly and candidly tells his life stories (the ups & downs) and shares his experience, strength and hope with the other members. The format they follow is "What was it like; What happened; and, What's it is like now." Although the audience may or may not benefit from his experience, they listen for the benefit of the speaker, who like Bill Wilson discovers the esteem and well being of telling his story in order to stay sober himself. The side benefit of the genuine nature of the speaker meeting, is that the audience often relates to the same encounters with EGO and often do not have to go to as great of lengths and disasters with EGO before they turn to HOLY SPIRIT. The story usually proceeds from youth down the road of ignorance and EGO until life becomes unbearable. The person turns to HOLY SPIRIT and describes the miracle that follows. It's an opportunity for any one at the fork of the road to evaluate both pathways. During the discourse about the relationship with EGO, the listener often identifies with similar experiences, but for some of the younger crowd, their experiences end at some point while the speaker continues on down the road to despair (and their bottom). Later when the speaker describes his life with HOLY SPIRIT it is nothing less than miraculous. In a moment of clarity the listener can choose which path they desire to follow: go down the path alone with EGO or join the group and the HOLY SPRIT life.

The Steps are not for everyone, but usually people looking for a better way or a way out can benefit greatly from the process, no matter how haphazard or faulty their first attempt may be. People pursuing ACIM most likely are in this category. If you walk through the door of an AA meeting, it is assumed that you have agreed to listen; likewise if you are pursuing a better way, you must be willing to go to great lengths to achieve what the steps are asking. I initially wanted to know "What do I get" and an elderly gentleman opened the AA Big Book to page 83 and read "If we are painstaking about this phase of our development, we will be amazed before we are halfway through. We are going to know a new freedom and a new happiness. We will not regret the past nor wish to shut the door on it. We will comprehend the word serenity and we will know peace. No matter how far down the scale we have gone, we will see how our experience will benefit others. That feeling of uselessness and self pity will disappear. We will lose interest in selfish things and gain interest in our fellows. Self seeking will slip away. Our whole attitude and outlook upon life will change. Fear of people and fear of economic insecurity will leave us. We will intuitively know how to handle situations which used to baffle us. We will suddenly realize that HOLY SPIRIT is doing for us what we could not do for ourselves." (AA) At the time, I didn't have a clue what they meant, but I was content knowing that I was going to get something for my effort.

In order to do the first Step, you must recognize how powerful EGO really is presently in your lives and admit to your innermost self that by yourself you are powerless over the temptations of EGO. (I can resist almost anything, but temptation). To do this you must write your life story (at least gather some notes, so that you can tell it to another trusted person). Go to different eras of your life (e.g. elementary, adolescence, teens, early twenties, etc.) and ask what did you plan to happen and then write down what actually happened. Be prepared and responsible to tell only what you feel comfortable with to another trusted person. This step can be done over and over again and more will be revealed each time. Do not take any unnecessary chances or reveal anything that you are not ready for. The process is to help you feel better about yourself and not to bring you down or embarrass you. Do not get hung up on the autobiography and listen to EGO (self loathing, shame, self pity, etc) and fail to continue with the process of cleaning house in order to live a more rewarding life experience. When ready and prepared, you should go through the Steps in a rather expeditious manner in order to receive the miracle of Spiritual Enlightenment. Miracles are often fleeting and you may have to go back to the steps time and time again to reach that state of mind.

To get an idea of the process, this excerpt is from one of the stories (autobiographies, drunk-a-logs) from the AA book: "...it was Dr. Bob's afternoon off - he had me to the office and we spent three of four hours, formally going through the Six Step program as it was at that time. The six steps were:

1. Complete Deflation; (from EGO)
2. Dependence and guidance from a Higher Power; (HOLY SPIRIT)
3. Moral Inventory;
4. Confession;
5. Restitution;
6. Continued work with other alcoholics

Dr. Bob led me through all of these steps. At the moral inventory, he brought up several of my bad personality traits or character defects, such as selfishness, conceit, jealousy, carelessness, intolerance, ill temper, sarcasm, and resentments. We went over these at great length, and then he finally asked me if I wanted these defects of character removed. When I said yes, we both knelt at his desk and prayed, each of us asking to have these defects taken away. This picture is still vivid. If I live to be a hundred, it will always stand out in my mind. It was very impressive, and I wish that every AA could have the benefit of this type of sponsorship today. Dr. Bob always emphasized the religious angle very strongly, and I think it helped. I know it helped me. Dr. Bob then led me through the restitution step, in which I made a list of all the persons I had harmed and worked out the ways and the means of slowly making restitution." (AA)

Now before you get too far ahead of yourself, it is important that you get the right person to listen to your story and work with you through the steps. The first step in this process would be to ask HOLY SPIRIT to lead you to the right person. (If you don't believe that the HOLY SPIRIT will help you out, this will be a good test to see what happens.) In order to screen out someone not right for you, ask the candidate if they wouldn't mind sitting down with you somewhere, and within an hour or so tell you their life story as candidly and honestly as they are able to at the time.

From the AA book in the above example, prior to the man working the steps with Dr. Bob, the man met with many AA members and listened to their life story: "I can still remember very distinctly getting into Akron at eleven P.M. and routing this same Howard out of bed to do something about me. He spent two hours with me that night telling me his story. He said he had finally learned that drinking was a fatal illness made up of allergy plus an obsession, and once drinking had passed from habit to obsession, we were completely hopeless and could look forward only to spending the balance of our lives in a mental institution - or to death. He laid great stress on the progression of his attitude toward life and people, and most of his attitudes had been very similar to mine. I thought that I was completely different from other people, that I was beginning to become a little balmy, even to the point of withdrawing more and more from society and wanting to be alone...Here was a man with essentially the same outlook on life, except that he had done something about it. He was happy, getting a kick out of life and people and beginning to get his medical practice back again. As I look back on that first meeting, I realize that I began to hope, then for the first time, and I felt that if he could regain these things, perhaps it would be possible for me too. The next afternoon and evening, two other men visited me, and each told me his story and the things that they were doing to try to recover from this tragic illness. They had a certain something that seemed to glow, a peace, a serenity combined with happiness. In the next two or three days the balance of the handful of men contacted me, encouraged me and told me how they were trying to live this program of recovery and the fun they were having doing it." (AA)

Now about that other human being; being that ACIM students do not have the experience with the Steps, I would suggest you contact someone in AA (or Alanon, NA, etc.). To go about this, the AA phone number for the local central office is in most phone books. You would have to find and go to an open meeting (as opposed to a closed "alcoholic only" meeting) and ask someone if they wouldn't mind telling you their story. Be sure to tell them that you are not an alcoholic. Some may be biased or feel inadequate to deal with someone who is not alcoholic. However, AA is like a Toast Masters club and most members are very proficient speakers and just love telling their story. Ask if they can limit their talk to one hour, maximum and be very careful to stay in control and not have them start to give you directions for running your life. There are many good and upright people in AA and there are also many flakes. It is very hard to distinguish who's who from the outside.

This idea of contacting an AA may seem too absurd or risky, and understandably so. You could ask a fellow ACIM student, a close friend, a family member, a counselor or a member of the clergy. We all have the experience of EGO in our lives. The idea is that once they have heard your story, it will be difficult to deny certain truths about EGO that we tend to hide from our consciousness. Once your story is told, you should then review the story and ask where in my life have I been powerless over EGO. Your friend can help you get through the denial. With alcoholics, we usually had some serious problems with EGO before we began drinking, and when we started drinking, it was to block out of our consciousness the problems and dissatisfactions with our lives. However when we talk to someone else we tend to cover it up, saying that we only became alcoholic a year ago or so. We go back through our story again with

STEVE H.

the help of our aid and identify where in our story was our life unmanageable. It will become evident, that most of our life was managed by EGO with not so very good consequences. What we had expected and what resulted where quite different. And finally (the scary part), we look over our story and identify where in our life had our behavior or our thinking been insane. (A mild definition of insanity used in AA is "doing the same thing over and over again and expecting different consequences".)

Don't throw your story away quite yet, you will need it for some of the other steps. But make sure that you safeguard any written material, so that it doesn't get in the hands of the wrong person. And don't jump ahead and make a confession to your wife, your boss or a jury. We can get a spiritual high, which can create some earthly problems. We can later review our story for fears, resentments, sex conduct, personality traits, etc. We will also make a list of names of the characters in the story, to determine whether any amends or restitution is necessary. This step process does not require perfection and improvement will occur with practice. The first few times may take a little longer, but do not get hung up with EGO anywhere in the process. EGO is easy to spot. If you are unhappy, you are listening to EGO. If you have to leave off the step work during its conception, do it at a point
where you are feeling content and satisfied (buzzed). But, beware, EGO is a jealous god and can twist your thinking around in a heart beat. It is a good idea to have a group of people you can call or visit. When ever two or more are gathered in HOLY SPIRIT's name, EGO is powerless. And stay prayed up. (At this point the editor would also like to recommend that you read Appendices G thru J to gain the concept of what the editor of this document is referring to by using the word EGO in this step.)

STEP 2: WE (HUMBLY) CAME TO BELIEVE THAT HOLY SPIRIT COULD RESTORE US TO SANITY. (AA)

In AA, the requirements for terminology about God are very liberal and are designed at introducing a concept of God to the person where ever they may be in their spiritual development or regression. Often alcoholics are spiritually bankrupt. AA emphasizes that you develop a concept of God as you understand Him (or don't understand Him). The idea is "Easy Does It - But Do It". Give it a chance and experiment with it. Listen to the testimony of others and try it. See what happens. Start somewhere. This proposal however, will use the term "HOLY SPIRIT" to remain in alignment with the text of ACIM. You can still experiment. Ask HOLY SPIRIT and see what happens. The concept of God and the concept of HOLY SPIRIT are often hard to fathom. What ever ideas you start with, they will inevitably change and grow as we proceed. In Step 2, AA starts with the term "Power Greater Than Yourself" and in this proposal it will start right off with the term "HOLY SPIRIT". A saying used in AA (rephrased to better suit ACIM) might well be applied here: "If the term HOLY SPIRIT drives you out the door, maybe EGO will drive you back in". Anyway, EGO is often a power greater than our self too and even a speeding locomotive is a power greater than our self.

Where ever we start, we usually bring our past along with us. AA has a story about a man who carried a rock (his past) with him wherever he went. He was aboard a ship when it went down, he wanted to get on board the life boat, and everyone was willing to have him board provided he "Drop the Rock". When I came to this step, I was unaware that I was filled with bias, prejudice and contempt toward the words "Jesus", "God", "Holy Spirit" etc. and was very stuck in my ways. AA recommends spiritual progress and not spiritual perfection; but, unfortunately for me, because of my stubborn know-it-all nature, I progressed very slowly and often regressed. For me it was the pain of mental and emotional insanity that drove me to use the Steps and when the pain left, so did my desire to proceed. I had no idea how insane I was then. And I said that every year, until I brought that statement into the present "I have no idea how insane I am right now". (Well maybe if I work the percentages, I may not be as insane as I was.) It can take a lot of time to realize that we are not well. At age 40 and ten years into my way of doing the Steps (after all I was a college graduate), my life once again bottomed out and I sought psychological help. I previously had great successes with hypnosis. The person I saw explained to me that the subconscious mind serves us and it will do what we ask it, but sometimes we ask it to do things that later are not in our best interest. Without asking it to stop, it will repeat the behavior over and over despite the unfavorable results (and we won't know why). She also explained that we recreate our childhood relationships (that we had with our parents and siblings) in our adult life and are unaware of doing so. Hypnosis is very much like guided meditation, but instead of going to the super conscious mind, we visit the subconscious mind. I always enjoy it tremendously (It is like taking a trip and never leaving the farm and the side effects are beneficial rather than detrimental). Once I am in the altered waking state (confirmed by rapid eye movement), I answer questions honestly and directly (I trust this person immensely). What ever problem I discussed with her prior to going under hypnosis, she asks me again and asks me where did this begin? I go directly to the age and situation that created the problem. She wanted to know why I had such problems with Spiritual concepts and I went to eighth grade. My mother was angry with my father, and removed me from Catholic catechism and made me go to Lutheran catechism, but I was several years older than the rest of the class. She didn't care. I was always angry with her and I would often repeat to myself, "I hate you, I hate you, I hate you...." In the class was a picture of Jesus and I would sit through the class, embarrassed and angry, and say to the picture of Jesus, "I hate you, I hate you, I hate you..." The therapist asked, that since I was now forty, did I still need to hate Jesus and I said no. She allowed me to re-create a protective device in my subconscious mind with a more mature understanding conscious mind. I write about this, because shortly afterwards I was intuitively led to the ACIM book and the terms Holy Spirit, Jesus, and God no longer had that negative effect on my attitude. I realized that I had a great resentment against these words and I could now read Christian literature, (which is what AA is actually based upon) and gain a great deal of spiritual knowledge that I had previously blocked out.

In discussing Step 2 in AA, we often say: "First we came, then we came to, and then we came to believe". There is also a cliché: "Belief is hanging on and Faith is letting go", but I always imagine the cartoon caricature of Beetle Bailey hanging on to a small branch over a very high cliff--until I later heard God is the net below. My faith and belief wax and wane with the moon. Often when I realize that I am with EGO (which is most of the time), I become aware of the warning bells and the pain of the insanity brought on by EGO. I begin working the steps in my mind or on paper in order to experience a spiritual awakening (I go back to spiritual sleep a lot). I often realize that I don't even believe that there is a HOLY SPIRIT or that this system will work. In AA, they also say that as we watch a man on a tightrope with a wheel barrel, we may believe that he will make it to the other side, but faith is getting into the wheel barrel. As long as there is a net below (HOLY SPIRIT) I can take greater experimental spiritual risks with the Steps.

How to work this Step is to ask yourself if you believe. If you don't believe, pray for willingness to believe. Willingness, open mindedness and honesty are the AA essentials in working the steps. If you don't have them, ask (HOLY SPIRIT). If you are afraid, ask for courage. Now, review your life story and ask your self where your thinking and behavior might have been insane. Then in each situation, ask yourself what you would have preferred your thinking and behavior to have been like. (This second concept is very useful in later steps.) If you make the discovery that you have been or may be insane, pray for sanity. Sanity is synonymous with Spiritual Experience, Spiritual Awakening, Truth, and healthy thinking. We are not bad people but we sometimes do get sick (not only physically, but emotionally, mentally and spiritually). If we correct the spiritually malady, the others will follow.

STEP 3: WE (HUMBLY) MADE A DECISION TO TURN OUR WILL AND OUR LIVES OVER TO THE CARE OF HOLY SPIRIT (AS WE UNDERSTOOD HIM). (AA)

Now, how hard can this be? If we are sick or hurting, we have no problem turning our will and our life over to the care of a physician. If we have trouble with the law, we turn our will and lives over to the care of an attorney. We often turn or will and our lives over to the care of our spiritual leaders and lecturers, or the author of a book. So why not get the best in the business, HOLY SPIRIT. To paraphrase an AA prayer "HOLY SPIRIT, I offer myself to Thee - to build with me and to do with me as Thou wilt. Relieve me of the bondage of self (EGO), that I may better do Thy will. Take away my difficulties, that victory over them may bear witness to those I would help of Thy Power, Thy Love, and Thy Way of life." (AA) Try it, you'll like it.

This is what AA literature has to say about the whole deal; "The first requirement is that we be convinced that any life run on self-will (EGO) can hardly be a success. On that basis we are almost always in collision with something or somebody, even though our motives are good. Most people try to live by self-propulsion. Each person is like the actor who wants to run the whole show; is forever trying to arrange the lights, the ballet, the scenery and the rest of the players in his own way. If his arrangement would only stay put, if only people would do as he wished, the show would be great. Everybody, including himself would be pleased. Life would be wonderful. In trying to make these arrangements our actor may sometimes be virtuous. He may be kind, considerate, patient, generous, even modest and self-sacrificing. On the other hand he may be mean, egotistical, selfish and dishonest. But, as with most of us, he is more likely to have varied traits. What usually happens? The show doesn't come off very well. He begins to think that life doesn't treat him right. He decides to exert himself more. He becomes, on the next occasion, still more demanding or gracious, as the case may be. Still the play does not suit him. Admitting that he may be somewhat at fault, he is sure that other people are more to blame. He becomes angry, indignant, self-pitying. What is his basic trouble? Is he not really a self-seeker even when trying to be kind? Is he not a victim of the delusion that he can wrest satisfaction and happiness out of this world if he only manages well? Is it not evident to all the rest of the players that these are the things he wants? And do not his actions make each of them wish to retaliate, snatching all they can get out of the show? Is he not, even in his best moments, a producer of confusion rather than harmony? Our actor is self-centered - egocentric, as people like to call it nowadays. He is like the retired business man who lolls in the Florida sunshine in the winter complaining of the sad state of the nation, the minister who sighs over the sins of the twentieth century, politicians and reformers who are sure all would be Utopia if the rest of the world would only behave; the outlaw safe cracker who thinks society has wronged him and the alcoholic who has lost all and is locked up. What-ever our protestations, are not most of us concerned with ourselves, our resentments, or our self pity? Selfishness-self-centeredness! That, we think, is the root of our troubles. Driven by a hundred forms of fear, self-delusion, self-seeking, and self-pity, we step on the toes of our fellows and they retaliate. Sometimes they hurt us, seemingly without provocation, but we invariably find that at some time in the past we have made decisions based on self which later placed us in a positions to be hurt. So our troubles, we think, are basically of our own making. We arise out of ourselves, and the "EGO" creates an extreme example of self will run riot, though we usually don't think so. Above everything, we

STEVEH.

must be rid of selfishness. We must, or it kills us! "HOLY SPIRIT" makes that possible. And there often seems no way of entirely getting rid of self without His aid. Many of us had moral and philosophical convictions galore, but we could not live up to them even though we would have liked to. Neither could we reduce our self-centeredness much by wishing or trying on our own power. We had to have "HOLY SPIRIT's" help. This is the how and why of it. First of all, we had to "quit EGO". It didn't work. Next, we decided that hereafter in this drama of life, "HOLY SPIRIT" was going to be our Director.....Most good ideas are simple, and this concept was the keystone of the new and triumphant arch through which we passed to freedom. When we sincerely took such a position, all sorts of remarkable things followed. We had a new Employer. Being all powerful, He provided what we needed, if we kept close to Him and performed His work well. Established on such a footing, we became less and less interested in ourselves, our little plans and designs. More and more we became interested in seeing what we could contribute to life. As we felt new power flow in, as we enjoyed peace of mind, as we became conscious of HOLY SPIRIT's presence, we began to lose our fear of today, tomorrow or the hereafter. We were reborn". (AA)

That's a lot to say in one breath. I took the liberty to rephrase a few words and omit a sentence or two. Another way we can address this is with another story: "A man is allowed to see both Heaven and Hell before he has to make a choice. He visits hell first, and it is a large buffet with all the imaginable trimmings. There is one catch, to everyone's arm's are tied long spoons and although they can scoop up the food, they can not get it to their mouth. He then visits Heaven and finds the same situation, except that instead of everyone trying to feed themselves, they are feeding each other. But the man chooses hell. Why? He must be insane! Without the help of HOLY SPIRIT, we will be doomed to choose hell over and over again. We do not have the power alone to match our good intentions. The road to hell is paved with good intentions.

(With a little editing on my part) Dr. Bob put it this way: "If you think you are an atheist, and agnostic, a skeptic, or have any other form of intellectual pride, which keeps you from accepting what is in this book, I feel sorry for you. If you still think you are strong enough to beat the game alone, that is your affair. But if you really and truly want what we have, and are willing to go to any length to get it, and sincerely think you must have some help, we know we have an answer for you". (AA) Notice that each step is the plural, 1st person pronoun, "We". United we stand, divided I fall. We join with HOLY SPIRIT and each other. No one goes to Heaven by themselves, we either all go together or no one goes at all.

Remember not to get hung up on this process. These steps are not to be taken as a bitter pill. They are to improve your well being, emotions, and health; satisfaction and contentment should be the signs that you are doing them right. The next steps, 4, 5, 6, 7, 8 can be done in rapid succession

STEP 4 : WE (HUMBLY) MADE A SEARCHING AND FEARLESS MORAL INVENTORY OF OURSELVES. (AA)

AA text states: "A business which takes no regular inventory usually goes broke. Taking a commercial inventory is a fact-finding and a fact-facing process. It is an effort to discover the truth about the stock-in-trade. One object is to disclose damaged or un-saleable goods, to get rid of them promptly and without regret. If the owner of the business is to be successful, he cannot fool himself about values. We did exactly the same thing with our lives. We took stock honestly. First, we searched out the flaws in our make-up which caused our failure. Being convinced that self (EGO), manifested in various ways, was what had defeated us, we considered its common manifestations." (AA) One way to perform an inventory is to list the credits and debits. An example is as follows:

Credit	%	Debit	%
HONESTY		DISHONESTY	
FORGIVENESS		RESENTMENT	
PEACE		WAR	
LOVE		HATE	
HUMILITY		ARROGANCE	
GENEROSITY		SELFISHNESS	
ESTEEM		JEALOUSY	
CONTENTMENT		ENVY	
GENUINESS		SARCASM	
PATIENCE		INTOLERANCE	
GRATITUDE		INGRATITUDE	
UNITY		REBELLIOUS	
SERVICE		AMBITION	
MERCY		GUILT	

The list is yours, so honestly identify your values (not someone else's). The words can be found in any self help or spiritual literature. If it is a debit you identify (e.g. lust, greed, gluttony, pride, sloth, etc.), think of and put down its opposite. If it is a credit do the same. In order to build esteem, you must do estimable things. This list helps us point out the direction we want to go. Honesty leads the list in the above example, because the AA Text says, "Those who do not recover are people who cannot or will not completely give themselves to this simple program, usually men and women who are constitutionally incapable of being honest with them selves. There are such unfortunates. They are not at fault; they seem to have been born that way. They are naturally incapable of grasping and developing a manner of living which demands rigorous honesty. Their chances are less than average. There are those, too, who suffer from grave emotional and mental disorders, but many of them do recover if they have the capacity to be honest." (AA) Honesty is an abstract with many diverse concepts and is often unattainable. AA meetings discuss many types of honesty (e.g. cash register honesty, self honesty, an honest days work, etc.). Some go as far to say if you took a pen home from work, you should put down on your inventory that you are a thief. Trying to obtain perfect honesty may be similar to walking halfway to the wall. Each time you go halfway, you get closer, but you will never reach the wall. Going from 0% toward 100% may require a good deal of time and effort. We often discover that although our intentions are good our discipline is often lacking. Besides without consultation from a sponsor or teacher, it is quite easy to make some large often irreversible mistakes in attempting to be honest. A plane reaches its destination by making very minor adjustments to its route. Instant 90 and 180 degree turns are not always recommended. At this point we are just taking inventory, so we ask our-self, how honest are we? With the Credit/ Debit list, we can use percentages. If I evaluate myself and say that I am 70% dishonest and 30% honest, I can identify the shortcoming and begin to improve to a goal such as 35% honest. As we go through the list, we will discover that some may be more glaring than others. Those items may be a source of emotional pain and life failures. Originally, I didn't understand how things such as pride, lust and envy could be defects. In the process of working the steps, I discovered that envy of others possessions and skills was a great source of resentment, self pity and pain. If I was to be free of pain, I had to find ways to reduce the amount of envy in my life. I couldn't tackle them all at once and didn't have the tools or skills to do anything about it at first, so beware not to go into morbid depression and guilt over your short comings. Put guilt, depression, self pity on the debit side and start to think about the opposite and begin to head in that direction. In order not to think of the color blue, think of the color red. In order not to think about the word Hippopotamus, think of the word Giraffe. In order not to think about your debit, think about your credit. The AA text goes on to say, "Resentment is the number one offender. It destroys more … than anything else. From it stem all forms of spiritual disease, for we have not only been mentally and physically ill, we have been spiritually sick. When the spiritual malady is overcome, we straighten out mentally and physically. In dealing with resentments, we set them on paper. We listed people, institutions or principles with whom we were angry. We asked ourselves why we were angry. In most cases it was found that our self esteem, our pocketbooks, our ambitions, our personal relationships (including sex) were hurt or threatened. So we were sore. We were burned up. On our grudge list we set opposite each name our injuries". (AA)

Write a grudge list. Use the names from your personal story. List each name and put down next to it your injuries. Put down what they did to you. Then go back through the list and cross their name out and put down yours; see what you did to yourself. We discover the enemy and it is our EGO. First we blame others; then we blame ourselves. Later we learn to take blame out of our vocabulary. (A gentleman I knew in AA would suggest, "Never say that you are proud to be a member of AA; instead say that you are grateful." His concept was to remove the word proud from our vocabulary.)

The AA books tells us: "It is plain that a life which includes deep resentment leads only to futility and unhappiness. To the precise extent that we permit these, do we squander the hours that might have been worth while. But with" us "whose hope is the maintenance and growth of a spiritual experience, this business of resentment is infinitely grave. We found that it is fatal. For when harboring such feelings, we shut ourselves off from the sunlight of the Spirit. The insanity"… "returns"…"If we were to live we had to be free of anger. The grouch and the brainstorm were not for us. They may be the dubious luxury" of EGO "but for" us "these things are poison. We turned back to the list, for it held the key to our future. We began to see that the world and its people really dominated us. In that state, the wrong-doing of others, fancied or real, had power to actually kill. How could we escape? We saw that these resentments must be mastered, but how? We could not wish them away"…"This was our course: We realized that the people who wronged us were perhaps spiritually sick. Though we did not like their symptoms and the way these disturbed us, they, like ourselves, were" spiritually "sick too. We asked" HOLY SPIRIT "to help us show them the same tolerance, pity and patience that we would cheerfully grant a sick friend. When a person offended we said to ourselves, "This person is spiritually sick. How can I be helpful?" HOLY SPIRIT "save me from being angry. Thy will be done. We avoid retaliation or argument. We wouldn't treat" spiritually "sick people that way. If we do, we destroy our chance of being helpful. We cannot be helpful to all people, but at least" HOLY SPIRIT "will show us how to take a kindly and tolerant view of each and every one. Referring to our list again; putting out of our minds the wrongs others had done, we resolutely looked for our own mistakes. Where had we been selfish, dishonest, self-seeking and frightened? Though the situation had not been entirely our fault, we tried to disregard the other person involved entirely. Where were we to blame? The inventory was ours, not the other man's. When we saw our faults we listed them. We placed them before us in black and white. We admitted our wrongs honestly and were willing to set these matters straight." (AA)

This is how we get through this seemingly large task. With each name from our life story, put down the story in one sentence. In another sentence, identify your behavior. Not too hard, except keeping it to one sentence (two or three at the most). You will begin to see a pattern and some repetition of your behavior and emotions. You may see how you have recreated relationships that you had as a child with your parents or siblings. You may have tried to create a father-son relationship with someone who didn't meet your expectations. You may discover that you have an inferiority-superiority complex. You may discover that jealousy, envy and pride cause you all kinds of pain and trouble. Now go back in each situation and write one sentence on how you would have liked your behavior to have been. (Remember it is your inventory, so be honest with yourself and put down what you honestly would have liked your behavior to be and not what your think others would have wanted or expected.) Although we cannot change the past, we will, as time goes by begin to be aware and identify such behavior in the present (the warning bells). When we become aware, we can ask HOLY SPIRIT to lead us from temptation and deliver us into the new desired behavior. (Congratulations, in this one paragraph, you just completed an abbreviated version of steps 4, 5, 6 & 7.)

Now about fear, AA text says: "...we think fear ought to be classed with stealing. It seems to cause more trouble. We reviewed our fears thoroughly. We put them on paper, even though we had no resentment in connection with them. Wasn't it because self-reliance failed us? Self reliance was good as far as it went, but it didn't go far enough. Some of us once had great self-confidence, but it didn't fully solve the fear problem, or any other. When it made us cocky, it was worse. Perhaps there is a better way -- we think so. For we now are on a different basis; the basis of trusting" HOLY SPIRIT "We trust infinite" HOLY SPIRIT "rather than our finite selves. We are in the world to play the role" HOLY SPIRIT "assigns. Just to the extent that we do as we think" HOLY SPIRIT "would have us and humbly rely on" HOLY SPIRIT, "does" HOLY SPIRIT "enable us to match calamity with serenity. We never apologize to anyone for depending upon" HOLY SPIRIT. "We can laugh at those who think spirituality the way of weakness. Paradoxically, it is the way of strength. The verdict of the ages is that faith means courage. All men or faith have courage. They trust" HOLY SPIRIT. We never apologize for" HOLY SPIRIT. "Instead we let' HOLY SPIRIT "demonstrate through us, what" HOLY SPIRIT "can do. We ask" HOLY SPIRIT "to remove our fear and direct our attention to what" HOLY SPIRIT "would have us be. At once, we commence to outgrow fear." (AA)

STEVE H.

The AA text also has a section beginning with: "Now about sex.", but it has little to do with sex. It should probably say, now about the guilt and shame we carry about our sexual desires and behavior. Personally, I thought that I was addicted to sex, but later discovered that I was addicted to the mental sensations of pre-orgasm, orgasm and post orgasm. With the courage to discuss these issues with a professional, certain medications and age, the problem is no longer as intense and the percentage of guilt and shame have been greatly diminished. AA text says, "We are not the arbiter of anyone's sex conduct." "We want to stay out of this controversy." (AA) Especially after the problem has been alleviated to a certain degree, we forget the intensity of the sex drive and the obsessions that often accompany it and tend to lecture the young. As with parenting, we try to cram twenty or thirty years of our life experience into any open orifice (of the newcomer) that will receive it. He asks for a drink of water and we get out the fire hose.

This section of the AA text is more about the development of sound (HOLY) relationships. "We reviewed our own conduct over the years past. Where have we been selfish, dishonest, or inconsiderate? Whom have we hurt? Did we unjustifiably arouse jealousy, suspicion or bitterness? Where were we at fault? What should have been done instead? We got this all down on paper and looked at it. In this way we tried to shape a sane and sound ideal for our future sex life. We subjected each relationship to the test -- was it selfish or not? We asked" HOLY SPIRIT "to mold our ideals and help us to live up to them."... "Whatever our ideal turns out to be, we must be willing to grow toward it. We must be willing to make amends, provided we do not bring about more harm in doing so. In other words, we treat sex as we would any other problem. In meditation, we ask" HOLY SPIRIT "what we should do about each specific matter. The right answer will come, if we want it." HOLY SPIRIT "alone can judge our sex situation. Counsel with persons is often desirable, but we let" HOLY SPIRIT "be the final judge. We realize that people are as fanatical about sex as others are loose. We avoid hysterical thinking or advise." ..."To sum up about sex: We earnestly pray for the right ideal, for guidance in each questionable situation, for sanity, and for the strength to do the right thing." The AA text also suggests, "If sex is very troublesome, we throw ourselves the harder into helping others. We think of their needs and work for them. This takes us out of ourselves. It quiets the imperious urge, when to yield would mean heartache." (AA)

The AA 12 & 12 text adds, "...it is from our twisted relations with family, friends and society at large that many of us have suffered the most. We have been especially stupid and stubborn about them. The primary fact that we fail to recognize is our total inability to form a true partnership with another human being. Our egomania digs two disastrous pitfalls. Either we insist upon dominating the people we know, or we depend upon them far too much. If we lean too heavily on people, they will sooner or later fail us, for they are human, too, and cannot possible meet our incessant demands. In this way our insecurity grows and festers. When we habitually try to manipulate others to our own willful desires, they revolt, and resist us heavily. Then we develop hurt feelings, a sense of persecution, and a desire to retaliate. As we redouble our efforts at control, and continue to fail, our sufferings become acute and constant. We have not once sought to be one in a family, to be a friend among friends, to be a worker among workers, to be a useful member of society. Always we tried to struggle to the top of the heap, or hide underneath it. This self-centered behavior blocked a partnership relation with any one of those about us. Of true brotherhood we had small comprehension." (AA)

Remember not to entertain EGO with guilt, shame and remorse. They are on the debit side of the list. Concentrate on their opposites and stay in close contact with HOLY SPIRIT. A gentleman I once knew in AA would say, "I may not be able to pray better than some of you, but I can pray more often". From the AA text it says: HOLY SPIRIT "did for us what we could not do for ourselves. We hope that you are convinced that" HOLY SPIRIT "can remove whatever self will (EGO) has blocked off. If you already have made a decision and an inventory of your grosser handicaps, you have made a good beginning. That being so you have swallowed and digested some big chunks of truth about" EGO. (AA)

Rewording the A, B, C's of AA to ACIM terminology:
    A. EGO can't
    B. HOLY SPIRIT can.
    C. Ask & let HOLY SPIRIT

STEP 5 : WE (HUMBLY) ADMITTED TO HOLY SPIRIT, TO OURSELVES, AND TO ANOTHER HUMAN BEING THE EXACT NATURE OF OUR WRONGS. (AA)

In the process of working the steps, great revelations come to us. Often the things we learn by doing the steps could never have been calculated by just proselytizing intellectual philosophies. In order to keep the knowledge and feelings that we acquired, we share our experience with others. The AA slogan is "You have to give it away in order to keep it". We share what we learned as we did the steps. For each step, it is not very difficult to tell a chronological life story of our progress, experience and happenings over the years of our spiritual journey. With repetitive discussion meetings, we develop a repertoire of candid stories of the positive and negative experiences (from both our successes and our mistakes) we have had growing spiritually which we readily share with the group. The benefit for those who listen is they can hear the do's and don'ts and maybe be able to apply the process a bit sooner or in an easier manner. We usually don't share from spiritual roof tops, but with rigorous honesty and candidness, tell the truth to the best of our ability up to the present. Spiritual activists from other teachings often find this method wanting because they claim we are reinforcing the negative as well as the positive. They advise us not to say anything negative after the expression "I am". It's hard to tell if this advise comes from EGO or HOLY SPIRIT, but in AA the process of telling our story has years of success helping ourselves and others. In another congregation I could possibly explain how all my relationships are holy and actually believe it. I could experience the shear joy in doing so. But in AA, there is a different audience, and this genuinely candid method allows the listeners to relate, bond and participate in the process. "We do not wish to shut the door on the past. No matter how far down the scale we have gone, we see how our experience can benefit others." (AA)

There are various ideologies on this confession matter. Some say never show your dirty laundry in public. Some advise that what you say may be used against you later. This proposal's advice is to consult with the HOLY SPIRIT. A poem I once memorized has assisted me greatly in this process. Before speaking pray, "HOLY SPIRIT, grant what I say be of Thy word, so others shall be blessed for having heard" and in helping others pray "HOLY SPIRIT grant that my path be Thy chosen way, so those who hold my hand will not be led astray." (Unk) You will be amazed at what comes out of your mouth and the actions you perform past EGO. ACIM points out that giving and receiving are the same, so when we share, we take (and vice versa). When we listen, we speak. When we teach, we learn. When we help others, we help ourselves.

With my first attempt in confessing my life story, I followed a drinking autobiography outline provided in the alcohol Recovery Center that I was in. I resented being told to do it and in my story, I frequently went past the instructions to vent and blame others for my predicaments. It was my mother's, father's, boss', wife's, etc. fault and if you had my problems you would drink too. I told my story to my group therapy session and got a lot of feed back in which I paid absolutely no attention to (because I was so much better than the rest of these slobs). I also decided that since I would probably never see these people again in my life, I would take the opportunity to share all my sexual exploits. It was not bragging, because I was very ashamed of many of my sexual fantasies and my attempts to enact them. They did not match the manly, macho character that I tried so hard to display. One of the doctors at the facility shared his story and it gave me the courage to start with mine. (This particular problem did not go away quite as easily as drinking and smoking, and I have been spending much of my sobriety still working on this issue.) About three months into my sobriety, I was asked to be the speaker at an AA meeting, so I got out my notes from rehab. When I read them I realized what a whiny baby I had been, and I decided to put the whole world of blame onto my shoulders. I shared my story taking the blame for everything. Each subsequent time I shared my story, I would attempt to be very honest but a different theme would surface. On one occasion, I was this tough, rebellious, run away juvenile delinquent and on the next occasion I'd share what a cry baby sissy I had been growing up. Each was true, but told from a different perspective and attitude. I began to realize that honesty and the truth may be two different things and the Truth may be much larger than I can comprehend. Especially when I tell my story and then I listened to my daughter's version. They are like day and night. I know that we are both trying to be honest, so why the difference. Maybe EGO altered things a bit, making me the hero or the goat of the story. Maybe details got exaggerated, or details forgotten got filled in with a better sounding story. I didn't always get A's in school, even if I studied and tried, so maybe I didn't always retain the information correctly and indefinitely. (This concept made forgiveness and letting it go easier for me, since I really didn't know the story, why lock up so much emotion and feelings into it).

When I got out of rehab, I was terrified to share my sexual issues with anyone, especially another man (but I had no problem dumping my problems onto my wife). A woman in AA suggested that I see a priest that she knew, and I visited the poor celibate young fellow three or four times to vent all of it. Also a guy in AA suggested that I go home and write down all the people I hate. I liked this guy because here was someone who understood. I enjoyed the assignment and couldn't wait to come back to tell him my story. He listened patiently and offered no advice. What a great guy. I felt absolutely great for about two days (then EGO returned to take control). I also discovered that the AA meetings were a great place to dump my troubles. For year's I used it as a confessional, repeating the same issues over and over again (because I failed to do the rest of the steps and ask for this behavior to be removed). When my wife divorced me, I finally decided to ask someone for help. The guy I asked was another someone who had listened to me often without giving any advice. However as we worked the steps, he told me I was afraid of rejection, abandonment and criticism. I stopped seeing this guy immediately and it took me about two more years to comprehend what he said was true. After each subsequent divorce or traumatic event, I sought out AA sponsorship and professional counseling, but never stayed with it once the pain was gone. I have never been an AA "A" student. (Many of us who were raised in abusive families are more motivated by punishment than rewards; once the pain of punishment is reduced or removed, we tend to revert to our old ways and repeat the undesirable behavior again.)

The AA text has about four pages of information and directions on this step. "This is perhaps difficult -- especially discussing our defects with another person. We think we have done well enough in admitting these things to ourselves. There is doubt about that. In actual practice, we usually find a solitary self-appraisal insufficient. Many of us thought it necessary to go much further. We will be more reconciled to discussing ourselves with another person when we see good reason why we should do so. The best reason first: If we skip this vital step, we may not over come" EGO. "Time after time newcomers have tried to keep to themselves certain facts about their lives. Trying to avoid this humbling experience, they have turned to easier

STEVE H.

methods"..."Having persevered with the rest of the program, they wondered why they fell. We think the reason is that they never completed their housecleaning. They took inventory all right, but hung on to some of the worst items in stock. They only thought they had lost their egoism and fear; they only thought they had humbled themselves. But they had not learned enough of humility, fearlessness and honesty, in the sense we find it necessary, until they told someone else their entire life story."...EGO "leads a double life. He is very much the actor. To the outer world he presents his stage character. This is one he likes his fellow to see. He wants to enjoy a certain reputation, but knows in his heart he doesn't deserve it. The inconsistency is made worse by the things he does on sprees. Coming to his senses, he is revolted at certain episodes he vaguely remembers. These memories are a nightmare. He trembles to think someone might have observed him. As fast as he can, he pushes these memories far inside himself. He hopes they will never see the light of day. He is under constant fear and tension -- that makes for more" EGO. "Psychologists are inclined to agree with us. We have spent thousands of dollars for examinations. We know but few instances where we have given these doctors a fair break. We seldom have told them the whole truth nor have we followed their advice. Unwilling to be honest with these sympathetic men, we were honest with no one else."..."We must be entirely honest with somebody if we expect to live long or happily in this world. Rightly and naturally, we think well before we choose the persons with whom to take this intimate and confidential step. Those of us belonging to a religious domination which requires confession must, and of course, will want to go to the properly appointed authority whose duty it is to receive it. Though we have no religious connection, we may still do well to talk with someone ordained by an established religion. We often find such a person quick to see and understand our problem. Of course, we sometimes encounter people who do not understand"... "If we cannot or would rather not do this, we search our acquaintance for a close-mouthed, understanding friend. Perhaps our doctor or psychologist will be the person. It may be one of our own family, but we cannot disclose anything to our wives or our parents (or our children) which will hurt them and make them unhappy. We have no right to save our own skin at another person's expense. Such parts of our story we tell to someone who will understand, yet be unaffected. The rule is we must be hard on ourself, but always considerate of others. Not withstanding the great necessity for discussing ourselves with someone, it may be one is so situated that there is no suitable person available. If that is so, this step may be postponed, only, however, if we hold ourselves in complete readiness to go through with it at the first opportunity. We say this because we are very anxious that we talk to the right person. It is important the he be able to keep a confidence; that he fully understand and approve what we are driving at; that he will not try to change our plan. But we must not use this as a mere excuse to postpone. When we decide who is to hear our story, we waste no time. We have a written inventory and we are prepared a long talk. We explain to our partner what we are about to do and why we have to do it. He should realize that we are engaged upon a life and death errand. Most people approached in this way will be glad to help; they will be honored by our confidence. We pocket our pride and go to it, illuminating every twist of character, every dark cranny of the past. Once we have taken this step, withholding nothing, we are delighted. We can look the world in the eye. We can be alone at perfect peace and ease. Our fears fall from us. We begin to feel the nearness of" HOLY SPIRIT. "We may have had certain spiritual beliefs, but now we begin to have a spiritual experience. The feeling that" EGO "has disappeared will often come strongly. We feel we are on the Broad Highway, walking hand in hand with" HOLY SPIRIT. Returning home we find a place where we can be quiet for an hour, carefully reviewing what we have done. We thank" HOLY SPIRIT "from the bottom of our hearts that we know Him better. Taking this book down from our shelf, we turn to the page that contains the Twelve Steps. Carefully reading the first five proposals, we ask if we have omitted anything, for we are building an arch through which we shall walk a free man at last. Is our work solid so far? Are the stones properly in place? Have we skimped on the cement put into the foundation? Have we tried to make mortar without sand? If we can answer to our satisfaction, we can then look at Step Six". (AA)

In the AA text, in the Chapter: The Family Afterwards, it states, "Henry Ford once made a wise remark to the effect that experience is the thing of supreme value in life." That is only true if one is willing to turn the past to good account. We grow by our willingness to face and rectify errors and convert them into assets. The" EGO's "past thus becomes the principal asset"... "The painful past may be of infinite value to other families still struggling with their problem (EGO). We think each family which has been relieved owes something to those who have not, and when the occasion requires, each member of it should be only too willing to bring former mistakes, no matter how grievous, out of their hiding places. Showing others who suffer how we were given help is the very thing which makes life seem so worth while to us now. Cling to the thought that in" HOLY SPIRIT's "hands, the dark past is the greatest possession you have -- the key to life and happiness for others. With it you can avert death and misery for them." (AA)

STEP 6: WE WERE ENTIRELY READY TO HAVE HOLY SPIRIT REMOVE ALL THESE DEFECTS OF CHARACTER. (AA)

Beware of the "ly" words, such as entirely, absolutely, completely, etc. (Even Bill Wilson couldn't accept all the tenets of the Oxford groups, especially the concept of absolute). The "ly" words don't leave any room for error; Nor does the HOLY SPIRIT. The spiritual concept is that we cannot serve two masters. HOLY SPIRIT leaves no room for EGO. We can drag out this step, and take the rest of our life getting ready. But do I really want to go back to being subservient, or do I want to keep my separation and freedom, no matter what the cost. This is a very difficult dilemma to be in and can keep us in indecision indefinitely. Sounds like the works of EGO to me (can you hear the warning bells). In the EGO system that we presently are experiencing, there are two methods of motivation, reward and punishment. They train dolphins by rewarding them for swimming over the bar and ignoring them if they swim under the bar. Eventually they can do all sorts of fantastic tricks based on a reward system. It is a method recommended for raising children, but unfortunately most of us didn't have the benefit of that method growing up. As for myself, growing up in a family with parents lacking education and being exposed to a rapidly changing world of affluence, entertainment, alcohol and drugs (prescription valium, diet pills, etc.) my sisters and I lacked attention. They sought out positive, rewarding attention and I chose the opposite. As we now pass middle age, the results still aren't in as to which direction proved to benefit us the most. We do however get set in our ways and find it very difficult to change the mold. Pain has been my motivator. I'll do most anything to get out of the emotional pain I have created, but once it is gone, I'll search it out again and again and again. I'll throw away my peace for more pain. Sounds like the world of EGO. The rewards of EGO are pain, misery and death. Like I said previously, I can resist almost anything, except temptation. I can certainly resist what is good for me. With this unending addiction cycle there is no hope. We can get lost in the many experiments of trial and error. It didn't work in Dallas, so let me move to Las Vegas and see if it works there. Or, "OK, HOLY SPIRIT, I'll let you have this, this and this, but I'll keep this and that". Who are we really dealing with? A rose by any other name is still a rose. EGO by any other name is still EGO.

We have ascertained that our defects of character cause us pain and failure and we have decided what we want in their place. We ask HOLY SPIRIT to remove the defect and replace it with the asset. We reserve the right to choose what the asset is and if it isn't as rewarding as we expected, we can choose again. Maybe it wasn't the money I wanted to make me happy; I'll just pray for happiness the next time. But after years of listening to this nonsensical approach of EGO we become disillusioned and once again are hopeless and desperate. (Which isn't necessarily a bad thing, because we often have to reach a bottom before we are entirely ready.)

There is a story shared in AA meetings about a boy wanting a horse from his father. On his 16th birthday he got his horse and was so excited, but his father remained calm and said, "Son, I don't know if this is good or bad, it just is". The next morning the boy went outside to play with his horse, but the corral gate was open and the horse was gone. The boy went to his father very upset and his father said, "Son, I don't know if this is good or bad, it just is". That afternoon, the boy spotted his horse with several mares and was successfully able to get them all back into the corral. The elated son by went to his father and his father calmly said, "Son, I don't know if this is good or bad it just is". The boy went back out to the corral and one of the mares kicked him and broke his leg. The hired hand brought the boy into the house in a great deal of pain and anguish, but the father just remained calm and said, "Son, I don't know if this is good or bad it just is". Well the next morning a government man came to the ranch to draft his son into the military, but because of his broken leg.... The story can go on indefinitely, but by now you get the point.

Paramahansa Yogananda in his interpretation of THE BHAGAVAD GITA, Chapter 5, Verse 20 -The knower of Spirit, abiding in the Supreme, with unswerving discrimination, free from delusion, is thus neither jubilant at pleasant experiences nor downcast by unpleasant experiences says "The ordinary man never analyzes the lessons inherent in the cinema of daily life; he remains identified with those pictures, grieving or rejoicing as the case may be. The yogi who roasts in a fire of wisdom all seeds of new desires becomes free from the thralldom of reincarnation. Nevertheless, not having finished the effects of all past actions, he encounters in his present life good and evil happenings, health or disease, flowing from past karma. Possessing inner tranquility and the joy of Spirit, he is not excited at the advent of good fortune; neither is he depressed by calamities. He watches with a calm indifferent attitude the joyous and sorrowful scenes of his life. What have they to do with him? And Chapter Five Verse 21 states – "Unattracted to the sensory world, the yogi experiences the ever new joy inherent in the Self. Engaged in divine union of the soul with Spirit, he attains bliss indestructible. He says, "The Yogi learns to control his chitta (primordial feeling), overcoming all likes and dislikes relative to external objects. Detaching his attention from the outer world into his true inner Self, he perceives the ever-existing, ever conscious, ever-new joy of the soul. When the Self is fully established in union with Spirit, his ever new joy becomes immutable." (SRF)

Not all the truths are found in the first 164 pages of the AA text. There are many revelations shared in the stories. Dr. Paul discovered that "My serenity is inversely proportional to my expectations. The higher my expectations of Max and other people; the lower is my serenity. I can watch my serenity level rise when I discard my expectations. But then my rights try to move back in and they too can force my serenity level down. I have to discard my rights as well as my expectations, by asking myself, "How important is it? How important is it compared to my serenity, my emotional sobriety?" And when I place more value on my serenity and sobriety than on anything else, I can maintain them at a higher level..." (AA, Third Edition, Chapter entitled Doctor, Alcoholic, Addict).

ACIM provides a third way of motivation that can be applied to the Steps. It never happened. Sin is impossible. We have already been forgiven. There are no such things as defects of character. We are perfect creation of God. ACIM offers us another way out. From the ACIM Workbook <u>I am not a body. I am free. I am still as God created me</u>, it goes on to explain, "...The EGO holds the body dear because it dwells in it and lives united with the home that it has made. It is a part of the illusion that has sheltered it from being found illusory itself." <u>I walk with God in perfect holiness</u> explains, "Today's idea but states the simple truth that makes the thought of sin impossible. It promises there is no cause for guilt, and being causeless it does not exist. It follows surely from the basic thought so often mentioned in the text; ideas leave not their source. If this be true, how can you be apart from God? How could you walk the world alone and separated from your Source?" The HOLY SPIRIT teaches the principle of Atonement that

STEVEH.

separation from God never occurred. (ACIM)

This is all pretty heavy to be slammed with, especially when we are told in the AA text that "…We are not saints. The point is that we are willing to grow along spiritual lines. The principles we have set down are guides to progress. We claim spiritual progress rather than spiritual perfection." (AA) In an earlier edition of the AA text, a gentleman wrote, "I used to think I was God, now I know I am." Somewhere along the line EGO participated with AA sayings such as "I hope I never get what I deserve". If we are Gods, I hope I get what I deserve. I was told a story that God only says "Yes". If I say I don't deserve anything but bad things, God says, "Yes". If I say, "I deserve everything wonderful and holy", God says, "Yes". You can choose what works best for you. The above view of step 6 may be what the AA book <u>12 Steps & 12 Traditions</u> means when it says, "This is the Step that separates the men from the boys." After years of experience Bill says, "Let's dispose of what appears to be a hazardous open end we have left. It is suggested that we ought to become entirely willing to aim toward perfection. We note that some delay may be pardoned. That word, in the mind of the rationalizing" EGO "could certainly be given a long term meaning. He could say, "How very easy! Sure, I'll head toward perfection, but I'm certainly not going to hurry any. Maybe I can postpone dealing with some of my problems indefinitely". Of course, this won't do. Such a bluffing of oneself will have to go the way of many another pleasant rationalizations. At the very least, we shall have to come to grips with some of our worst character defects and take action toward their removal as quickly as we can." He also states earlier, "All of AA's 12 Steps ask us to go contrary to our natural desires…they deflate our ego." (AA)

OK, so are you entirely ready to do this step. The ACIM Workbook can greatly assist. Sayings such as: I am a blessed Son of God; My mind is part of God's; I am very holy; There is nothing my holiness cannot do; God goes with me wherever I go; God is the strength in which I trust; There is nothing to fear; I am sustained by the love of God; can get you through this. The following is a somewhat rephrased healing prayer from and organization called "Teaching of Inner Christ": "I call on the HOLY SPIRIT to heal and dissolve any negative thoughts and emotions that influence me adversely. I now ask that you remove _____, _____, _____, etc. and replace them with _____, _____, _____, etc. I now accept that I am healed and forgiven. Thank you. " (TIC)

STEP 7: WE HUMBLY ASKED HOLY SPIRIT TO REMOVE OUR SHORTCOMINGS. (AA)

The AA Text uses this prayer (the editor has changed the tense to plural, 1st person "we" to achieve a certain effect): HOLY SPIRIT "We are now willing that You have all of us, good and bad. We pray that You now remove from us every single defect of character which stands in the way of our usefulness to you and our fellows. Grant us strength, as we go from here, to do Your bidding". The AA text warns, "We ask especially for freedom from self-will, and are careful to make no request for ourselves only... We are careful never to pray for our own selfish ends. Many of us have wasted a lot of time doing that and it doesn't work. You can easily see why." (AA) The gender has been changed because we don't have to do this alone anymore. The highest spiritual position we can ever achieve is equal. We are one with everyone and everything else. As we forgive, we are forgiven. (We can now detach from the drama and pray for the murderers and forgive our enemies with ease; it's no longer personal.) The word "we" has been used with all the steps, but it's hard to get away from I (EGO). However, now as a group, we experience our power (when ever two or more are gathered). The last step laid it on thick and heavy and it is important to trudge through it and get to a place of peace. When we use the word "we", we see that our fears were only an illusion. What appeared to be a mountain was only a molehill. Here is a poem that has always been helpful (sorry cannot remember the author):

There is a special art to living and you need a frame of mind.
To overlook the showers till the sun begins to shine

There is a special art to living and you have to understand, That things don't always function in the way that they were planned.

There is a special art to living, and the challenge must be met. The longer that we try it the better we get.

Don't be caught waiting for the world to come to you. *We have to climb the mountain to appreciate the view. (Unk)*

The word humbly has also been used throughout the steps in parenthesis. But it is not until now that we should discuss the word because humility is not a singular, first person action. We are one in the great sea of God. HOLY SPIRIT was designed specifically to lead us away from temptation (EGO). EGO is first person singular and HOLY SPIRIT is first person plural. Humility is a spiritual concept and a very illusive word to comprehend on the playing field of EGO. It is often synonymous with open-minded, willing and honest. Others throw in teachable. Some of us grew up with a false sense of modesty that limits us from experiencing our good. In search of more information with an open mind, new concepts of humility were thrust upon me. Channeled works from the Teachings of Inner Christ (TIC) state: "...step forth into the acknowledgment of who and what you are, and no longer hold back, with reticence or some form of modesty, to wait until it is thrust upon you or provided to you. But search deep within you for the knowledge of your identity, and proclaim it to yourself and to the world. It has been said, "Do not hide your light under a bushel." No longer hide yourselves, but be yourselves and step out. Affirm it and claim it and know it, thereby helping all to know themselves. If you hide your faith shall you help another gain faith? If you hide your joy do you help another be joyful? Therefore, if you hide your awareness do you help another to know for himself his

STEVEH.

godhood? All are sons of the Most High God. You know it. Be it, claim it, say it, do it and help those around you to do the same... Do not try to seem less than you are for fear someone may think you proud. True humility is to be what you are....You are all equal with each other and with God, -- for you are God. There is no one on this earth who is not equal to Jesus. He who dares to claim Christhood shall have it. The love of God is such that He places you with Himself in love, gives you free will, showers upon you His love, His blessings, according to your claim and your acknowledgment; for He also gives you freedom to bind yourself as long as you wish." Remember "We are one with the Father". (TIC)

STEP 8: WE (HUMBLY) MADE A LIST OF ALL PERSONS WE HAD HARMED AND BECAME WILLING TO MAK AMENDS TO THEM ALL. (AA)

Amends are not apologies, begging for forgiveness or saying, "I'm sorry". Amends are not getting it off your chest and dumping it on another. Amends are not heroic actions or Herculean tasks. Amends are not a sack cloth and stick to beat ourselves with. Amends are permanent repairs for the betterment of all concerned. Amends are not necessarily aimed to help another as much as to help yourself (There are later steps for helping others). Amends clear up any misgivings and resentments about the past and bring the person into a healthy present. Note that this is another preparatory step which requires no outside action. We became willing. The "became" part may require some time. If fear and resentment linger, go back through the steps. Ask HOLY SPIRIT to remove them and replace them with forgiveness and courage. Also put the results into HOLY SPIRIT's hands. Much of the world is still dominated by EGO and may not applaud your actions. There is a story in the AA text entitled FREEDOM FROM BONDAGE which goes, "I've had many spiritual experiences (miracles) since I've been in the program, many that I didn't recognize right away, for I'm slow to learn and they take many guises. But one was so outstanding that I like to pass it on whenever I can in the hope that it will help someone else as it has me. As I said earlier, self-pity and resentment were my constant companions and my inventory began to look like a diary, for I seemed to have a resentment against everybody I had ever known. All but one responded to the treatment suggested in the Steps immediately, but this one posed a problem. It was against my mother and it was 25 years old. I had fed it, fanned it and nurtured it as one might a delicate child, and it had become as much a part of me as my breathing. It had provided me with excuses for my lack of education, my marital failures, personal failures, inadequacy, and of course, my alcoholism, and though I really thought I had been willing to part with it, now I knew I was reluctant to let it go. One morning, however, I realized I had to get rid of it, for my reprieve was running out, and if I didn't get rid of it I was going to get drunk -- and I didn't want to get drunk anymore. In my prayers that morning I asked HOLY SPIRIT to point out to me some way to be free of this resentment. During the day a friend of mine brought me some magazines to take to a hospital group I was interested in, and I looked through them and a banner across the front of one featured an article by a prominent clergyman in which I caught the word resentment. He said, in effect: "If you have a resentment you want to be free of, if you will pray for the person or the thing that you resent, you will be free. Ask for their health, their prosperity, their happiness, and you will be free. Even when you don't really want it for them and your prayers are only words and you don't mean it, go ahead and do it anyway. Do it everyday for two weeks and you will find you have come to mean it and want it for them, and you will realize where you used to feel bitterness and resentment and hatred, you now feel compassionate understanding and love." It worked for me then, and it has worked for me many times since, and it will work for me every time I am willing to work it. Sometimes I have to ask first for the willingness, but it too always comes. And because it works for me, it will work for all of us." (AA) Martin Luther King in his acceptance speech in Oslo, Norway for receiving the Nobel Peace Prize said, "I have chosen forgiveness because hatred is too much of a burden to bear." (MLK)

So we have a list of people in our lives, taken from our life story. We put the names down on paper. After each name, we write one sentence (we should be able to keep to one by now) for:
1 What happened?
2 What was my behavior?

3   What was the underlying cause (Was it our self-esteem, our ambitions, our security, our pride, jealousy, envy, competition, lost relations, which had been interfered with)?
4   When and if this situation arises with the same person (or surrogate) what would I like my behavior and emotions to be?

When you recognize that you are into the old emotions and behavior ask HOLY SPIRIT to bring you into the new desired action. Going into the new behavior and emotions with the help of HOLY SPIRIT is the amend. We don't have to pay back the IRS or College tuition unless it makes major improvements in our life and consciousness. We don't have to go back and confess crimes or subject ourselves to the retaliation of others. Follow the guidance of HOLY SPIRIT and not EGO. HOLY SPIRIT's ways are easy, effortless and joyous. The way of EGO will be a major and unrewarding task and you will remain unsatisfied. Ask HOLY SPIRIT if there is any restitution required and be prepared to hear that the answer is "NO".

STEP 9: MADE DIRECT AMENDS TO SUCH PEOPLE WHEREVER POSSIBLE, EXCEPT WHEN TO DO SO WOULD INJURE YOURSELF OR OTHERS. (AA)

The preparatory steps are quite the deal, but when we get ready to take action, we find that the HOLY SPIRIT has passed judgment, "NOT GUILTY". The object of the step is to be rid of guilt. If you feel you must go and perform some great and noble deed of amends, by all means do so. But later you may find out it wasn't necessary. Consult with someone before doing this step and as in the story "The Richest Man in Babylon" don't go to a brick layer and ask questions about jewels. In my own personal experience, the alcoholism rehab center I attended in Washington D.C. took us out daily to various types of AA meetings. (In the early 80's, there were more than 700 AA meetings a week in the D.C. area.) I went to a meeting that was discussing amends and I asked about my going back to my home and making restitution for things I did over ten years ago as a juvenile delinquent. (I was presently married and had a child.) Most everyone that commented advised me that I should do so. I said to myself, "Yea, sure, looks like I won't be hanging around this AA thing for too long". After the meeting two guys came up to me and shared with me some of their exploits. They asked how long I had been working the steps. I told them that I had been in rehab for 29 days. They explained that I had the rest of my life to do them and that is where they warned me about asking questions in the meetings and gave me the "drink of water -fire hose" slogan. So I waited (for about 5 years). I was in a meeting one day and this guy really sounded good about what he knew about amends, so afterwards I told him my story and asked him about making restitution for my juvenile delinquency. He thought that I should, so I wrote my sister asking her for some addresses of some of our neighbors. She wrote back and asked if I had gone mad. In the mean time my advisor had gone back to drinking and I found out that he wasn't sober for very long. He had a lot of knowledge about AA from his numerous attempts at sobriety and he sure talked a good game. Amends are ongoing and later I did go to my 25th high school reunion and also visited some of the neighbors and talked. All had forgotten and it was just me carrying around the rock. I also learned that drunks often do have some excellent advice; it's just that they can't live by it because they never have developed the discipline.

The amends aren't any big deal but developing discipline and vigilance to stay with the HOLY SPRIT is on the other hand, quite a task, for EGO is a subtle foe. Many of us come from an undisciplined background and find that it is something that cannot be developed overnight. But fear not, the memory of this rewarding experience will register and we will be brought back with the desire to experience the miracle again. Like in AA, daily meetings and joining with peers and like souls and sharing of your strengths and weakness can be of great benefit. The AA text says: "It is easy to let up on the spiritual program of action and rest on our laurels. We are headed for trouble if we do, for" EGO "is a subtle foe. We are not cured of" EGO. "What we have is a daily reprieve contingent upon the maintenance of our spiritual condition. Every day is a day when we must carry the vision of God's (HOLY SPIRIT's) will into all of our activities. "How can we best serve Thee--Thy will (not ours) be done." These are the thoughts which must go with us constantly. We can exercise our will power along this line all we wish. It is the proper use of the will". (AA) The ACIM text and workbook can be very beneficial with daily spiritual maintenance.

STEVE H.

Rewording some paragraphs from an AA story entitled THE KEYS TO THE KINGDOM, will let you know that this "is not a plan....that can be finished and done with. It is a way of life, and the challenge contained in its principles is great enough to keep any human being striving for as long as he lives. We do not, cannot outgrow this plan....we must have a program for living that allows for limitless expansion. Keeping one foot in front of the other is essential...retrogression can spell death for us. However it isn't as rough as it sounds, as we do become grateful for the necessity that makes us tow the line, and we find that we are compensated for a consistent effort by the countless dividends we receive." (AA)

From AA text, THERE IS A SOLUTION it says "Almost none of us liked the self searching, the leveling of our pride, the confession of shortcomings (and service to others) which the process requires for its successful consummation. But we saw that it really worked in others, and we had come to believe in the hopelessness and futility of life as we had been living it. When, therefore, we were approached by those in whom the problem (EGO) had been solved, there was nothing left for us but to pick up the simple kit of spiritual tools laid at our feet. We have found much of heaven and we have been rocketed into a fourth dimension of existence of which we had not even dreamed (HOLY SPIRIT). The great fact is just this and nothing less: That we have had deep and effective spiritual experiences (miracles) which have revolutionized our whole attitude toward life, toward our fellows and toward God's universe. The central fact of our lives today is the absolute certainty that our Creator has entered into our hearts and lives in a way which indeed is miraculous. He has commenced to accomplish those things for us which we could never do by ourselves." (AA)

The following is an account of Bill Wilson's experience, "There I humbly offered myself to God, as I then understood Him, to do with me as He would. I placed myself unreservedly under His care and direction. I admitted for the first time that of myself I was nothing; that without Him I was lost. I ruthlessly faced my sins and became willing to have my new-found Friend take them away, root and branch...My school mate visited me and I fully acquainted him with my problems and deficiencies. We made a list of people I had hurt or toward whom I felt resentment. I expressed my entire willingness to approach these individuals, admitting my wrong. Never was I to be critical of them. I was to right all such matters to the utmost of my ability. I was to test my thinking by the new God-consciousness within. Common sense would thus become uncommon sense. I was to sit quietly when in doubt, asking only for direction and strength to meet my problems as He would have me. Never was I to pray for myself, except as my requests bore on my usefulness to others. Then only might I expect to receive. But that would be in great measure. My friend promised when these things were done I would enter upon a new relationship with my Creator; that I would have the elements of a way of living which answered all my problems. Belief in the power of God, plus enough willingness, honesty and humility to establish and maintain the new order of things, were the essential requirements. Simple, but not easy; a price had to be paid. It meant destruction of self-centeredness (EGO). I must turn in all things to the Father of Light who presides over us all. These were revolutionary and drastic proposals, but the moment I fully accepted them, the effect was electric. There was a sense of victory, followed by such an utter confidence. I felt lifted-up, as though the great clean wind of a mountain top blew through and through. God comes to most men gradually, but His impact on me was sudden and profound. For a moment I was alarmed and called on my friend, the doctor, to ask if I were still sane. He listened in wonder as I talked. Finally he shook his head saying, "Something has happened to you I don't understand. But you had better hang on to it. Anything is better than the way you were." The good doctor now sees many men who have had such experiences. He knows that they are real." (AA)

Editor's note: Please know that the editor of this proposal has never entirely surrendered his EGO to HOLY SPIRIT nor has he had a complete psychic change. Nor in all my extracurricular spiritual studies have I met an avatar. I have studied the lives of some saints and my EGO mind has found them wanting. I even heard a rumor that Saint Theresa was very unkind to her co-workers. I am at battle with EGO on a daily basis and I hang on dearly to many defects of character. My experience has been on a slow learning process as explained in the AA Text under Appendix II entitled SPIRITUAL EXPERIENCES which (with some rewording) states: The terms spiritual experience and spiritual awakening are used many times in this book which, upon careful reading, shows that the personality change sufficient to bring about recovery from alcoholism (EGO) has manifested itself among us in many forms. Yet it is true that our first printing gave many readers the impression that these personality changes, or religious experiences, must be in the nature sudden and spectacular upheavals. Happy for everyone, this conclusion is erroneous. In the first few chapters a number of sudden revolutionary changes are described. Though it was not our intention to create such an impression, many…have nevertheless concluded that in order to recover they must acquire an immediate and overwhelming "God-consciousness" followed at once by a vast change in feeling and outlook. Among our rapidly growing membership of thousands…such transformations, though frequent, are by no means the rule. Most of our experiences are what the psychologist William James calls the "educational variety" because they develop slowly over a period of time. Quite often friends of the newcomer are aware of the difference long before he has undergone a profound alteration in his reaction to life: that such a change could hardly have been brought about by himself alone. What often takes place in a few months could seldom have been accomplished by years of self-discipline. With few exceptions our members find that they have tapped an unsuspected inner resource which they presently identify with their own conception of" HOLY SPIRIT. "Most of us think this awareness of" HOLY SPIRIT "is the essence of spiritual experience. Our more religious members call it "God-consciousness". Most emphatically we wish to say that any" one "can recover (from EGO), provided he does not close his mind to spiritual concepts. He can only be defeated by an attitude of intolerance or belligerent denial. We find that no one need have difficulty with spirituality of the program. Willingness, honesty and open mindedness are the essentials of recovery. But these are indispensable. " (AA)

"There is a principle which is bar against all information, which is proof against all arguments and which cannot fail to keep a man in everlasting ignorance--that principle is contempt prior to investigation" _ HERBERT SPENCER. (AA)

The purpose of this proposal is to provide the AA information for the benefit of others as they may see fit and perhaps assist ACIM (in the following Chapters) with getting their information out to others in a way that has worked for AA. I just didn't want to skip over a fantastic method of achieving miracles. We have discovered that no matter how poorly we have attempted these steps they have brought extraordinary good into our lives.

THE DISAPPEARANCE OF THE UNIVERSE provides some practical layman information about

STEVEH.

HOLY SPIRIT and forgiveness: "The HOLY SPIRIT takes the very device the EGO made to protect itself and uses it to undo it. HOLY SPIRIT devices can only be used for good. Don't worry about the results that may or may not be seen on the level of form. Be grateful for what forgiveness and the HOLY SPIRIT are doing for you. By forgiving your brothers and sisters ... you are rejoining with what you really are. You're telling the world and the bodily images you see that their behavior cannot have any effect on you, and if they can't have any effect on you, then they don't really exist separately from you. Thus, there is no separation of any kind in reality -- which brings us to the final major component of the attitude of forgiveness: Trust the HOLY SPIRIT and choose His strength. The peace of the HOLY SPIRIT will be given to you if you do your job. He will heal the larger, unconscious mind that is hidden from you, and give you His peace at the same time. This peace may not always come right away, and sometimes it will. Sometimes it may surprise you in the form of something happening that would usually upset you -- except this time it doesn't. All this will lead you the Kingdom of Heaven, for along with the HOLY SPIRIT, you are doing the work that leads to the condition of peace -- which is the condition of the Kingdom. Forgiveness is actually preparing you to re-enter the Kingdom of Heaven. (Renard)

ACIM says, "There is a very simple way to find the door to true forgiveness, and perceive it open wide in welcome. When you feel that you are tempted to accuse someone of sin in any form, do not allow your mind to dwell on what you think he did, for that is self-deception. Ask instead, "Would I accuse myself of doing this?" (ACIM)

Paramahansa Yogananda in his rendition of the Bhagavad Gita states: "The Gita instructs: the devotee dies fighting his evil impulses rather than to succumb to them and again be enmeshed in the miseries of incarnation. The yogi is advised not only to remain concentrated on the divine bliss during meditation but to feel it during activity, in order to successfully combat the prompting of past harmful impulses buried in the subconscious mind. A person who fails to carry over the bliss of meditation into the activities of his daily life is liable to be overwhelmed by sudden remembrances of past evil worldly experiences. The yogi who always feels the inner joy of the soul is able to subdue any erratic emotional urges." (SRF)

OH hell, why not one more AA story, too, just for good-measure: A father returns from Louisiana and gives his daughter some bright shiny white Mardi-Gras beads that look like pearls and the little girl is delighted. Everywhere she goes, she proudly wears the beads. She even sleeps with them. Every so often the father asks his daughter if he can have them back, but the little girl never wants to let go of the beads. One time, however after the girl has grown some, the father asks again if he can have the beads back and his daughter gives them back to him. The father then gives the girl a string of real pearls, much more beautiful and valuable than the plastic beads. That is what our Father wants for us. I hope you get what you deserve.

STEP 10: WE (HUMBLY) CONTINUED TO TAKE PERSONAL INVENTORY AND WHEN WE WERE WRONG (AND IN EGO) WE PROMPTLY ADMITTED IT (TO OUR-SELF, HOLY SPIRIT, AND ANOTHER HUMAN BEING [AND NOT NECESSARILY THE ONE SUPPOSEDLY WRONGED]). (AA)

I'm sorry usually doesn't work. Sometimes the amend is to remove yourself from interaction and take yourself out of the equation. Nothing needs to be said. Sometimes we need to represent ourselves. A psychological technique for constructive confrontation is to (again one sentence will do just fine): 1. Praise the person; 2. State what happened; 3. State your feelings; 4. (and if at all possible) ask what can we do about it, however these techniques can grossly backfire especially the first couple of trial runs. Ask for guidance, strength and courage from HOLY SPIRIT. No one rule applies. There is the "do nothing" technique and let the problem resolve itself. The whole idea of step ten is that once you cleaned house, keep it clean. Yes, we are sometimes wrong. There really isn't a hero and a villain. Things aren't so black and white. One person isn't right and the other is wrong. Neither party remembers or tells the story correctly. In EGO, both parties are wrong (guilty); in HOLY SPIRIT both are right (innocent). Current books about successful negotiation discuss "Win – Win" techniques. In the 80's when I took a computer programming class, the language (most likely very obsolete by now) had what was called a loop or a "IF _ THEN" statement and it would send you back to earlier functions if you met the conditions of the IF statement. Therefore, IF you are wrong, THEN go back to step 1 and work your way back through nine. "The longer that you try it the better you will get" Remember this is a come as you are party. HOLY SPIRIT can finance you no matter what your credit history has been. Don't let mistakes put you into EGO state of mind. Do not entertain guilt, remorse, shame, hopelessness, self pity, "what's the use" thinking. They are all on the negative side of the ledger. Work the steps to get your self back into a content state of mind and stay there, joined with us and HOLY SPIRIT, as long as you can. The EGO system is a design for failure, misery and hopelessness, so don't be surprised if EGO gets the best of you. EGO is cunning, baffling and powerful. Alone you stand little chance. You are lucky if 10% of the people you know are concerned for your well being, another 80% are only concerned about there own, but beware there is another 10% who may be glad you have troubles and enjoy making them worse. My EGO doesn't like me very well, but it doesn't like your EGO much better. Another warning is that EGO does not want to be smashed. It has a very strong sense of survival and believes it can continue living even if we die. It is not willing to surrender and is very capable of keeping a destructive pace with the corrections HOLY SPIRIT makes. Once you start on this path, many things will come your way to divert you, distract you and defeat you. Stay joined with us in meetings, prayer and meditation. Do not leave your mind idle for it is the devil's (EGO's) playground. Fill your waking hours with positive activity. Substitution is a very effective cure for addiction and bad habits and behavior. Some substitute alcohol for drugs, then antibuse for alcohol, then AA meetings, then spirituality. The substitute must have the desired effect or it will not make a sufficient substitute. The reward must register somewhere in the mind. If the AA meetings and the subsequent spirituality did not give me the same or better high that I was looking for in drugs and alcohol, I would by default seek out the old feelings to escape pain of EGO. We must find a sufficient substitute for EGO.

In lesson 136, ACIM says," No one can heal unless they understand what purpose sickness seems to serve. For then they understand as well its purpose has no meaning. Being causeless and without a meaningful intent of any kind, it cannot be at all. When this is seen, healing is automatic. It dispels this meaningless illusion by the same approach that carries all of them to truth, and merely leaves them there to disappear. Sickness is not an accident. Like all defenses, it is an insane device for self-deception. And like all the rest, its purpose is to hide reality, attack it, change it, render it inept, distort it, twist it, or reduce it to a little pile of unassembled parts. The aim of all defenses is to keep the truth from being whole. The parts are seen as if each one were whole within itself. Defenses are not unintentional, nor are they made without awareness. They are secret, magic wands we wave when the truth appears to threaten what we would believe. They seem to be unconscious but because of the rapidity with which we choose to use them. In that second, even less, in which the choice is made, we recognize exactly what we would attempt to do, and then proceed to think that it is done. Who but ourselves evaluates a threat, decides escape is necessary, and sets up a series of defenses to reduce the threat that has been judged as real? All this cannot be done unconsciously. But, so it seems to be external to our own intent, a happening beyond our state of mind, an outcome with a real effect on us. Instead of one effected by our self. It is this quick forgetting of the part we play in making our reality that makes defenses seem to be beyond our own control. But what we have forgotten can be remembered, given willingness to reconsider the decision which is doubly shielded by oblivion. Our not remembering is but a sign that this decision still remains in force, as far as our desires are concerned. Mistake not this for fact. Defenses must make facts unrecognizable. They aim at doing this and it is this they do. Every defense takes fragments of the whole, assembles them without regard to all their true relationships, and thus constructs illusions of a whole that is not there. It is this process that imposes threat, and not whatever outcome may result. When parts are wrested from the whole and seen as separate and wholes within themselves, they become symbols standing for attack upon the whole; successful in effect, and never to be seen as whole again. And yet you have forgotten that they stand but for your own decision of what should be real, to take the place of what is real. Sickness is a decision. It is not a thing that happens to us, quite unsought, which makes us weak and brings us to suffer. It is a choice we make, a plan we lay, when for an instant truth arises in our own deluded mind, and all the world appears to totter and prepare to fall. Now are we sick, that truth may go away and threaten our establishment no more. How do we think that sickness can succeed in shielding us from truth? Because it proves our body is not separate from us, and so we must be separate from truth. We suffer pain because our body does, and in this pain are we made one with it. Thus our 'true" identity preserved, and the strange, haunting thought that we might be something beyond this little pile of dust silenced and stilled. For see, this dust can make us suffer, twist our limbs and stop our heart, commanding us to die and cease to be. Thus the body is stronger than the truth, which asks we live, but cannot overcome our choice to die. And so the body is more powerful than everlasting life, Heaven more frail than hell, and God's design for the salvation of His Son opposed by a decision stronger than His Will. His Son is dust, The Father incomplete, and chaos sits in triumph on His throne. Such is our planning for our own defense. And we believe that Heaven quails before such mad attacks as these, with God made blind by our illusions, truth turned into lies, and all the universe made slave to laws which our defenses would impose on it. Yet who believes illusions but the one who made them up? Who else can see them and act to them as if they were the truth? God knows not of our plans to change His Will. The universe remains unheeding of the lies by which we thought to govern it. And Heaven has not bowed to hell, nor life to death. We can but choose to think we die, or suffer sickness or distort the truth, in any way. What is created is apart from all of this. Defenses are plans to defeat what cannot be attacked. What is unalterable cannot change. And what is wholly sinless cannot sin. Such is the simple truth. It does not command obedience, nor seek to prove how pitiful and futile our attempts to plan defenses that would alter it. Truth merely wants to give us happiness, for such its purpose is. Perhaps it sighs a little when we throw away its gifts, and yet it knows, with perfect certainty, that what God wills for us must be received. It is this fact that demonstrates that time is an illusion. For time lets us think what God has given us is not the truth right now, as it must be. The Thoughts of God are quite apart from time. For time is but another meaningless defense we made against truth. Yet what He wills is here and we remain as He created us. Truth has a power far beyond defense, for no illusions can remain where truth has been allowed to enter. And it comes to any mind that would lay down its arms, and cease to play with folly. It is found at any time; today, if we will choose to practice giving welcome to the truth. This is our aim today... And truth will come, for it has never been apart from us. It merely waits for just this invitation which we give today. We introduce it with a healing prayer, to help us rise above defensiveness, and let truth be as it has always been. Sickness is a defense against the truth. I will accept the truth of what I am, and let my mind be wholly healed today. Healing will flash across our mind, as peace and truth arise to take the place of war and vain imaginings. There will be no dark corners sickness can conceal, and keep defended from the light of truth. There will be no dim figures from your dreams, not their obscure and meaningless pursuits with double purposes insanely sought, remaining in our mind. It will be healed of all the sickly wishes that it tried to authorize our body to obey. Now is our body healed, because the source of sickness has been opened to relief; And we will recognize we practiced well by this: Our body should not feel at all. If you have been successful, there will be no sense of feeling ill or feeling well, of pain or pleasure. No response at all is in the mind to what our body does. Its usefulness remains and nothing more. Perhaps we do not realize that this removes the limits we had placed upon the body by purposes we gave to it. As these are laid aside, the strength our body has will always be enough to serve all truly useful purposes. Our body's health is fully guaranteed, because it is not limited by time, by weather or fatigue, by food and drink, or any laws we made, for sickness has become impossible. Yet this protection needs to be preserved by careful watching. If we let our mind harbor attack thoughts, yield to judgment or make plans against uncertainties to come, we may have again misplaced ourself, and made a bodily identity which will attack our body, for our mind is sick. Give instant remedy, should this occur, by not allowing our defensiveness to hurt us longer. Do not be confused about what must be healed, but tell ourself:

We have forgotten what we really are, for we mistook our body for our self. Sickness is a defense against the truth. But we are not a body. And our mind cannot attack. So we cannot be sick. (ACIM)

The steps are designed to restore your power and not leave you in a powerless state. Our emotions are the guidepost (and warning bells) that tells us how much power we have in the tank. The book "ASK AND IT IS GIVEN" by Jerry and Ester Hicks, points out, "...remember that our emotions indicate our degree of alignment with Source Energy and the better we feel, the more we are allowing our alignment with the things we desire, then it is easier to understand how to respond to our emotions. Absolute alignment with Source Energy means that we know we are free, powerful, valuable, happy and joyous. At any time that we are thinking thoughts that cause us to know our true nature, we are in alignment with who we really are....the way those thoughts feel is the ultimate emotion of connection."... "In terms of a fuel gauge on a vehicle, this state of alignment would be a full tank."... "Imagine a gauge or scale with graduations or degrees, which indicate the position of the fullest allowance of our connection with Source Energy all the way down to the emptiest, most resistant disallowance of our alignment with Source Energy." (Hicks) Use your own words to describe your feelings, but an example would be something like this:

Full empowerment Happy, Joyous, Free, Grateful

3/4 empowerment Optimism, Hopefulness, Positive Expectations

1/2 empowerment Complacent, Boredom, Coasting

1/4 empowerment Discouraged, Doubt & Worry, Pessimism

Empty Unworthy, Angry, Depressed, Powerless

We can fill up in increments or the whole tank. Inspirational books can fill us up. A massage, a movie or a nice walk can fill us up. Meetings can fill us up. AA warns not to get too hungry, too angry, too lonely or too tired (HALT). We need to watch our gauge and fill up routinely. By working the steps we reach for a higher state of mind. As you go up the steps, identify what thoughts cause what feelings, and choose thoughts that give you feeling of relief. Being complacent might be very good for you if you were coming from depression. From complacency you can optimistically set some goals and hope to become happy, joyous and free again. Try not to let anyone judge you or bring you back down, but if they do, turn back to the steps until your feelings improve again. Try to stay in gratitude as long as you can. There are many techniques from the above referenced book that you can try or just do the old standard - make a list of the things you are grateful for. If you stayed grateful for an hour, next time go for two; then a day, a week, a month. I knew a man that claimed he never had a bad day, he might sometimes have a few bad moments, but they are relatively short. I guess as the saying goes, we are as happy as we make up our mind to be. Remember that "Today is the future you created yesterday".

It's OK to be a Pollyanna, but don't be so naive to allow abuse to come your way. The AA text says (twice) that we have quit fighting everyone and everything. Well we may have quit fighting alcohol (and EGO), but not everyone else has stopped fighting and competing and their EGO may not like you just because you are so happy. Be careful not to make yourself the doormat or scape-goat in social settings. People not aspiring to be spiritual and still in EGO are often envious, greedy, jealous, conspiring, and outright hateful and spiteful. (And sometimes it comes out from the ones you trust the most.) The AA code is patience and tolerance of others. We are hard on ourselves, but we are considerate of others. Working the steps is not like the country western song played backwards that gets you the wife, the house and the truck back. The steps may not raise you above others for promotion, riches or fame. Pride is on the debit side of the inventory list. The highest position that you can obtain is equal to your brother (when EGO would tell us he is slob, criminal, or snooty snob). We place ourselves to be in maximum service to others. Our leaders serve, they never govern. The master washed the feet of his disciples.

STEP 11: WE (HUMBLY) SOUGHT THROUGH PRAYER AND MEDITATION TO IMPROVE OUR CONSCIOUS CONTACT WITH GOD (THROUGH HOLY SPIRIT) PRAYING ONLY FOR KNOWLEDGE OF HIS WILL FOR US AND THE POWER TO CARRY THAT OUT. (AA)

At this point, the editor's number one recommendation is to start ACIM, Text, Workbook or Teacher's Manual, which ever feels right for you. With ACIM we can learn anything and everything we might want to know about prayer and meditation. The book speaks for itself and can be done alone or with a group. The following chapters in this proposal are suggestions for developing groups and meetings to study, learn and teach ACIM by using the experience of AA. In AA it is said "The Steps prevent us from killing ourselves and the Traditions prevent us from killing each other". Ideas on how to hold and regulate meetings, where to hold them, etc. will be discussed later. It is best to get into the reading of ACIM by yourself and establish a relationship with the author, source of ACIM, first. However, for the benefit of the readers and for those who may not be ready for ACIM, the editor of this proposal would also like to discuss other concepts and teachings of prayer and mediation that he has encountered.

At age 40, my second wife left me, my daughter went back to live with her mother, I was demoted on the job, and I was very despondent. The AA text talks about a complete psychic change, which was obviously something that I had never experienced. I have always applied overkill for solving my problems (complete immersion). I returned to going to catholic mass, which was very beneficial. I continued with daily AA discussion meetings and AA book and step study meetings. I sought out professional help and I sought out other 12 step recovery groups for emotions and sexual addictions. Hypnotherapy opened the door for my exploration into the vast metaphysical world. I began reading ACIM and later started attending a class. In the class I met people who referred me to many other activities. Some of my favorites have been the First Church of Religious Science, Teachings of the Inner Christ and Effortless Prosperity (which I am sure more information can be obtained from the Web, if interested.) I also became interested in and attended several sessions with The Monroe Institute. I also read a tremendous amount of metaphysical literature and text books. (I have always had an intuitive sense that has led me to certain books or classes appropriate for me at the time; find yours). The reading lifted me and occupied my thoughts. I attended classes on prayer and meditation. I learned different methods of prayer and how to focus my thoughts. A friend of mine in AA would always say "There are two hungry dogs living inside of us and they are fighting each other. One is positive and one is negative. The one we choose to feed will be the one that wins." I read a book a while back called, GOD'S PRESCRIPTION, which said basically, that if we are not feeling well and go to a Doctor, he may give us a prescription to take something, several times a day, for several weeks, until we are better. The author suggested if we are not feeling spiritually well, why not use God's Rx; he suggested using a peaceful Psalm, such as the 23rd and take it in the morning, at lunch, dinner and when you go to bed; and take it for several weeks. I used a newer version of the Bible that had a modern translation of English (for easier reading and comprehension) and the prescription was very effective.

    Because the Lord is my Shepard,
       I have everything I need,
  He lets me rest in the meadow grass,
  He leads me beside the quiet streams,

STEVEH.

> He restores my failing health,
> He helps me do what honors
> Him most Even when walking
> through the shadow of death,
>
> I will not be alone,
> For He walks with me,
> Guarding and guiding the way,
> He has provided delicious food for me,
> In the presence of my enemies,
> He has anointed me as His son,
> Only goodness and mercy shall be with me,
> For the days of my life,
> And afterwards I will live with Him,
> Forever in His home.. (23rd Psalm)

The best book on prayer that I have encountered is THE SCIENCE OF MIND by Ernest Holmes: "The Science of Mind is based entirely upon the supposition that we are surrounded by a Universal Mind, into which we think. This Mind, in Its original state, fills all space. It fills the space that man uses in the Universe. It is in man, as well as outside him. As he thinks into the Universal Mind, he sets a law in motion, which is creative, and which contains within Itself a Limitless possibility. The Law through which man operates is Infinite, but man appears to be finite; that is, he has not yet evolved to a complete understanding of himself. He is unfolding from a Limitless Potential but can bring into his experience only that which he can conceive. There is no limit to the Law, but there appears to be a limit to man's understanding of It. As his understanding unfolds, his possibilities of attainment will increase." "Prayer does something to the mind of the one praying. It does not do anything to God. The Eternal Gift is always made. The Gift of God is the Nature of God, the Eternal Giving-ness. God cannot help making the gift, because God is the Gift." "There can be no gift without the receiver. It is said "To as many as received Him, to them gave He the power. We seek to uncover the science of prayer: the essence of the Spirit embodied in it. We find that the essence of the power of prayer is faith and acceptance. In addition to the law of faith and acceptance, the law of mental equivalents must be considered. These are the great laws with which we have to deal and we shall never get away from either. If prayer has been answered, it is not because God has been moved to answer one man and not another, but because one man has moved himself into a right relationship with the Spirit." "Since we are thinking beings and cannot stop thinking" (except through meditation) "and since Creative Mind receives our thought and cannot stop creating, It must always be creating something for us. What It will make depends wholly upon what we are thinking, and what we shall attract will depend upon that which our thoughts dwell. Thought can attract to us that which we first mentally embody, that which has become a part of our mental makeup, a part of our inner understanding. Every person is surrounded by a thought atmosphere. This mental atmosphere is the direct result of his conscious and unconscious thought, which in it turn, becomes the direct reason for, and cause of that which comes into his life. Through this power we are either attractive or repelling. Like attracts like and it is also true that we may become attracted to something which is greater than our previous experience." "Man must bring himself to a place in mind where there is no misfortune, no calamity, no accident, no trouble, no confusion; where there is nothing but plenty, peace, power, Life and

Truth. He should definitely, daily (using his own name) declare the Truth about himself, realizing that he is reflecting his statements into consciousness and that they will be operated upon by It. This is called, in mysticism, High Invocation: invoking the Divine Mind, implanting within It, seed of thought relative to oneself. And this is why some of the teachers of olden times used to instruct their pupils to cross their hands over their chests and say:" Wonderful, wonderful, wonderful, me!" definitely teaching them that as they mentally held themselves, so they would be held. "Act as though I am and I will be." One of the ancient sayings is that "To the man who can perfectly practice inaction, all things are possible." This sounds like a contradiction until one penetrates its inner meaning, for it is only when one completely practices inaction that he arrives at the point of the true actor, for he then realized that the act and the actor are one and the same: that cause and effect are the same: which is simply a different way of saying "Know the truth and the truth shall make you free." (SOM)

Like learning the piano or a foreign language, it will take most us many years to master the art of prayer. When my daughter was young, I just assumed that teaching her to tie her shoes would be a matter of a couple weeks, but parenting shows us just how long it takes us to learn things. (It took me a couple of years to teach her how to tie her shoes). For a child's first attempt at writing the letter A until it is accomplished is many years. We assume that as adults our learning abilities are different and we can learn these things rapidly, and if we can't do it like a master, then we quit or become distracted with something else. Worse yet is when we teach ourselves without the benefit of a master or teacher, we find that we have developed habits too difficult to overcome. We have many habits from our childhood education and experience that influence our concepts of God and how to pray. Some of us hold a view point that God is some far off being and we approach him with doubt wondering if by some luck we might be able to persuade or placate Him. In AA, we say the Serenity Prayer, "God grant me the courage to accept the things I cannot change...." and like the Lord's Prayer, it is a command. We don't say, "God, if you have the time and aren't too busy, could I please have some bread for this day?" We use the command form: "Grant me…", "Give us…", "Lead us…", etc.

Ernest Holmes' book SCIENCE OF MIND (SOM) says the following about prayer, "Nothing could bring greater discouragement than to labor under the delusion that God is a Being of moods, who might answer some prayers and not others. It would be difficult to believe in a God who cares more for one person than another. There can be no God who is kindly disposed one day and cruel the next; there can be no God who creates us …and then eternally punishes us when we make a mistake. God is a Universal Presence, and impersonal Observer, a Divine and impartial Giver, forever pouring Himself into His Creation. Most men who believe in God believe in prayer, but our idea of prayer changes as our idea of God changes; and it is natural for each to feel that his way of praying is the correct way. But we should bear in mind that the prayers which are effective--no matter whose prayers they may be-- are effective because they embody certain universal principles which, when understood, can be consciously used. If God ever answered prayer, he always answers prayer since He is "the same yesterday, today and forever". If there seems to be any failure it is in man's ignorance or misunderstanding of the Will and Nature of God. We are told that "God is Spirit, and they that worship Him must worship Him in spirit and truth." The immediate availability of the Divine Spirit is "neither in the mountain nor at the temple; neither lo, here, nor lo there, for behold the Kingdom of God is within". This is a true perception of spiritual power. The power is no longer I, but "the Father who dwelleth in me". Could we conceive of Spirit as being incarnate in us--while at the same time being ever more than that which is incarnated--would we not expand spiritually and intellectually? Would not our prayers be answered before they were uttered? "The Kingdom of God is within you." When we become conscious of our Oneness with Universal Good, beliefs in evil, sin, sickness, limitation, and death tend to disappear. We shall no longer "ask amiss," supplicating as though God were not willing, begging as though He were withholding. "If ye abide in me and my words abide in you, ye shall ask what ye will and it shall be done unto you." This gives great light on an important law governing the answering of prayer. Abiding in Him means having no consciousness separate from His consciousness--nothing in our thought which denies the power and presence of Spirit. Yes, we can readily see why prayers are answered when we are abiding in Him. Again we read, "Whatsoever ye shall ask in my name, that will I do". This sounds simple at first, but it is another profound statement like unto the first; its significance lies in the phrase: "in my name". In His name, means like His Nature. If our thought is as unsullied as the Mind of God, if we are recognizing our Oneness with God, we cannot pray for other than the good of all men. In such prayer we should not dwell upon evil," sickness or "adversity. The secret of spiritual power lies in a consciousness of one's union with the Whole, and of the availability of Good. God is accessible to all people." (SOM)

Why not try reading the above paragraph, twice a day for two weeks. At least you will get a Spiritual High, but be careful not to quit the day job. We often get so lofty with new spiritual ideas, that we can create some problems in our earthly existence. Don't run any red lights and it's a good idea to stay in touch and consult with someone before making any major decisions. (EGO will come up with some great escape plans that sound good but will leave you on the rocks and wanting: e.g. maybe I should quit my job and go to a monastery; I think that I'll leave my family and move to a new town; etc.) But don't succumb to fear and settle for less. Remember, you are responsible for your well being. It is, however, easy to develop some wrong ideas about prayer. If you are out to win the Lotto, get a new car or girlfriend, or levitate, you might be disappointed with prayer. If you win the Lotto, you would also have the spiritual responsibility to use the money for the betterment of all. Prayer does not satisfy greed, gluttony, jealousy, pride, envy, anger etc. Pantajali writes how to obtain all the same metaphysical qualities that his successor Jesus used, the catch is that when we become that spiritually advanced we will no longer have any need to do those things. With time we learn to pray for happiness rather than an object or condition that our EGO says will make us happy. And we learn to pray for everyone concerned. For instance a friend is having surgery: we pray for perfect divine goodness for the person, family and friends, the surgeon, anesthetist, nurses, lab techs, etc. and know whatever the result, it is Divine Will. Prayer does not make my will or the will of EGO to take place, but instead it makes our will coincide with God's will. If you are happy and content, no matter what your walk in life is, that is a sign that you are in God's will.

Another method of developing discipline with your thinking is called Spiritual Treatment. It is a form of prayer designed to align the mind into the Mind of God. It is taken from a formula that the Lord's Prayer provides: (1) Recognition of God, (2) Unification with God, (3) Claim and Accept our Good, (4) Thanksgiving and Release. The treatment is in the present tense and we state the facts. First we decide what it is that we wish to treat for. Remember it is called Spiritual Treatment and not Material Treatment. Some ideas are happiness, satisfaction, success, contentment, peace, truth, joy. The recognition is: Holy Sprit is happiness." (Try to stay in the

Absolute). Unification is "We are happy" (It's not much fun being happy alone). Claim: "We now claim and accept our happiness." (Ask HOLY SPIRIT to remove or dissolve any negative thought forms that would take away our happiness.) Thank Holy Spirit and "Don't worry, Be Happy". The following example is just to show how one can start with prayer treatment (unifying with Holy Spirit in the plural):

Title: This treatment is to express a deep and unconditional love

Recognition:
1. Holy Spirit expresses deep and unconditional love
2. Holy Spirit is True Love
3. Holy Spirit is Perfect Love
4. Holy Spirit is Absolute Love
5. Holy Spirit is Infinite Love
6. Holy Spirit is Abundant Love
7. Holy Spirit is Profound Love
8. Holy Spirit is Complete Love
9. Holy Spirit is Opulent Love
10. Holy Spirit is Eternal Love

Unification:
1. We express deep and unconditional love
2. We are True Love
3. We are Perfect Love
4. We are Absolute Love
5. We are Infinite Love
6. We are Abundant Love
7. We are Profound Love
8. We are Complete Love
9. We are Opulent Love
10. We are Eternal Love

Claim: We claim that we express deep and unconditional love

Acceptance:
1. We accept that we express deep and unconditional love
2. We accept that we are True Love
3. We accept that we are Perfect Love
4. We accept that we are Absolute Love
5. We accept that we are Infinite Love
6. We accept that we are Abundant Love
7. We accept that we are Profound Love
8. We accept that we are Complete Love
9. We accept that we are Opulent Love
10. We accept that we are Eternal Love
11. We ask Holy Sprit to remove anything in our thoughts and actions that does not express unconditional love

12. We ask the Holy Spirit to remove hate from our thoughts and actions
13. We ask the Holy Spirit to remove imperfection from our thoughts and actions
14. We ask the Holy Spirit to remove judgment from our thoughts and actions
15. We ask the Holy Spirit to remove limitations from our thoughts and actions
16. We ask the Holy Spirit to remove lack from our thoughts and actions
17. We ask the Holy Spirit to remove cynicism from our thoughts and actions
18. We ask the Holy Spirit to remove failure from our thoughts and actions
19. We ask the Holy Spirit to remove poverty from our thoughts and actions
20. We ask the Holy Spirit to remove death from our thoughts and actions

<u>Thanksgiving</u>:
1. We thank Holy Spirit for expressing unconditional love
2. We thank Holy Spirit for Perfect Love
3. We thank Holy Spirit for Absolute Love
4. We thank Holy Spirit for Infinite Love
5. We thank Holy Spirit for Abundant Love
6. We thank Holy Spirit for Profound Love
7. We thank Holy Spirit for Complete Love
8. We thank Holy Spirit for Opulent Love
9. We thank Holy Spirit for Eternal Love
10. We thank Holy Spirit for True Love.

<u>Release</u>: We now release unconditional, absolute, perfect, abundant, infinite, profound, complete, opulent and eternal love for Self.

"Holy Spirit is _____, We are _____, We claim _____, We accept _____, We thank you for _____" is perhaps an over-simplification of Spiritual Treatment. The process of speaking or writing more advanced treatments has a tremendous effect on the person praying and the effectiveness of the prayers, but we have to start somewhere. Naturally, the prayer treatment is better conducted using the plural 1st person "We". It has a better effect of joining as one with your brother (friend or foe). The method might be especially useful in praying for your enemies and those you resent. It may help you better see the Holy Spirit in them. From ACIM "Song of Prayer":

The secret of true prayer is to forget the things you may think you need. To ask for the specific is much the same as to look on sin and then forgive it. Also in the same way, in prayer you overlook your specific needs as you see them, and let them go into God's Hands. There they become your gifts to Him, for they tell Him that you would have no gods before Him; no Love but His. (ACIM)

Gary Renard provides the following example: "...when you meditate, you might visualize yourself taking the HOLY SPIRIT's hand and going to God. Then you might think of yourself as laying your problems and goals and idols on the altar before Him as gifts. Maybe you'll tell God how much you love Him and how grateful you are to be completely taken care of by Him -- forever safe totally provided for. Then you become silent. You have the attitude that God created you just like Him and to be with Him forever. Now you can let go of everything, join with God's Love and lose yourself in joyful Communion with Him. A couple of days later, you might be eating a sandwich or working and all of a sudden it hits you; an inspired idea comes to you. The word inspired, as you know, means "in SPIRIT". By joining with HOLY SPIRIT you are given the answer. People are always looking to God to answer their prayers. If they knew more about how to pray then they'd know how the answer is given. His answers don't come in the form of physical answers; they come to your mind in the form of guidance -- an inspired idea..." (Renard)

Remember our thoughts and beliefs are very powerful and create our experiences. If we experience the same thought over and over again, it becomes a belief or habit. Repeating a treatment can change our habits and beliefs. Choose wisely which new habits and beliefs you want. In order to receive our good, we must have the belief that we are worthy to receive our good. We must have the sensation of excitement and empowerment when we are through. In the book Science Of Mind by Ernest Holmes, it states, "Know, without a shadow of doubt, that as a result of your treatment, some action takes place in Infinite Mind. Infinite Mind is the actor and you are the announcer. If you have a vague, subtle, unconscious fear, be quiet and ask yourself, "Who am I?", "What am I?", "Who is speaking?", "What is my life?" In this manner think right back to Principle, until your thought becomes perfectly clear again. Such is the power of right thinking, that it cancels and erases everything unlike itself. It answers every question, solves all problems, it is the solution to every difficulty. It is like the sunlight or Eternal Truth, bursting through the clouds of obscurity and bathing all life in glory. It is the Absolute with which you are dealing." Spiritual treatment is very effective for treating resentment of people's actions and words and replacing it with forgiveness. In AA when disgruntled, we say, "This man is sick, how can I be useful or of service". (AA) ACIM calls it "a call for love". The Science Of Mind text tells us that the practitioner "must be able to look at the sick man who has come to him for help, and know that only perfection stands before him; he must see beyond the appearance to that which is basically perfect." "Truth knows no opposites. When we take away the belief in evil, the belief that the outward appearance is the same as the inner reality, evil flees. We must continually remind ourselves of the power of the Word, and of our ability to use it. We must know that Truth produces freedom because Truth is freedom." (SOM) Prayer is essential to our Happiness. Just as we can't go to Heaven alone, ACIM reminds us that we are not healed alone. "Healing, forgiveness, and the glad exchange for all the world of sorrow for a world where sadness cannot enter, are the means by which Holy Spirit urges you to follow Him. His gentle lessons teach how easily salvation can be yours; how little practice you need undertake to let His laws replace the ones you made to hold yourself prisoner to death. His life becomes your own, as you extend the little help He asks in freeing you from everything that ever caused you pain. And as you let yourself be healed, you see all those around you, or who cross your mind, or whom you touch or those who seem to have no contact with you, healed along with you. Perhaps you will not recognize them all, nor realize how great your offering to all the world, when you let healing come to you. But you are never healed alone. And legions upon legions will receive the gift that you receive when you are healed." (ACIM)

Prayer is a very powerful method of helping others. Helping others is altruism and not evangelism. With prayer we don't necessarily have to help others with our mouth, our backs, or our pocket books. (The latter is nice but can easily be a trap set up by EGO for self praise and adulation. "Hey everybody, look at me and what I have done!" On the other hand, this is not a recommendation to be stingy, selfish, callous and apathetic. We trust the power of God (HOLY SPIRIT) and try not to meddle. (On this plane of existence, we don't always know when we are being influenced by HOLY SPIRIT or EGO so therefore we don't always intuitively know what is best for someone else.) In prayer, stick with the basics (e.g. forgiveness, joy, sanity, health, correct thinking, etc) for yourself and others. Also, in this experience of time and space, it will take some time to develop prayer skills and understanding our inner voice and outer emotions. To paraphrase from Gary Renard's book, Pursah says, "You have work to do along with HOLY SPIRIT to uncover your eyes and get your mind into the condition where you can awaken from the dream and become aware of what you really are... Don't fall into the trap of thinking you can just pray to God and everything will be hunky-dory. Think forgiveness, don't say it; forgiveness is done silently....say the words, "I want the peace of God". To say these words is nothing. But to mean these words is everything (ACIM)... "Thus you demonstrate that you mean you want the peace of God not with your words, but by your forgiveness...practice true forgiveness on whatever comes up in front of your face on any given day. Those are the lessons the HOLY SPIRIT would have you learn. You won't always do them perfectly, or even well. Sometimes, you'll have to do them later...Forgive them and be free...concentrate on your own forgiveness lessons, not somebody else's. The law of forgiveness is this: Fear binds the world. Forgiveness sets it free (ACIM)." Through prayer, we can obtain the condition where we cannot suffer. "That is the destiny HOLY SPIRIT holds out to us when we forgive the fantasy episodes of our bodily addicted EGO." (Renard) Being a guiltless Son of God, our mind cannot suffer.

Back to the Science Of Mind book, it points out, "So we learn to go deeply within ourselves, and speak as though there were a Presence there that knows; and we should take the time to unearth this hidden cause, to penetrate this inner chamber of consciousness. It is most worthwhile to commune with Spirit - to sense and feel It. The approach to Spirit is direct...through our own consciousness. This Spirit flows through us. Whatever intelligence we have is this Spirit in us. Prayer" (and meditation) "is its own answer. To daily meditate on the Perfect Life, and to daily embody the Great Ideal, is a royal road to freedom, to that peace which passeth understanding, and is happiness to the soul of man. Let us learn to see as God must, with a Perfect Vision. Let us seek the good and the true and believe in them with our whole heart, even though every man we meet is filled with suffering, and limitation appears at all sides. We cannot afford to believe in imperfection for a single second, to do so is to doubt God; it is to believe in a Power apart from God, to believe in another Creator. Let us daily say to ourselves: "Perfect God within me, Perfect Life within me, which is God, come forth into expression through me as that which I am; lead me ever into the paths of perfection and cause me to only see Good." By this practice, the soul will become illumined and will acquaint itself with God and be at peace. "Be ye therefore perfect, even as your Father which is in Heaven perfect." (SOM)

Much has been said about prayer, but is by no means all encompassing or the only point of view about prayer. But I cannot share something I don't have. (We say in AA that you can't be angry with your parents because they didn't teach you Chinese. They just didn't know.) What I provided above about prayer is from my 11 Step search. Do your own and follow your conscious or inner voice. Another thing I learned in AA which facilitated my search was to look for the similarities and not the differences. I also observed very closely the characteristics of who was doing the teaching to make sure their behavior matched their words. For me it didn't have anything to do with whether or not I ate some bread and drank some wine in a certain way or if gays had the right of marriage. I also used my emotions to guide me. I found that spiritually attuned people can express their ideas in a very gentle, loving manner whereas those dominated by EGO cause an abrasive, repulsive feeling.

Now about Meditation (which, perhaps, should have been discussed first because effective prayer requires going within): Meditation is an altered state of consciousness. There are methods of meditation established that when followed allow us to release our normal waking state of consciousness, release our past troubles, release our worries about the future, our emotional disturbances and enter a place of peace and quiet. It is like a small vacation for the brain and body systems and just as rejuvenating as eight hours of sleep. Meditation provides the same feelings you get sitting by a mountain lake or walking through a forest or laying in the sun in a quiet cove by the beach. And after meditation you feel recharged and in a better state of mind than when you began. Hypnosis also has the same effect, but the purpose of meditation is to contact your higher self, a loving, all knowing side of yourself that can provide you answers and can answer prayer. Some call it super conscious mind; some call it the inner Christ; ACIM calls it HOLY SPIRIT. Also some have visual experiences; some auditory or a feeling nature; so allow yourself freedom to experiment and explore. There are many wonderful books, tapes and videos for meditation. Personally I took classes and found group meditation to be very powerful. I also met a wonderful quality of people to associate with.

An organization known as The Teaching of the Inner Christ provides information on meditation in their book entitled BEING A CHRIST - Inner Sensitivity (Intuitional) Training Course by Ann P. Meyer and Peter V. Meyer. The following is liberally transcribed from that book to provide the reader information on meditation (the editor recommends that the reader of this proposal read their text or take their courses in order to gain the specific information provided by their teaching and in order to gain a fuller experience with your inner Christ): "In this Teaching we define deep meditation as an awareness trance, in order to emphasize the fact that we are very much aware in the state of deep meditation. To an observer, a person sitting motionless in a deep meditation may appear to have lost conscious awareness, but they are actually keenly aware and very conscious of the inner levels of their Being, while oblivious to their outer environment. The word trance comes from the word transcend, which means go beyond. The prefix "trans" means to go across. This suggests a movement in consciousness. Awareness Trance is a movement in consciousness to the inner Being, taking awareness with us. When we are in an awareness trance we are not asleep or dreaming, but are alert, in an altered consciousness, at a deeper level of mind, a level which we are normally unconscious. The awareness trance or deep meditation is a state of relaxation and concentration -- that is relaxation of the outer levels of consciousness and concentration on the deep inner levels. During meditation the subconscious mind is not listening to the voice of another individual, nor to the voice of one's own outer self, but to the voice of Spirit inside (HOLY SPIRIT). Deep meditation is absolute, undivided, concentration upon the Inner Self. The practice of deep meditation is perfectly natural, as well as extremely beneficial. We are primarily intuitive beings, designed to draw forth from our inner resources of wisdom all the knowledge required for us to fulfill the needs of our lives. The flow of intuitive knowledge from deep within our minds would be constant and all sufficient if human beings had not for the most part, turned their attention outward upon the physical world, with the resulting loss of daily awareness of their Inner Selves. To pause to listen to the inner voice, to listen completely and intently, is the most natural and helpful practice a human being can engage in. In mind there is no space or time. All action of mind takes place anywhere and everywhere. "The Kingdom of Heaven is within you". The first step of this type of meditation is to remove all attention from our outer environment (where our attention is focused most of the time) by becoming still, closing the eyes (seeing, hearing, smelling and other senses) and being willing to let the world go by for a while. The second step is to remove attention from our physical body. (We do this by employing complete body relaxation methods as discussed in the TIC text.) Having relaxed all awareness of both the environment and the physical body, it is now possible to take the attention to the next level inward, the conscious mind (the intellect). By now we may begin to have the feeling that we are merely a mental being; we may have forgotten temporarily that we have a physical body. This level of trance, which may be called light-meditation is quite usual; many people reach it while deep in thought (or deep into the present work task in front of them). The next step of our journey inward is the relaxation of the intellect (the reasoning mind) which allows the attention to be drawn still deeper, to the subconscious mind. Now we are aware only of feelings, deep memories, or visualizations. This is the subliminal state, which you have experienced many times while drifting off to sleep or awakening. The difference here is that we are in conscious control and are able to maintain awareness on the subliminal level without going to sleep. We are awake and alert with deeply relaxed bodies. Next we relax the subconscious mind and thus are able to transfer awareness to the inmost level of Spirit (the super conscious, the Christ Self, the I AM, etc.). At this time there may be a temporary feeling of upheaval as we cross for the first time the psychic barrier composed of long-held beliefs in separation from the Inner Self. Going through it can cause a great vibrational change in the physical and mental bodies" (a spiritual experience or awakening, a psychic change, etc.) "As we approach the inner levels of our being by rendering ourselves completely relaxed and receptive, the Christ Self often takes the opportunity to reach out for us and draw us inward, through this mental barrier to Himself. The sudden vibration change may cause us to tremble, shake, weep, laugh", (see a bright light, etc.) as the case may be. After we have penetrated to the innermost levels, we feel a great sense of release and peace. At the Christ level we are aware only of the Christ Mind thoughts - Truth, Goodness, Love, Peace, Harmony, and Oneness with life. Spirit gives no recognition to the error thinking of the outer mind, or to the collective race mind consciousness. The Spirit within is our true identity. Having reached the depths of our being, through the process of relaxation and concentration, we now can feed upon the wisdom, love, life and power of the Universal God. We receive new truths, new solutions to our problems, and we are submerged into creative thought. From this inner reservoir many people receive healing, spiritual power and a replenishing of the life substance of mind and body." (TIC)

As it is said "there are many mansions", Ernest Holmes in <u>Science Of Mind</u> tells us that we may well have a body within a body to infinity, so each one of us has a Christ Self within a Christ Self and so on to the ultimate center of individualization, the I AM or God Self. If we are eternal, then we have many more dimensions to experience, but with the knowledge of prayer and meditation we have a choice as to which direction and what quality of experience we wish to have in this and the next experience. The TIC text goes on to describe the wonderful benefits of meditation: "A deep meditation, whether short or long, results in a lifting of consciousness for any person who goes into it with this intent. As you go deep within yourself there is a temporary merging of the outer levels of your mind (which are often influenced by error thinking) with the pure inner mind, which knows only reality - perfection now. Each time you lift your consciousness through meditation, you achieve a permanent change in your beliefs and attitudes. You become more like your true inner Self. As you learn to engage in deep meditation regularly, you will experience an entirely new way of viewing life, enjoying high ideals and ideas, harmonious thinking and living, peace of mind and physical health. The benefits of deep bodily relaxation are in themselves most important, for many people today are not able to completely relax the body, even in sleep. Improved relaxation results in better health, balance of living, poise, and sense of well being, agility, flexibility, and a prosperous life. The relaxed body is vibrating on a higher frequency and more attuned to the inner bodies, and thus more able to be fed the universal energy (prana) through these inner bodies. The relaxed person is more receptive to Truth and better able to enjoy living. A deep meditation furnishes a temporary relief or refreshment from the sea of race-mind error thinking (a.k.a. EGO) in which we live in daily. Although each of us is an individual center of awareness, we are in the one mind, and the error beliefs (a.k.a. EGO) of fear, lack, illness, disharmony, etc. which exist in the composite memory of the human race often influence our individual minds. We achieve dominion over these error beliefs by making regular visits into pure, fresh consciousness of the Inner Christ Mind. Practicing meditation on a regular basis also deepens the life expression. We become less emotionally embroiled in our problems and the trouble of others; we become more objective, thus achieving command over them. The outer personality keeps in closer touch with the Inner Being, allowing the outward flow of Christ love which feeds the mind, the feeling nature and the body. False personality facades disintegrate and the real person begins to express the self at last. Those who meditate regularly are aware of many sensations of power feeding, spiritual quickening, surges of energy,--and they actually begin to require less and lighter foods to maintain bodily health and vigor. The physical body functions more efficiently and becomes more youthful, lighter, more beautiful and more like the perfect inner bodies." (TIC) The Teachings of Inner Christ organization has much more quality information on prayer and meditation and spiritual development for those interested.

Some of my first experiences in meditation where like drug induced trips on LSD, with visualizations of Jesus and Mary. (Addicts and alcoholics are mostly very adept and have some wonderful experiences with meditation because of the years of experience they gained in altered states of consciousness. However, please note that the editors comments about alcoholics and drug addict's altered conscious state skills is not an endorsement for the use of drugs or alcohol to achieve these states. Most drugs and alcohol have an addictive quality, mostly because the initial effect is usually very pleasing, which is the "reward" that creates a conditioned response or habit. Besides the addictive and progressive nature of using drugs and alcohol, they also have many undesirable side effects, whereas prayer and meditation do not. This is especially true when the progression leads to the ingestion of toxic quantities to the human body, organs, brain and central nervous system. Also, drugs and alcohol can alter one's personality and psychic, sometimes negatively and irreversibly, even after the drugs and alcohol have dissipated from the body). My meditation experiences remained a meteor storm of events for quite awhile, but eventually it settled down to routine spiritual maintenance. For me one of the reasons the quality of my meditation and prayer experiences may diminish is because of my inability to resist temptation. I revisit areas and activities of EGO that would better be left alone and the result is that I often have less than desirable consequences. Sometimes, the 12 Steps have been more like the game of Shoots and Ladders for me.

Meditation did improve my parenting skills and my relationship with my daughter. I was divorced for the second time (after trying my best to make it work this time) and became emotionally instable, again. My daughter was 13 experimenting with marijuana and 18 year old boys. I learned my method of parenting from my German mother, which is yelling and screaming to get the desired behavior. Needless to say I was pushing my daughter, who I loved dearly, far away from me (just like I did with everyone else). A lady at the meditation group (who I haven't seen since) told me a similar story about her daughter and she said that meditation greatly improved their relationship. She suggested that I try it for six months and see what happens. She said go into meditation and send her your love. I went to a group meditation every Monday and Wednesday night for six months and my relationship with my daughter improved drastically. I learned that meditation was more powerful than my big, know it all mouth. So I adapted this experience with meditation for my daughter to use in many other situations with other people and found it to work (but not as fast as I would like). Sometimes with someone (such as myself) that has a very obstinate EGO, persistence is necessary and it may take a while, maybe six months to get acceptable results. I am sure with more routine practice, the time factor can be greatly reduced to something more in correlation with the Spiritual Readings. Sloth, laziness, rationalization and procrastination are also on the negative side of the ledger and inhibit spiritual growth. We want to play the piano like a master, but we don't want to take the lessons. It is easy to get caught up with the concept that if we are eternal, maybe I'll just rest and take it easy in this life. Sometimes pain is a blessing to keep us going in the right direction. As I advance Spiritually, I find that my tolerance for pain is less. If I keep advancing, maybe someday, I'll no longer need pain as a motivational force and I can be motivated by receiving the rewards of doing things right. In AA they say, "In order to develop self esteem, you have to do estimable things".

The Self-Realization Fellowship founded in the U.S. in 1920 by Paramahansa Yogananda also provides some excellent information on meditation, however the information must be obtained from their office (for a nominal fee) and it is requested not to disperse their information (probably because of editors such as myself, who only take the portions they see fit and pass on diluted or misconstrued information). The following information which is available comes from Yogananda's commentary of The Bhagavad Gita and I will extract it to this proposal word for word as it is written for the benefit of the fellowship and the reader: "By the special technique of Kriya Yoga, the ingoing breath of prana and the outgoing breath of apana are converted into cool and warm currents. In the beginning of the practice of Kriya Yoga, the devotee feels the cool prana current going up the spine and the warm apana current going down the spine, in accompaniment with the ingoing and outgoing breath. The advanced Kriya Yogi finds that the inhaling breath of prana and the exhaling breath of apana have been evened, neutralized or extinguished; he feels only the cool current of prana going up through the spine and the warm current of apana going down through the spine"..."In successful meditation, the Kriya Yogi converts the two distinct impulses of inhalation and exhalation into two life currents, the cool prana and the warm apana, felt in the spine. He then realizes the truth of Jesus' saying -- that a man is not required to depend on external breath (or on "bread" or any other outward sustenance) as a condition of bodily existence. The yogi perceives the cool and warm currents in the spine to be constantly and magnetically pulling an extra voltage of current from the omnipresent cosmic life force ever flowing through the medulla. He gradually finds that these two spinal currents become converted into one life force, magnetically drawing reinforcements of prana from all the bodily cells and nerves. This strengthened life current flows upward to the point between the eyebrows and is seen as the tricolored spherical astral eye: a luminous sun, in the center of which is a blue sphere encircling a bright scintillating star. Jesus referred to this single eye in the center of the forehead and to the truth that the body is essentially formed of light, in the following words: "If therefore thine eye be single, thy whole body shall be full of light…" "By practice of Kriya, the yogi scientifically detaches his mind from gross sensory perceptions and realized that consciousness and life force (prana or cosmic light) are the basis of all matter. The Kriya Yogi adopts a scientific method to divert his mind and reason from his perception of physical flesh; he perceives the body as light and consciousness by rising above the gross perception of breath. All inner experiences like that of subconscious sleep can only take place when the consciousness of breath disappears. The Kriya Yogi has no need or desire to withhold breath forcibly in the lungs; he becomes mentally so calm that he feels himself to be aloof of breath. By the practice of Kriya Yoga he can consciously and at will attain the breathless state and sustain life in his body solely by the cool and warm currents flowing through the spine and trickling down from the spiritual eye"…"When the devotee is convinced by Kriya Yoga that he can live solely by the inner source of cosmic energy, he realized that the body is a wave of the all-sufficing cosmic ocean of life. By the special technique of Kriya Yoga, the devotee--through perfect calmness, though a greater supply of energy distilled from oxygen in the Kriya breath, and through enhanced flow of cosmic energy coming into the body through the medulla-is less and less subject to the necessity for breathing. By deeper Kriya Yoga the bodily life, ordinarily dependent on reinforcement by life force distilled from gross outer sources, begins to be sustained by the cosmic life only: then breathing (inhalation and exhalation) ceases. All the trillions of bodily cells become like regenerating dry batteries needing nothing but the inner "electricity" recharged from the cosmic source of life. In this way the bodily cells remain in a suspended state -- that is, they neither grow or decay. They are sustained and vitalized directly from the life-energy dynamos in the brain and spine. When the cells cease to grow, they are not required to depend on the life current distilled from oxygen, sunshine, solids and liquids but on the inner source of cosmic life. Kriya Yoga pranayama withdraws life force from the activities unnecessary--and unites that bodily prana with the cosmic life force; man's slavish dependence on breath is thus realized to be delusory. When the yogi expert in pranayama can thus disengage at will the life force from its bondage of oxygen and so on, he can immortalize it by uniting with Cosmic Life"… "The prana and apana currents flowing in the spine become calm and even, generating a tremendous magnetic power and joy. As meditation deepens, the downward-flowing apana current and the upward flowing prana current become neutralized into one ascending current, seeking its source in the cerebrum. Breath is still, life is still, sensations and thoughts are dissolved. The divine light of life and consciousness perceived by the devotee in the cerebrospinal centers becomes one with the Cosmic Light and Cosmic Consciousness. Acquisition of the power of this realization enables the yogi to consciously detach his soul from identification with the body. He becomes free from the distressing bondage of desires (the body's attachment and longing for sensory gratification), fears (the thought of possible nonfulfillment of desires), and anger (the emotional response to obstacles that thwart fulfillment of desires). These three impelling forces in man are the greatest enemies of soul bliss; they must be destroyed by that devotee who aspires to reach God. Life force is the connecting--and disconnecting--link between matter and Spirit, between body consciousness and soul consciousness. The ordinary man does not know how to get at the bodily prana directly. Therefore, this life force works automatically to enliven the body and senses and by the medium of breath ties man's attention solely to his physical existence. But by the use of Kriya Yoga the devotee learns how to distill life force out of breath and how to control prana. With this control, the life force can be switched off at will from the five sense channels and turned inward, thus diverting the soul's attention from the perception of material phenomena to the perception of Spirit. By the scientific step by step method, the yogi ascends from the senses in actuality and not by a mere ineffectual mental diversion from them. He completely disconnects mind and reason and attention from the body, by switching off the life force from the five senses. He learns scientifically to divert to the spine and brain the currents from his five sense channels and thus unite his consciousness with the joy of higher spiritual perceptions in the seven centers" (Chakras). "When he is able to remain immersed in divine bliss even in his active state, he does not become further involved in desires to enjoy external objects. Radiating the calmness of divine realizations, he is not disturbed by the springing up of fear and anger from non-fulfillments of material desires. He finds his soul no longer tied to matter but forever united to the cosmic bliss of Spirit."..."Methods of spiritual freedom are various, but the actual attainment of liberation by ascent through the spine is universal. Whether through: (1) Bhakta - intense devotion and prayer, (2) Jnani - pure discrimination, (3) Karma Yoga - nonattached selfless actions, or (4) Kriya Yoga; the consciousness purified and concentrated thereby still makes its final ascent to God through the subtle spinal channels through which it descended into flesh. The principle of Kriya Yoga therefore is not a formula of a sectarian rite, but a science through the application of which the individual may realize how his soul descended into the body and became identified with the senses and reunited with Spirit by a scientific method of meditation. This route of descent and ascension is the one universal path that every soul must travel. Kriya Yoga teaches first to withdraw the mind from sensory objects by self control, and then scientifically to disconnect the mind and intelligence from the senses by switching off the life force from the five sense channels, and then take the ego, mind and intellect through the five astral centers in the spine, through the sixth center (the medulla, which is magnetically connected with the spiritual eye in the middle of the forehead), and finally into the seventh center of omniscience in the middle of the cerebrum. The Kriya Yogi then attains perception of his self as soul, and finds his ego, intellect and mind to be dissolved in soul ecstasy. He then learns how to take his soul from the prisons of the physical, astral, and causal bodies and to reunite the soul with Spirit. As the physical eyes through frontal vision, reveal a portion of matter, so the omnipresent spiritual eye, through its boundless spherical visions, reveals the entire astral and ideational cosmoses. In the beginning, when the yogi is able to penetrate his mind through the astral eye, he sees his astral body; by further advancement he sees the entire astral cosmos of which his body is but a part. Without entering the spiritual (astral) eye, no one can know how to take his life force and consciousness through the astral plexuses in the spine. After entering the spiritual eye he passes, in a step by step way, through the perception of the physical body; the perception of the astral eye; the perception of the astral body; the perception of the astral cerebrospinal tunnel with the seven astral plexuses; and through the casual body into final freedom. It requires intricate scientific explanation to interpret Kriya Yoga, but the art itself is very simple. Kriya Yoga, practiced deeply, will dissolve breath into mind, mind into intuition, intuition into the joyous perception of soul, and soul into the cosmic bliss of Spirit. The Yogi then understands how his soul descended into matter and how his prodigal soul has been led from matter back to the mansion of omnipresence, there to enjoy the fatted calf of wisdom"... "(Detailed instruction in the actual techniques of Kriya Yoga is given to students of the Self Realization Fellowship who fulfill the requirements of certain preliminary spiritual disciplines"...Paramahansa Yogananda wrote: "In a book available to the general public I cannot give the techniques themselves; for they are sacred, and certain ancient spiritual injections must first be followed to insure that they are received with reverence and confidentiality, and thereafter practiced correctly..."). (SRF)

Try to say the above paragraph seven times real fast. That information was awfully deep and naturally not for everyone. (However, when Bill wrote his chapter on prayer and meditation in the "12 Steps & 12 Traditions", his access to such information on advanced prayer and meditation might have been very limited). It was provided for the benefit of any aspirants (maybe one in a million) who can speed up the process. That used to be the odds for the chances of an alcoholic getting and staying sober for the rest of his life. Bill Wilson even prophesized in the chapter WE AGNOSTICS that someday they will land on the moon. He accurately describes our agnosticism: "Some of the contempories of Columbus thought a round earth preposterous. Others came near putting Galileo to death for his astronomical heresies. We asked ourselves this: Are we not some of us just as biased and unreasonable about the realm of spirit as were the ancients about the realm of material?"..."We were having trouble with personal relationships, we couldn't control our emotional natures, we were prey to misery and depression, we couldn't make an enjoyable living, we had a feeling of uselessness, we were full of fear, we were unhappy, we couldn't seem to be of real help to other people--was not the basic solution of these bedevilments more important than whether we should see newsreels of lunar flight? Of course it was. When we saw others solve their problems by a simple reliance upon the Spirit of the Universe, we had to stop doubting the power of God. Our ideas did not work. But the God idea did".(AA) Understand that many of us are set in our ways and learning a new language can be too difficult of a task this lifetime. My father had a 7th grade education and joined the military (underage) during World War II. The military gave him a skill and he successfully retired at age 52. I went in the military service at age 18 and not only received a skill but the college door was opened to me. In the military service, part of my job was to educate airman who worked in hazardous noise areas to wear earplugs. I caught hell from the old-timers, but the younger men were willing to listen. In a period of about five years, earplugs were common place. In the story, The 100th Monkey (Unk): Scientists went to an island to study the behavior of a certain monkey and in order to observe them they put sweet potatoes in a central area. The older ones just grabbed the potatoes and selfishly ate them. Some of the younger ones discovered that they could wash the potato in a stream before eating them. As they grew they taught their children to wash the potatoes. Eventually the entire tribe of monkeys washed their potatoes. And what was even more remarkable was that scientists on another island studying the same monkey suddenly observed that overnight the entire tribe was washing their potatoes, without being shown. The critical mass of race consciousness builds up to a certain level where suddenly everyone changes. Who knows maybe at one time the world really was flat, until enough people believed that it was round.

STEP 12: HAVING HAD A SPIRITUAL AWAKENING (A MIRACLE) AS THE RESULT OF WORKING THESE STEPS, WE CONTINUE TO STUDY AND PRACTICE SPIRITUAL PRINCIPLES; AND WE HELP TO TEACH OTHERS SPIRITUAL PRINCIPLES AND FORGIVENESS (WITH THE GUIDANCE FROM THE ACIM TEXT, WORKBOOK AND MANUAL FOR TEACHERS AND OTHER SIMILAR INFORMATION). (AA)

The words have been changed and are more secular towards ACIM. Feel free to change the words again. As the editor, I am not highly qualified to discuss this Step from experience because, although, I have had many spiritual awakenings in my life, I also have the tendency to fall back asleep again. I am rather skilled at starting the steps over again (without having to take a drink to do so) and working myself back up the steps of enlightenment. Some choose not to use the analogy of steps and call them the 12 pillars (that surround them so they can't fall down). Although my honestly sharing how EGO interferes in my life plans often helps others or when I am really down and out and pressed to the wall, I will do some service work, or sometimes I even buy the guilt tickets the zealots are selling, the word altruism has always seemed to be a bitter pill and I have been unwilling to swallow. (I only recently discovered that all they were saying about tithing is true.) I have always been the naive sucker, who lends out money and never gets paid back, who befriends the con-artist, who puts his hand out and gets bit. When my first wife left, I said, "If you love someone, set them free, if they love you they'll return". She didn't come back and after a three year depression, I wasn't too willing to let a poem make decisions for my life. When my second wife left, she asked me if I could change and I honestly replied, "I've been in AA for ten years trying to change and I have changed very little." After a year of self pity, I wished that I would have lied to her. For promotions I prayed for my competitors and said, "Thy will not mine be done." And after getting passed over more than twelve times for failure to lie adequately and conspire with others, I regretted taking the moral high ground. In fact taking the moral high ground has made me an outsider in many social settings and created many unnecessary enemies. Gossip and hearsay are very strong opponents to compete with. People do unknowingly project their guilt onto others and often they unite to feel justified in doing so. I have no idea where to tell someone to balance spiritual concepts with the world we live in. Rather than becoming altruistic, I have sought half measures and easier softer ways. I have spent the last twelve years hiding out in the 11th step, maybe it is about time that I got into the 12th (I could easily study altruism for the next 12 years). I have observed many do the "two step" (steps 1 then 12) with seeming impunity. They satisfy their EGO with their great deeds and go on to live happy and content lives. It is jealousy and envy that bring me down. Why do I have such grave emotional and mental disorders and reek with self pity. I get condolence from knowing that all the information we use from the first 164 pages of the AA text was written by someone who was only about three years sober. Although the founder of AA and author of the text and the "12 Steps & 12 Traditions" (12 + 12) had a profound Spiritual Experience, he lost it after about three years (probably from cheating on his wife; there wouldn't be an AA organization or text if it weren't for the steadfast strength of Lois Wilson). He later used psychedelic drugs to try to regain the experience (he even tried to persuade his wife to try it). And although he received a heroes welcome throughout the US, he was seriously depressed for the next thirteen years, during which time he wrote the 12 + 12 text and developed spiritual traditions and concepts par none that have kept the organization (that is not organized) of misfits (and benign anarchists) together for seventy years. (Maybe it is just OK if I feel motivated to write a book too. In my readings about Helen Schumann, she was not too willing or always cooperative in channeling the ACIM information).

AA has always been able to provide a perspective that allows for spiritual progress. Someone said in a meeting, "If you can't surrender, then begin fighting in a new direction". Bill's statement in HOW IT WORKS that "We are not saints", may have been a self fulfilling prophesy. But, we should not say "No never". Everything I have read so far indicates that we are saints (or working towards it). Analee Skarin wrote a book "Ye are God's", indicating that we are. An old-timer sang the line from a song, "You have to accentuate the positive and eliminate the negative". Faith is a bridge from our mind to the Mind of God. We help others on the faith that it is a bridge to God Mind (HOLY SPIRIT), regardless of the consequences in the world of EGO. I have been committed to institutions, so the word commitment to me is a life sentence. I am committed to living by these spiritual principles on the good days as well as the bad. The consequences of EGO are much more severe and when people share their life experiences in dealing with EGO, it not only motivates them, but us as well to lead a spiritual as well as a moral life. There really isn't much of a choice, as in the military, do it our way, or the stockade way. If you want what we have for a day, do this for a day. If you want it for a week, do it for a week. If you want it for a year, do it for a year and if you want it for a lifetime, do it for a lifetime. AA has a policy that if you are not satisfied, they will refund your misery. And beware of the elite and fascists who want to force a particular brand of spirituality down your throat (or any other orifi ce they find available); they only thought they lost their egoism. Throughout the ages, people practicing certain spiritual beliefs have been persecuted. The orthodox wiped out the heretics. The conservatives have no tolerance for the liberals. Many Europeans came to this continent after hundreds of years of religious persecution and censorship to gain freedom of speech, the right to assemble and a God of their own understanding. Yet there are still those in any society that will use the techniques of shunning and scolding (and much more severe methods) to force people to believe and do as they do. This step is about altruism and not evangelism. We are not promoting world dominance with this particular spiritual belief system. With this step we are promoting maximum service to others. We try to see what we can bring to the occasion, rather than what we can take from it. We are hard on ourselves, but considerate of others.

Dr. Bob's view on this step is as follows (from the AA text, chapter entitled DOCTOR BOB's NIGHTMARE): "I spend a great deal of time passing on what I learned to others who want it and need it badly. I do it for four reasons:
1	Sense of duty
2	It is a pleasure
3. Because in so doing I am paying my debt to the man who took time to pass it on to me.
4. Because every time I do it I take out a little more insurance for myself"... "It is a most wonderful blessing to be relieved of the terrible curse with which I was afflicted. My health is good and I have regained my self-respect and the respect of my colleagues. My home life is ideal and my business is as good as can be expected in these uncertain times. " (AA)

Today is the first day of the rest of your life. So begin to live in the present, "One day at a time". Paraphrased from HOW TO HANDLE SOBRIETY: "We avoid the festering mental attitude of self pity and resentment by working the steps and sharing in meetings. We rid ourselves of guilt and remorse as we clean out the garbage from our minds by working Steps 1 thru 10. We learn how to level out the emotional mood swings that got us into trouble both when we were up and when we were down. We are taught to differentiate between our wants (which are never satisfied) and our needs (which are always provided for). We cast off the burdens of the past and the anxieties of the future, as we begin to live in the present. We are granted "the serenity...the courage..., and the wisdom..." and thus lose our quickness to anger and our sensitivity to criticism. Above all we reject fantasizing and accept reality". From INTO ACTION: "Are these extravagant promises? We think not. They are being fulfilled among us--sometimes slowly--sometimes quickly. They will always materialize if we work for them". And A VISION FOR YOU says: "Still you may say: "But I will not have the benefit of contact with you who write this book." We cannot be sure. God (HOLY SPIRIT) will determine that, so you must remember that your real reliance is upon Him. He will show you how to create the fellowship you crave. Our book is meant to be suggestive only. We realize we know only a little. God (HOLY SPIRIT) will constantly disclose more to you and to us. Ask Him in your morning meditation what you can do each day for the man who is still sick. The answers will come, if your own house is in order. But obviously you cannot transmit something you haven't got. See to it that your relationship with Him is right, and great events will come to pass for you and countless others. This is the Great Fact for us. Abandon yourself to God (HOLY SPIRIT) as you understand God (HOLY SPIRIT). Admit your faults to Him and to your fellows. Clear away the wreckage of your past. Give freely of what you find and join us. We shall be with you in the Fellowship of the Spirit and surely you will meet some of us"... "May God (HOLY SPIRIT) bless you and keep you--until then." (AA)

In order to do the rest of step twelve, one ought to have had a spiritual awakening; however in AA the only requirement for membership was a desire to stop drinking. When AA was presented to me, I had a great desire to stop drinking, but I had very little desire to have a spiritual awakening (let alone understand what it really meant). AA provided me a spiritual education in a very enjoyable, easily digestible and work-at-your-own- pace method. It took quite a long time to understand and then later how to apply spiritual concepts and principles in my life. At first I was elated that by the power of going to AA meetings, I magically no longer drank and I was driven to carry that message to others. Unfortunately you can't transmit something you don't have. Therefore I only managed in keeping myself sober (and enlarging my EGO). I also managed to irritate a large number of people, many that were friends and family members. Time after time, hopelessness and despair would return into my life as a result of hanging on to my EGO and failing to develop spiritually. However each event would end up being a life or death situation, where I would choose life and in order to live in comfort I would have to apply spiritual principles. When I achieved satisfactory or mediocre results I would always ease up on my spiritual progress and then eventually regress back to EGO and selfish and self-centered motives. One time when I was in great despair, I sought out an AA sponsor who discussed priorities with me. Naturally I responded that God, AA and my daughter were my main priorities in life and I wrote them down and put the note in my wallet to remember what my priorities were. What I discovered was that I did not spend a great deal of time during the day on my priorities but instead in other interests and desires. The most time I spent was trying to find another sexual partner and a mother for my daughter. I also spent a great deal of time watching NFL games. What this sponsor was able to point out to me was that I needed to spend a proportional amount of time on my priorities. He helped me make a schedule with a 24 hour clock diagram. First we put down the mandatory events that take place, such as work, sleep, eating, self - care, etc. Then we put in the priorities such as prayer, meditation, meetings, reading, and family. He also emphasized that there should always be a certain amount of time set aside for leisure. We made a schedule for weekdays and one for week-end days. The times rapidly filled up and it was very simple to see how easy it is to overbook your day especially if you are a compulsive personality. He also pointed out how substitution can replace less desirable behaviors and activities with better ones because there are just so many hours in a day. If you spend the time doing the activities you had planned, there won't be any time to do the activities that have less than desirable results. In order to build self esteem, you must do estimable things.

Tom Johnson, a SOM author of TO LOVE OR BE LOVED says, "Nearly everyone wants to be loved but there are so few who want to love or even know how to love. If your motivation is to be loved, you will never be happy because happiness, freedom, life, health, all comes from your expressing love. Wanting to be loved indicates your insecurity, it indicates your lack of self-awareness, and possibly your self-hatred and condemnation, and these ideas cause you to reach outside of yourself and look for someone else to give to you what you are not willing to give to yourself. Love has nothing to do with anyone else. Love is never what you receive. Love is always what you give and express. As you know this, you can put your attention where it belongs, not on someone else, receiving from them, but on who and what you are, the expression which is now going forth from you". (Johnson - SOM)

What ACIM teaches is equality. From THE DISSAPPEARANCE OF THE UNIVERSE (with some minor changes): "...we are all Christ. The idea will at least help us think about people the way we should. Remember if they are not expressing love, then they must be calling out for it. Even that won't stop us from reacting to people and situations in a judgmental way, because EGO is clever (and baffling, cunning and treacherous). Except when we have something like a sulking resentment, full of self pity, most things that bother us happened suddenly. The EGO loves unpleasant surprises. When the next rude awakening comes your way, here is a tip that might help. Any kind of upset, from a mild discomfort to outright anger, is a warning bell. It tells you that your hidden guilt is rising up from the recesses of your unconscious mind and coming to the surface. Think of that discomfort as the guilt that needs to be released by forgiving the symbol you associate with it. The EGO is trying to get you to see the guilt as being outside of you by projecting the reason for it onto an illusionary image. The EGO thought system is trying to put some distance in between yourself and the guilt, and any suitable object or person who comes along will suffice. Projection always follows denial. People have to project this repressed guilt onto others, or correctly forgive it. Those are the only two choices available, no matter how complex the world may seem. If you want to outplay EGO and successfully trim the tables on it, you have to be alert for that warning bell of discomfort or anger, and then stop reacting and start forgiving. That's how you'll win."... "People won't agree with you on that if they're not ready to forgive. People always resist the truth; the EGO wants to make it real." (A friend in AA told me that we always call the truth a lie and a lie the truth; so start lying.) "Forgive those who think you are a moron for not buying into the EGO system and stick to spiritual principles."..."You've got to understand that if the Course is teaching there is no hierarchy of illusions, and if a miracle is a shift in perception where you switch over to HOLY SPIRIT's script, then one miracle (spiritual experience, spiritual awakening) is no less important than another."... "I learned that it is just as important to forgive a cold as it is to forgive a physical assault, and just as important to forgive a subtle insult as it is to forgive the death of a loved one.

If you think that sounds heartless, you're wrong. It hurt when my parents died, and it hurt when my husband died. Yet what is perceived as tragedy can be forgiven just as quickly as we are willing to recognize that the separation from God never occurred, so it's only a dream, nobody is guilty"… "the purpose of time is to forgive. That is the only viable answer to life. Act accordingly, child of God." (Renard)

The following is taken from the AA TWELVE STEPS AND TWELVE TRADITIONS (although most of the sentences are taken word for word, they are taken out of context of the book and may construe something other than what was intended by Bill Wilson): "When the Twelfth Step is seen in its full implication, it is really talking about the kind of love that has no price tag on it. The persistent use of meditation and prayer, we found, did open the channel so that where there had been a trickle, there now was a river which led to sure power and safe guidance from God (HOLY SPIRIT) as we were
increasingly better able to understand Him. So practicing these Steps, we had a spiritual awakening about which finally there was no question. What we have received is a free gift, and yet usually, at least in some small part" (e.g. usually praying "God (HOLY SPIRIT) help me" is all it takes), "we have made ourselves ready to receive it." (AA)

You might want to know how to identify someone who has had a Spiritual Awakening (filled with HOLY SPIRIT rather than EGO). From the AA text: "When a man or a woman has had a spiritual awakening, the most important meaning of it is that he or she has now become able to do, feel, and believe that which he or she could not do before on their unaided strength and resources alone. He or she has been granted a gift which amounts to a new state of consciousness and being. He or she has been set on a path which tells them they are really going somewhere, that life is not a dead end, not something to be endured or mastered. In a very real sense he or she has been transformed, because he or she has laid hold of a source of strength which, in one way or another, they have previously denied themselves. They find their selves in possession of a degree of honesty, tolerance, unselfishness, peace of mind, and love of which they had thought themselves quite incapable." These are the road signs that you might want to look for to determine whether someone is genuine or faking. Beware of false prophets. They are filled with EGO and may lead you down the wrong road. "They only thought they lost their egoism". From the editor's experience, when you are enlightened, you will see a bright aura around those who are also enlightened and know that what they say is something to pay attention to. Their eyes shine and they have a profound peace of mind. Someone spiritually enlightened does not demand anything from you (or sell you guilt tickets). Their method of teaching is through praise and not critique. Because Spiritual principles are paradoxical to this world, their methods may not make sense (to the EGO). "This is indeed the kind of giving that demands nothing. He does not expect his brother… to pay him, love him (or even obey him). And then he discovers that by the divine paradox of this kind of giving, he has found his own reward…he senses that he stands at the edge of new mysteries, joys, and experience of which he had never dreamed." (AA)

If you have not had such a spiritual awakening, your attempts at helping others may go awry and not feel so wonderful, but such attempts will always benefit the giver in some wonderful way. Our growth lessons in this world of EGO, don't always feel so spectacular. However, you will have much greater experiences if you hook up with HOLY SPIRIT first, instead of riding along with EGO. The core of Step Twelve is: Freely ye have received, freely give. Use the spiritual principles of, non-judgment, equality and unconditional love. Not all 12 Step work is helping the new comers (he might just have come for a "drink of water"). Give him some space and time to adjust (and keep the fire hose on the wall). Don't chase them back to spiritual starvation, while trying to fatten your own EGO. Meetings are usually a spiritual buffet and not all the items can be consumed; the newcomer might not want a lecture before or after the meeting, or to be cross talked to during the meeting. Wait patiently for someone to ask, and pay close attention to what they are asking for so that you can provide it (with the help of HOLY SPIRIT and not EGO). We often pee all over ourselves trying to unconditionally save the newcomer, and treat our fellow members with judgment and disdain (sounds like EGO to me). The highest position that we can spiritually obtain is equal. Honestly and candidly sharing your life experience (both the good and the bad), whether with one or many, is the basis of how we help others; knowing in our prayers that the person who shared their difficulties and trials with life to us is in the hands of HOLY SPIRIT and that their outcome will be God's perfect divine plan. Praying for God's divine and perfect outcome in other's lives is extremely powerful (especially praying as a group - one or more gathered in his name). Instead of holding business meetings to organize and control everyone (EGO business), prayer and meditation meetings might serve the greater good (HOLY SPIRIT business).

So congratulations, you are now ready to take the final exam to determine whether you are with HOLY SPIRIT or EGO. (I bet you didn't think that there would be a test):

Circle the correct answer

1   YES NO   Can we love the whole pattern of living (as eagerly as we do the small segment of it)? (AA)
2   YES NO   Can we bring the same spirit of love and tolerance into our family lives that we bring outside our family (and vice versa)? (AA)
3   YES NO   Can we have the same kind of confidence and faith in our family, loved ones, friends and co-workers as we do in our idols? (AA)
4   YES NO   Can we carry the HOLY SPIRIT into our daily work and jobs (and driving in traffic)? (AA)
5   YES NO   Can we bring new purpose and devotion to our ACIM studies (or a spiritual teaching or religion of our choice)? (AA)
6   YES NO   Can we bring a new joy in living trying by doing something about all these things? (AA)
7   YES NO   Can we accept and adjust to seeming success and failure without despair or pride? (AA)
8   YES NO   Can we accept poverty, sickness, loneliness, and bereavement with courage and serenity? (AA)
9   YES NO   Can we steadfastly content ourselves with the humbler, yet sometimes more durable satisfactions when the brighter, more glittering achievements are denied us? (AA)

The answers to the above questions are YES. IF you (honestly) answered NO to any of the above, THEN go to Step 1. (That's if you can admit that you were wrong) See what you are powerless over and what you are managing with the help of EGO. Work your way back up through the Steps to HOLY SPIRIT and then continue with the test. For the following situations, can you,

STEVE H.

with the help of HOLY SPIRIT, handle the following situations bravely and transform calamities into assets making them sources of growth and comfort:

10 YES NO   We fail to get a worked for promotion at work? (AA)
11 YES NO   We lose a good job? (AA)
12 YES NO   We have serious domestic difficulties at home? (AA)
13 YES NO   We lose a great sum of money or property? (AA)
14 YES NO   We get dumped, rejected or divorced? (AA)
15 YES NO   There is a death, murder, suicide or military casualty? (AA)
16 YES NO   We failed miserably at one or many attempts to live by spiritual principles (HOLY SPIRIT) and succumbed to temptation (EGO)? (AA)

If you answered NO to any of the above, perhaps instead of pontificating to the newcomer and your fellows how things should be done, you could share your weaknesses and gain strength from doing so. Don't worry, no matter how far down the scale you may go, you will see how with HOLY SPIRIT your experience will benefit others. You are just becoming more qualified to help others (through extracurricular and post graduate work with EGO). We're not done with the test:

Fill in the Blanks ; On the following two columns, give four examples of "Playing God" and four examples of "Being God":

<u>Playing God</u>   <u>Being God</u>

example A:
    Dominating Others   Serving Others
example B:
    Demands Attention   Unconditional Love
17 _____   _____
18 _____   _____
19 _____   _____
20 _____   _____

Oh, and I couldn't quite let you loose with out an essay question.

20 - 40 Write two paragraphs (10 sentences each) of how you learned that the satisfactions of our instincts cannot be the sole end and aim of our lives, and that we must be willing to place spiritual growth first:

Extra Credit: Write a "Gratitude List" of ten things you are grateful for in your present situation.

[Editor's note: I have been writing much of this test in a light hearted manner, and it's not to be taken too seriously. There is no intent to create any unworthy feelings. The "12 + 12" tells us, "without exception, we all pass through times when we can practice" spiritual principles "only with the greatest exertion of will. Occasionally we go even further than this. We are seized with a rebellion so sickening that we simply won't…When these things happen we should not think too ill of ourselves. We should simply resume…as soon as we can, doing what we know to be good for us….out of every season of grief or suffering, when the hand of God seemed heavy or even unjust, new lessons for living were learned, new resources of courage were uncovered, and finally, inescapably, the conviction came that God does move in a mysterious way His wonders to perform". (AA) Remember you can come to God (or HOLY SPIRIT) as you are, you don't have to clean up first; He will wash you, dress you, feed you and restore you.

The HOLY SPIRIT takes care of me. I have everything I need. He lets me rest in the meadow and leads me beside the quiet stream. He restores me to sanity. He helps me do what honors us most. Even when living in this seeming world of EGO (unfairness, hatred, war and death), I will not be afraid, because he is there guarding and guiding the way. HOLY SPIRIT has provided delicious food and drink for me along with my brothers and sisters. He has anointed me as His son. Surely goodness and mercy shall be with me in the presence of EGO, and I will dwell in the house of HOLY SPIRIT, forever. Amen (23rd Psalm changed liberally by the editor). Now try saying that five times a day!

(From the AA book "12 Steps + 12 Traditions") Remember, "true leadership depends upon example and not upon vain displays of power and glory. We shipwreck upon the reefs of personal importance, power, prestige, and ambition...We do not have to be specially distinguished among our fellows in order to be useful and profoundly happy...Service gladly rendered, obligations squarely met, troubles well accepted or solved with HOLY SPIRIT's help, the knowledge that at home, (in the work place) or in the world, we are partners in a common effort" (Equality, Non-judgment, Unconditional Love) ... "We are no longer isolated and alone in self-constructed prisons." (Some say the acronym of EGO stands for Edging God Out.) "The surety that we need no longer be square pegs in round holes, but can fit and belong in God's scheme of things -- these are the permanent and legitimate satisfactions of right living... True ambition is a desire to live usefully and walk humbly under the grace of God (HOLY SPIRIT)." (AA) God (HOLY SPIRIT) works anonymously, therefore our service and helpfulness to others should be anonymous, too.

The editor would like to close this chapter with several quotes which hopefully may encourage the reader to pursue a spiritual way of life:

"...although he came to scoff, perhaps he may remain to pray." Wm D. Silkworth, M.D.

"Tell him exactly what happened to you. Stress the spiritual feature freely. If the man be agnostic or atheist, make it emphatic that he does not have to agree with your conception of God (or HOLY SPIRIT). He can choose any conception he likes, provided it makes sense to him. The main thing is that he be willing to believe in a Power greater than himself and that he live by spiritual principles." Bill Wilson

"...if by one or two divings into the ocean of divine perception you do not find the pearls of God-communion, do not blame the ocean as lacking in the Divine Presence! Rather find fault with your skill in diving! Again and again sink into the ocean of meditation and seize there the pearls of blessed communion." Paramahansa Yogananda

HOLY SPIRIT, "I offer myself to Thee—to build with me and to do with me as Thou will. Relieve me of the bondage of" EGO, "that I may better do Thy will. Take away my difficulties, that victory over them may bear witness to those I would help of Thy Power, Thy Love, and "Thy Way of Life. May I do Thy will, always!" AA Third Step Prayer

CHAPTER 2 - THE TWELVE TRADITIONS TO PROTECT THE INDIVIDUAL AND COMMON WELFARE OF ACIM (AA)

The Traditions were written and established by Bill Wilson over a course of time after AA was fully operating and growing rapidly and the experiences of AA groups indicated their need. They were first formulated in 1946. Bill also had to spend about five years trying to sell and convince elders, groups and boards of their value and necessity. Then they were adopted by the substantial unanimity of a conference of AA delegates in 1950 at the 1st International Convention in Cleveland, Ohio. (Note that this is a much abbreviated version; much greater detail is available from AA literature such as <u>THE AA SERVICE MANUAL</u>, <u>PASS IT ON</u>, <u>LANGUAGE OF THE HEART</u> and <u>AA COMES OF AGE</u>.) The AA Concepts were developed much later after many other events, significant growth and functional development (they are copyrighted 1962). The editor has very little actual experience with the AA service structure and the AA fellowship has a large population of many wise fellows (men and women) who could provide much greater assistance and knowledge of its operation. This information is provided and outlined in this manner (by perhaps a novice) only as a proposal for the benefit of ACIM study groups. Other organizations have used and adopted the structure as well as some of the spiritual ideas of AA to develop their fellowships and there are presently many other 12 step fellowships available for a wide demand of special needs.

The editor did have a lot of fun recreating and rewording the AA information to better suite ACIM, but in the process many errors, omissions, misconceptions, new inventions and just pure untested theory may have occurred. Please take head that although I had fun creating this, it is not to be taken as a strict doctrine but only as a proposed guideline that may help ACIM study groups in their founding and growing phases. The Traditions are worded mostly to members, meetings, business discussions and groups, but after finishing the Concept chapter of this proposal, the editor had to rework and edit many ideas presented in this Tradition chapter because the Traditions do apply to all AA service functions. The reason for reworking this chapter was to attempt to eliminate any confusion that might occur for the different perspective views of the readers (be it new members or Board members). However the editor may not have achieved satisfactory results and there may be some procedural ambiguities that will obviously need further work and revision (which would be best to be done by a collective ACIM conscience with HOLY SPIRIT). Being that this document is not intended to be law, the editor is comfortable that sufficient information is provided and perhaps some of the errors and ambiguities may present different alternatives and provide the freedom to create and amend as the need arises.

As a novice and untrained writer, it is very difficult for me to express the great respect and awe that I hold for the entire written work of A COURSE IN MIRACLES. I believe that it is self explanatory, simple and understandable, if one has the persistence to stick with it enough to get through the initial confusion and resistance presented by EGO. It is in that same light that I hold the 12 Traditions of Alcoholics Anonymous. It is the AA Bill of Rights, which adequately protects the individual from other individuals or groups of people, thereby allowing him sufficient breathing space to remain, learn and continue to return to the well. The traditions also make sure that there is always enough room for the next person entering (without having to put up the "Members Only" sign on the door). The new person does not have to swear allegiance to the steps or traditions (nor do they have to get down or their knees or take a public bath to receive the same rights that all the other members have). Loyalty is strictly voluntary. AA has only one requirement for membership; the newcomer must have a desire to stop drinking (this does allow the group chairman to ask someone to leave if they are disrupting the meeting or it is apparent that they have a different agenda, such as panhandling or preaching the gospel, Koran, etc.). This prerequisite can be transposed to ACIM as "the only requirement for membership is a desire to learn and live ACIM". (My high school motto was "Live to learn; learn to live".) The process of protecting the individual and providing them with respect and concern creates a spiritual paradox; first, the individual feels welcome and part of a group. From that they develop a desire to align, serve and give back what is so freely given (which no amount of scolding, guilt producing lectures and finger waving could ever produce). The traditions protect the individual from the other people at the meeting; they protect the meeting from the sway of the group, they protect the group from other groups and higher organizational leadership, therefore the organization is protected from itself. (We presently live in a free society that provides and protects the rights of an individual and of spiritual assemblies. Hopefully AA, ACIM or any other spiritual organization will never need protection from government or other outside forces).

From the book AA COMES OF AGE: "Today we in AA are together, and we know we are going to stay together. We are at peace with each other and with the world around us. So many of our conflicts are resolved that our destiny seems secure. The problems of yesterday have produced the blessings of today. Ours is not the usual success story; rather it is the story of how, under God's grace, an unsuspected strength has arisen out of great weakness; of how, under threats of disunity and collapse, world-wide unity and brotherhood have been forged. In the course of this experience we have evolved a set of traditional principles by which we live and work together and relate ourselves as a fellowship to the world around us. These principles are called the Twelve Traditions of AA. They represent the distilled experience of our past, and we rely on them to carry us in unity through the challenges and dangers which the future may bring." (AA) Alcoholics Anonymous also has Three Legacies: Recovery, Unity and Service (represented in their emblem in the three sides of the triangle which create a structure of great strength). ACIM could use them as follows:

1	Recovery (AA) - We recover from EGO and return to HOLY SPIRIT
2	Unity (AA) - We stay together in unity. "United we stand, divided I fall."
3	Service (AA) - We serve our fellowship which provides the message of ACIM to all who need it or want it.

AA has also kept one rule: Rule 62 - Don't take yourself too damn seriously. From the AA "12 + 12" text: "At one time every AA group had many membership rules. Everybody was scared witless that something or someone would capsize the boat and dump us all back into the sea of alcohol. Our Foundation office asked each group to send in its list of protective regulations. The total list was a mile long. If all those rules had been in effect everywhere, no one could have possibly joined AA at all, so great was the sum of our anxiety and fear...isn't fear the true basis of intolerance? Yes, we were intolerant. How could we then guess that all those fears were to prove groundless? How could we know that thousands of these sometimes frightening people were to make astonishing recoveries and become our greatest workers and intimate friends? ...Could we foresee that troublesome people were to become our principal teachers of patience and tolerance? Could any then imagine a society which would include every conceivable kind of character cut across the barrier of race, creed, politics and language with ease? Why did AA finally drop all its membership regulations? Why did we leave the newcomer to decide himself whether...he should join us? Why did we dare to say, contrary to the experience of society and government everywhere, that we would neither punish nor deprive any AA of membership, that we must never compel anyone to pay anything, believe anything or conform to anything? ..Who dared to be judge, jury and executioner of his own sick brother? As group after group saw these possibilities, they finally abandoned all membership regulations." In another setting, "the elders, stargazing, dreamed of innovations. They figured that the town needed a great big alcoholic center, a kind of pilot plant AA groups could duplicate everywhere." "There was a promoter in the deal ... who allayed all fears ... despite the advice from the AA Foundation that other ventures which mixed an AA group with medication and education had come to sticky ends... To make things safer, the promoter organized three corporations and became president of them all ...To insure foolproof, continuous operation, sixty-one rules and regulations were adopted. But alas, this bright scene was not long in darkening. Confusion replaced serenity...and confusion compounded...and then came the inevitable explosion. When the smoke lifted, a wonderful thing had happened. The head promoter said...he wished he'd paid some attention to AA experience. Then he did something else that became an AA classic", he created rule # 62: "Don't take yourself so damn seriously" which also provides members and the membership the right to be wrong. (AA)

So then, why would an ACIM group wish to adopt a set of twelve traditions taken from the experiences of AA. Well perhaps the primary purpose should be listed first. The traditions provide ground rules for students and teachers of ACIM to better disseminate the ACIM information to the masses. AA information is passed on by word of mouth and anonymous "meetings" are held in almost every town in the U.S. and conducive to almost any schedule. The traditions provide a format that creates an enjoyable ambience and a desire to return for more information. (The AA slogan above the door is "Keep coming back" which is a great rule for success.) We like the meetings so much we return again and again for more (free) information. Some of us come daily or even twice a day, because the experience is so wonderful. We check our EGO's at the door (which we can readily retrieve after the meeting). There are no bosses or dictators to deal with. It is an atmosphere of true democracy, where everyone's perspective is valued. I wish my fellow ACIM students could benefit from the democracy of AA. From some of my exposure to ACIM groups, they appeared to me to be benign autocracy with a ministry of leaders. (I don't know if this is good or bad, it just is.) Some of the leaders expounded about how all their relationships were "HOLY" but ours were not. Other sessions appeared to be introductory therapy sessions that used the title ACIM to draw in people. Some used the title of ACIM to draw you into their particular belief system with all sorts of supplemental literature (not that some of the supplemental literature isn't awesome, but just a bit staggering sometimes). I often felt entrapped and with these kinds of experiences; and I didn't have an overwhelming desire to return (unless of course there were a lot of pretty women attending the class). Naturally this perspective is coming from EGO, but then again so it will be for most newcomers. With the AA traditions, that have been tried and tested, ACIM doesn't have to re-invent the wheel. The traditions work by some power greater than its individual parts. We ask you to "Keep it simple". Decisions to accept the traditions and afterwards decisions for the group are made by a collective conscious with a consensus of substantial unanimity. Some will agree with parts and disagree with other sections of the traditions. Some will hold it in disgust or feel betrayed. Some will make cynical jokes. But the tie breaker that can always bring things back to HOLY SPIRIT is to ask "What would the Master do"? The traditions must be accepted by the individual, then the members of the meeting, the members of the meeting can form a routine of scheduled meetings and activities and call themselves a group, the groups can interact with other groups in their central district or geographic area, on the Internet or in other locations (e.g. sister groups, brotherhoods, etc.), and if services are necessary or wanted at a higher level they can then be formed as needed. An AA tradition is that our leader's serve, they never govern.

The traditions (reworded from AA to compensate for ACIM) are as follows:

1 ACIM depends upon unity; individual welfare as well as our common welfare are of the highest priority. All ACIM members and service staff (paid or unpaid) are equal. No one person or group of persons should have supreme rule or perspective over others; we only share our opinion, wisdom and insight (experience, strength and hope).

2 There is one Ultimate Authority, an Unconditional Loving God - we ask HOLY SPIRIT first before any decisions or votes - decisions are expressed through a collective conscience by the immediate participants and a consensus is represented by a substantial unanimity or majority. We respect the majority as well as the minority opinion. A "No Decision" can be resolved by random pick from the "hat" of all the presented solutions or candidates.

3 ACIM should be, whenever possible, inclusive and not exclusive. The only requirement for membership is a desire to learn and live ACIM; we live to learn and we learn to live. Prior to speaking in an ACIM meeting, business discussion, group or service function, the speaker should qualify by stating their name and that they have a desire to learn and live ACIM. (Paid and unpaid service staff, landlords or consultants should be welcome to participate in any meeting or group business discussion pertinent to their duties and responsibilities and they should introduce themselves appropriately; service functions, offices and boards operate within the specifications of their charter, bylaws and the 12 concepts, always respecting the spirit of the 12 traditions).

4 Each member is autonomous, each meeting is autonomous, and each group is autonomous. With autonomy, each member, each meeting and each group must be responsible to the authority of their conscience (HOLY SPIRIT), treating all other members, meetings, groups and service functions with respect, dignity and consideration.

5 Each member, each meeting and each group has but one primary purpose, which is to learn and live ACIM and to assist other members, meetings and groups to learn and live ACIM.

6 An ACIM member, meeting or group, service worker, teacher or representative should never endorse, finance or lend the ACIM name to any related facility or outside enterprise - lest problems of money, property, prestige and authority divert us from our primary spiritual aim. The material assets should be divided from the spiritual;

 a. Considerable property of genuine use should be separately incorporated and managed;
 b. Meetings and groups should never go into an ACIM business;
 c. Meeting halls, clubs and group service offices ought to be incorporated and set apart from ACIM membership, meetings, groups, and business discussions, but the financial support and administration ought to be provided by ACIM members whenever possible.

d. An ACIM meeting, group, service function should bind itself to no one.

7. Every ACIM meeting, group or service office ought to be fully and voluntarily self supporting by its own members, declining outside contributions or fund raising activities. Experience has shown us that futile disputes over property, money and authority can destroy our spiritual heritage. ACIM treasuries should not continue beyond prudent reserves. The method of dispersing the excess shall be decided by a collective conscience of the immediate participants representing their convention of members (after each participating member consults with HOLY SPIRIT). ACIM membership is asked to support the ACIM service functions accordingly.

8. ACIM should remain nonprofessional - we never charge a fee for our assistance in teaching ACIM to others, however anyone providing necessary services for the benefit of ACIM members, meetings, groups or service functions can receive adequate compensation, when appropriate and deemed necessary. Complaints and disputes are submitted to the applicable leadership and are handled by a collective conscience of those leaders and members present for the discussion (after each consults with HOLY SPIRIT).

9. Each ACIM meeting, group, or service function should require the least amount of organization practical. All leaders are trusted servants to the whole and should be experienced with guidance from the HOLY SPIRIT. Rotating leadership is recommended. Two or more members may form meetings, meetings may form groups, groups may form central district service functions, central district service functions may form geographic area service functions and geographic area service functions may form a national service function and national service functions may form world service functions. Service functions are only authorized to provide service to the ACIM membership and to maintain the integrity of ACIM (e.g. in our overall public relations, our publications and literature, etc.) being always responsible to the ACIM membership. The contributions and authority they receive comes directly from the membership convention level that created the service function (the service function does not govern). Meetings and groups should have positions such as chairman, treasurer, representatives, etc. filled by volunteers (ratified with a substantial unanimity or majority by a collective conscience of the immediate participants after each participating member consults with HOLY SPIRIT. Ties, close decisions, and a "No Decision" should be resolved by the "hat" method).

10. ACIM has no opinion on outside issues. ACIM neither supports nor opposes any causes. No ACIM member, leader, representative, meeting, group or service function should ever, in such a way as to implicate ACIM, express any opinion on outside controversial issues.

11 ACIM ought to set an example of attraction rather than promotion (whenever practical) in their meetings, groups, service functions and public relations. The spiritual principle is to practice genuine humility in representing ACIM.

12 Anonymity is a spiritual principle that excludes EGO. Members ought check their titles, histories, heroics, pocket books, etc., as well as their EGO at the door prior to ACIM meetings and business or group discussions, ACIM service work or ACIM public relations. Spiritual principles take priority over personalities. Always ask HOLY SPIRIT for direction prior to speaking or acting for ACIM. (AA)

TRADITION 1 :

ACIM depends upon unity; individual welfare as well as our common welfare are of the highest priority. All ACIM members and service staff (paid or unpaid) are equal. No one person or group of persons should have supreme rule or perspective over others; we only share our opinion, wisdom and insight (experience, strength and hope). (AA)

The traditions, (steps and concepts) are suggestions and not commands. (The word "suggestion" should never be redefined to mean command). The traditions never use the word "Don't (and primarily uses the words: "should" or "ought to"). No ACIM member can compel another member to believe or practice a certain way. We are all equal (regardless of tenure or accomplishment) and we guard the individual's right for autonomy in their speech and actions. No one who expresses the desire to learn and live ACIM may be expelled or punished. Each member has the right to speak or refrain on any issue or discussion, however each member must conform to the particular meeting, group, and service function ground rules for participation. Anyone who cannot conform to acceptable standards for public behavior will be asked (usually by the chairman, who has the responsibility for the common welfare of the members) to leave the meeting, business discussion, group, or service function until such time that they are willing to conform. Unity and equality are cherished spiritual qualities; each member should be considerate and respectful to the other members, convention of members and service functions. (AA)

The traditions guarantee ACIM unity. The spiritual paradox is that when ACIM members are treated with dignity and respect, they treat ACIM meetings, conventions and service functions with dignity and respect. The member learns that their desires and ambitions (of EGO) must be silenced whenever it would damage ACIM. The member becomes aware that they are a part of the whole and that service to the whole ensures its continuity. The member discovers ACIM to be a way of life. The member finds that they cannot keep their miracle of forgiveness unless they give it away.

TRADITION 2:

There is one Ultimate Authority, an Unconditional Loving God - we ask HOLY SPIRIT first before any decisions or votes - decisions are expressed through a collective conscience by the immediate participants and a consensus is represented by a substantial unanimity or majority. We respect the majority as well as the minority opinion. A "No Decision" can be resolved by random pick from the "hat" of the presented solutions or candidates. (AA)

During meetings and business discussions each immediate participant has the right to be heard (within the constraints of the ground rules and specified time) and their perspective is valued and treated equally. In all matters of ACIM business, administration, or representation all decisions should consider the common welfare of ACIM first. Decisions should be made by each participating member (present for the discussion) consulting with HOLY SPIRIT in their own way and then voting. A certain amount of quiet time or intermission should be provided prior to voting. Members not present for the actual discussion should refrain from voting or participating in making the decision. Passing votes should be a substantial unanimity (80% or greater), including the abstained votes as part of the tally and "no decision" may be an acceptable solution, whenever possible. When a decision must be made, a "No Decision" can be resolved by random pick from the "hat" of the presented solutions or candidates. Meetings, business discussions and ground rules should not be designed to exclude other members from participating. This above method of decision making is what is referred to as the collective conscience (except that service functions above the group level use a substantial majority of 67% or higher, and do not count abstained votes).

Leaders, representatives and service officers are servants, not senators. These members have the altruistic privilege of doing the service chores. Such simple voluntary services that enable meetings, business discussions and groups to function are chairman, treasurer, secretary, and representatives. At the meeting level usually the chairman, treasurer and secretary roles can be fulfilled by one person unless the population of the meeting or group requires more assistance. The representatives are elected from one convention of members to participate in service function conventions requiring general membership representation; they also should participate actively and routinely in the routine meetings and group business discussions from which they were elected as representative to the higher service functions and likewise present the service function activities and decisions back to the group and meeting members. The trusted servants should not use their service position as status to go outside the function of that position in issuing orders, scolding or judging others. In no sense what ever should a sole member or group of members govern. (AA)

TRADITION 3:

ACIM should be, whenever possible, inclusive and not exclusive. The only requirement for membership is a desire to learn and live ACIM; we live to learn and we learn to live. Prior to speaking in an ACIM meeting, business discussion, group or service function, the speaker should qualify by stating their name and they have a desire to learn and live ACIM. (Paid and unpaid service staff, landlords or consultants should be welcome to participate in any meeting or group business discussion pertinent to their duties and responsibilities and should introduce themselves appropriately; service functions, offices and boards operate within the specifications of their charter, bylaws and the 12 concepts always respecting the spirit of the 12 traditions). (AA)

People are attracted to crowds and for various reasons. Some are trying to take care of the lonely heart. Some are looking for a loan or "someone to take care of me". Some are evangelizing and trying to convert others. Some are looking for customers. And some are just naturally giving and caring people. Often our motives are mixed. Since the traditions do not provide for judges in ACIM then no one can say who can attend a meeting of ACIM and who can't. However, each meeting should have established ground rules to prevent disruption, anarchy and chaos. It would be the meeting chairman's responsibility to identify what would be considered disruptive and take action by requesting order. Membership should be declared by the member prior to speaking: something similar to, "My name is _____, and I have a desire to learn and live ACIM." If they cannot qualify, they should just listen and learn.

When it is a member's turn to share their experience, strength and hope in a meeting or business discussion, they should be alert to their EGO and the concerns and needs of others to share also. Preferably they should consult with HOLY SPIRIT prior to sharing. They should try to be concise and to the point in order to limit their time of sharing and not repeat themselves. They should not use the time for self glorification or egotism. Their concern is to see what they can bring to the occasion and where might they be helpful. Under no circumstances should a member or anyone speaking be allowed to filibuster the meeting or activity by continuous sharing and not allowing other members sufficient time to express their perspective and opinion. In such an event, the chairman should take action accordingly.

Desire is an interesting word that can be looked at from many perspectives. In some realms of spiritual development, sensual desires should be overcome. The word desire as used in this tradition will be used through the HOLY SPIRIT which takes all things made of EGO to return us to Truth. Some success book authors (e.g. Napoleon Hill, Clement Jones) indicate that desire must be strong and foremost in our thought in order to achieve our goals. Therefore if your goal is a miracle, spiritual enlightenment, atonement, etc., we suggest that your desire be top priority in order to deal with the many other desires of EGO that will come your way. Vigilance will require a strong, persistent desire. A story told in AA goes, "A man asked his teacher about salvation and the teacher took him down to the river. They walked a ways into the water and the teacher turned to the man, put his hands on his shoulders and slowly pushed him down until the man's head was beneath the water. There the teacher held the man, steadfast. In a short while the man began to struggle and fight to get out of his teacher's grasp. When he finally made it to the surface with a large gasp for air, he looked at his teacher very puzzled and

STEVEH.

the teacher replied, "When you want salvation as much as you just wanted air, then it shall be yours." Therefore, your desire to learn and live ACIM should be as great as the above example in order to benefit yourself and others. "Seek first the Kingdom of God, and all else shal be provided unto you."

TRADITION 4:

Each member is autonomous, each meeting is autonomous, and each group is autonomous. With autonomy, each member, each meeting and each group must be responsible to the authority of their conscience (HOLY SPIRIT), treating all other members, meetings, groups and service functions with respect, dignity and consideration. (AA)

Good sense would recommend keeping rules and regulations to a minimum; however unfortunate situations arise before, during, and after meetings that should be addressed in business discussion later and added or subtracted from the ground rules to prevent reoccurrence of more unfortunate events. Each meeting or group will evolve differently and for different reasons. Eventually there may be quite a disparity between meetings. One may be ultra conservative as the other is liberal. One group should not try to infiltrate, corrupt, slander or change the other in order to have it conform to their perspective of how meetings and groups shall run things. In a sparsely populated area, you are more or less stuck with the collective conscience and must try to work within the system. In larger populated areas, you can shop around for the meetings and groups that suit your needs. If you don't think that your meeting or group is the best one, you should probably shop around for another. Ask HOLY SPIRIT for help; HOLY SPIRIT may either help you change your attitude or your location.

When I was younger, an AA elder (self appointed) came to our downtown AA meeting and lectured us that we should not talk about drug use in an AA meeting. We let him have his say, then, when the next person had the floor, they explained the traditions and the word autonomy. The traditions prevented chaos and the event turned into only a matter of difference of opinion, instead of a fist fight. What puzzled me more was, after the meeting the two shook hands, laughed and went their way. (Many times in meetings, EGO wanted to leave and I had to hold onto my chair to keep my body in the meeting. If you bring the body to meetings, the mind will follow.)

TRADITION 5:

Each member, each meeting and each group has but one primary purpose, which is to learn and live ACIM and to assist other members, meetings and groups to learn and live ACIM. (AA)

Do I need to say more; for whatever motives brought us to meetings, we soon learn that there is something loving and caring going on in the meeting that keeps us coming back. (Personally, I try not to go longer than 24 hours without a meeting in order to recharge my spiritual battery.) EGO recovers much faster than anything else and although we may have been deflated, soon temptations of every sort (especially the one's you have the greatest weakness for) will come your way. You may leave a meeting sure of your spiritual path and trip over your feet out the door. Do not be discouraged, although we think that we are or can be honest (if only we make up our mind to be) we may find that practicing it may be as difficult as getting into the major leagues. Our desires for relationships, power, money, prestige, recognition, etc. return to our blind side full force. Alone, we once again become the zombies of King EGO. The best way to defend against depression and self loathing after our disappointments and failures is to love ourselves. One of the best ways to love our self is to return to meetings. (A friend told me at a meeting to say after each defeat, "I love you my name , and I'm on your side".) In the meetings we share our defeats as well as our victories (miracles). We tell others what we learned in ACIM and how it applied to our lives. We tell others in order to help ourselves and laugh at EGO.

TRADITION 6 :

An ACIM member, meeting or group, service worker, teacher or representative should never endorse, finance or lend the ACIM name to any related facility or outside enterprise - lest problems of money, property, prestige and authority divert us from our primary spiritual aim. The material assets should be divided from the spiritual;

a. Considerable property of genuine use should be separately incorporated and managed;
b. Meetings and groups should never go into an ACIM business;
c. Meeting halls, clubs and group service offices ought to be incorporated and set apart from ACIM membership, meetings, groups, and business discussions, but the financial support and administration ought to be provided by ACIM members whenever possible.
d. An ACIM meeting, group, service function should bind itself to no one. (AA)

Somehow, when we are big fish in a small pond, we seem to know what to do; but put us into a larger lake or sea and our appetites grow. We can get fat off the smaller fish until a bigger one comes along and devours us. As we become fearless, our appetites and ambitions can often balloon. This is where the "shoemaker should stick to his trade". Our focus and vigilance should be on ACIM. It is enough to keep us busy for a lifetime. These other extravagant and grandiose ideas may be a distraction by EGO and diversion from our spiritual path toward HOLY SPIRIT.

Arranging for meetings and renting the space does not have to be too difficult, but in the world of EGO, unforeseen difficulties do arise. Troubles with landlords, fellow tenants, parking, etc will have to be addressed the ACIM way. Sometimes it is best to establish a meeting hall. There will be many ACIM members with experience and trades in these sorts of matters and we can use the help of HOLY SPIRIT and collective conscience to sort things out. The idea of this tradition is to not let the membership get tied up into the material assets. Congregations flock and grow during the financial good times and scatter rather quickly when times get tough, leaving a few leaders strapped to the building.

Remember that common sense in the world of EGO doesn't make dollars or sense in the world of HOLY SPIRIT. We must rely on infinite HOLY SPIRIT rather than our finite selves. An AA sponsor (teacher of another newer member) told his sponsee to call before acting on any bright ideas, and if he had any really good ones, to come over to his house right away. The power of EGO dissolves "whenever two or more are gathered in His (HOLY SPIRIT's) name". This includes on the telephone.

Likewise, the traditions suggest that ACIM does not get into any ties with outside companies, corporations or institutions, etc. We have no opinion on issues outside the scope of what is in the ACIM literature; therefore we neither endorse nor oppose anyone. The ACIM name should only be used in reference to the ACIM literature and to the convention of members trying to learn and live the philosophies presented in the ACIM literature. (AA)

TRADITION 7:

Every ACIM meeting, group or service office ought to be fully and voluntarily self supporting by its own members, declining outside contributions or fund raising activities. Experience has shown us that futile disputes over property, money and authority can destroy our spiritual heritage. ACIM treasuries should not continue beyond prudent reserves. The method of dispersing the excess shall be decided by a collective conscience of the immediate participants representing their convention of members (after each participating member consults with HOLY SPIRIT). ACIM membership is asked to support the ACIM service functions accordingly. (AA)

The management principle used is a reverse pyramid system. Although through the eye of EGO it would appear that we are building the pyramid from bottom to top, actually the membership will always be on top and the added structure will be subordinate to the membership. Such an organizational structure is something like the board having to answer to the stock holders; or politicians having to answer to the voters; with such analogies, it makes it simple to see how easy it would be for someone or a group to try to reverse that order and unknowingly dominate the membership. Funding comes from voluntary donations of members during all meetings, convention of members or business discussions by passing the hat. Elected treasurers for each convention of members handle the financial responsibilities. The funds go first to paying the rent and bills to keep the meeting halls open. If it is found necessary by collective conscience to add more administrative structure, then the added organization is financed and maintained by the members of that collective conscience and their representative convention of members. At meeting and group levels, the newly formed administration and staff answer only to the convention of members that created it, but when required, serve the general membership and public. Within reason, the newly formed administration performs only the job it was created to do. When these meeting and group structures get old or topple, unless a new convention of members takes action by collective conscience to do something, the "no decision" alternative takes effect and we let the chips fall were they may. And sometimes by the act of collective conscience it may be required to reassemble or disassemble the structures built by previous members. At the service functions above the group level, service responsibilities and activities are carried out in accordance with the established charters, bylaws and the 12 concepts always respecting the 12 traditions. (AA)

Likewise, ACIM should not horde money, property or material assets. A collective conscience of each convention of members will decide as to what is prudent and what is extravagant and will disperse the funds according to the decisions of the collective conscience. (AA)

TRADITION 8:

ACIM should remain nonprofessional - we never charge a fee for our assistance in teaching ACIM to others, however anyone providing necessary services for the benefit of ACIM members, meetings, groups or service functions can receive adequate compensation, when appropriate and deemed necessary. Complaints and disputes are submitted to the applicable leadership and are handled by a collective conscience of those leaders and members present for the discussion (after each consults with HOLY SPIRIT). (AA)

"Freely ye have received, freely give". And this shall be true within the confines of ACIM meetings, business discussions and groups. There should be no charge for any altruistic endeavor we perform in teaching or sharing the ACIM information that we have with our fellows or someone newly interested. At all meetings and business or group discussions, the treasurer passes the hat (or basket) for voluntary contributions. At the time when the hat is passed something similar to the following is announced: "ACIM is self supporting through its own voluntary contributions. The funds are handled by the treasurer to pay the costs of the meeting hall and to support the service functions and administration of ACIM. ACIM is not affiliated with any outside agency, which includes the landlords of the meeting hall. Freely ye have received, freely give."

Anyone providing outside services for ACIM (whether a member or not) is entitled full and fair compensatory pay and reimbursement. It would be difficult to list all the types of services rendered, but the staff of the ACIM service offices and boards would be included. (AA)

ACIM does not have the authority to tell anyone how they should live their personal life or how they should make a living. To do so would be a breach of that person's anonymity. No one swears allegiance to the traditions. How they choose to use their name or the name of ACIM or choose to pass on the information of ACIM to others outside of the meetings, business discussions and facilities is their affair. We ask all ACIM members to respect the traditions and the common welfare of ACIM.

The traditions are guidelines and naturally will not encompass every imaginable situation that could occur, therefore, complaints and concerns should be submitted to the leaders (preferably the chairman) for debate in scheduled and announced business discussions (usually held immediately after a regular ACIM meeting). The format for discussion should be something as follows:

1   Chairman leads opening prayer (and invites HOLY SPIRIT), reads the ground rules and opens discussion;
2   Complainants voice concerns and possible solutions;
3   Floor is open going in a clockwise circle around the room asking each member for discussion of the presented solutions or other possible solutions. The member who has the floor should not be interrupted except by the Chairman for matters of procedure. The circle continues until no one has anything left to say (or the Chairman closes the discussion for the sake of time and the common welfare);
4   A solution is submitted to the floor for voting in a YES (in favor) or NO (against) format;
5   A silent period or intermission is held for prayer and meditation, asking HOLY SPIRIT

for direction;

6   The vote is taken, counted and written down as number of YES, the number of NO, the number abstained and the total number participating in the discussion. A substantial unanimity (80%) should be reached for either YES or NO (counting the abstentions); otherwise a "No decision" is reached.

7   With a "No decision", if a decision is necessary, then prior to adjournment each participating member writes their solution on a piece of paper and puts it in a hat and the chairman randomly pulls one from the hat which will be the new resolution or ground rule.

8   The Chairman or Secretary incorporates the decision into the regular ACIM meeting ground rules, which are always read at the beginning of every meeting.

TRADITION 9:

Each ACIM meeting, group, or service function should require the least amount of organization practical. All leaders are trusted servants to the whole and should be experienced with guidance from the HOLY SPIRIT. Rotating leadership is recommended. Two or more members may form meetings, meetings may form groups, groups may form central district service functions, central district service functions may form geographic area service functions and geographic area service functions may form a national service function and national service functions may form world service functions. Service functions are only authorized to provide service to the ACIM membership and to maintain the integrity of ACIM (e.g. in our overall public relations, our publications and literature, etc.) being always responsible to the ACIM membership. The contributions and authority they receive comes directly from the membership convention level that created the service function (the service function does not govern). Meetings and groups should have positions such as chairman, treasurer, representative, etc. filled by volunteers (ratified with a substantial unanimity or majority by a collective conscience of the immediate participants after each participating member consults with HOLY SPIRIT. Ties, close decisions, and a "No Decision" should be resolved by the "hat" method). (AA)

By not taking ourselves do damn seriously, we will find that often things don't go in the way that they were planned. People don't keep their commitment, no one shows up for the meeting, the treasurer didn't handle the money correctly, etc. On the other hand some will do all the work and later be rejected by a group of new comers. We find with experience that things work out just fine and in the way they were intended. ACIM should not reserve the right to direct or govern its members, but the members by their own omission should be willing to obey spiritual principles. HOLY SPIRIT provides the rewards and EGO provides the punishment. ACIM represents HOLY SPIRIT and is animated by the spirit of service.

At the time of this writing, the ideas presented for this ACIM tradition are just speculative. The above structure is taken from AA, but AA did not initially form in the above manner. The AA founders were wise enough to create the Traditions and Concepts later so that they could turn the organization back to its members for posterity. It worked so it may work again. The Traditions should be subject to amendment by collective conscience and substantial unanimity only at the highest established convention of members (e.g. national conference, world conference).

TRADITION 10:

ACIM has no opinion on outside issues. ACIM neither supports nor opposes any causes. No ACIM member, leader, representative, meeting, group or service function should ever, in such a way as to implicate ACIM, express any opinion on outside controversial issues. (AA) We mind our own business. We are concerned with the matters of HOLY SPIRIT and not the world of EGO. That goes for the good as well as the bad. We shouldn't rush to champion or defend any causes. We never have sufficient information from EGO to know the truth of these issues, therefore we trust in the Truth provided to us from HOLY SPIRIT and the ACIM literature. Our action is through prayer, meditation, forgiveness, and service to others. We allow the collective conscience of ACIM membership to guide our actions.

TRADITION 11:

ACIM ought to set an example of attraction rather than promotion (whenever practical) in their meetings, groups, service functions and public relations. The spiritual principle is to practice genuine humility in representing ACIM. (AA)

AA is a society that wishes to publicize their principles and not their personalities, therefore if we
were to adopt these traditions, personal ambitions should have no place in ACIM. Each member becomes an active guardian to protect ACIM by using the spiritual principle of attraction. Actions speak louder than words. We neither shun press, radio, television or films nor do we try to sell ACIM. For us pride is a debit and we replace the word pride with gratitude. Our advertisement campaign is one of genuine humility. Anonymity at the public level is protection against our selves (EGO) and becomes the sentinel of the traditions. (AA)

From the book AA COMES OF AGE: "As never before, the struggle for power, importance, and wealth is tearing civilization apart--man against man, family against family, group against group, nation against nation. Nearly all those engaged in the fierce competition declare that their aim is peace and justice for themselves, their neighbors, and their nations. "Give us power," they say, "and we shall have justice; give us fame and we shall set a great example; give us money and we shall be comfortable and happy." People throughout the world believe such things and act accordingly. On this appalling dry bender, society seems to be staggering down a dead-end road. The sign at the end of the road is clearly marked, "Disaster" (EGO). We of AA know. Nearly every one of us has traversed this identical dead-end path. Powered by ... self-justification, many of us had pursued the phantoms of self-importance and money right up to the "Disaster" sign. Then came AA" (or HOLY SPIRIT). "We faced about and found ourselves on a new high road where the direction signs never said a word about ...fame...The new signs read "This way to sanity and serenity"..."Anonymity is the greatest protection our society can ever have". (AA)

Does this mean we hide our heads in the sand and never try to disseminate this great message and wonderful ACIM way of life; by no means! "Faith without works is dead!" We just want to avoid the pitfalls of frenzy and delirium" (EGO) "and pay attention to the warning signs where others have crashed at high speed on the winding turns of the road. We allow the collective conscience of HOLY SPIRIT to guide our way. What was once common sense is now uncommon sense. It may take some us a while to develop our intuitive sense and maybe even longer to listen to it. So we should trust infinite" HOLY SPIRIT "to lead in the collective conscience of" ACIM, "rather than our finite selves." In genuine humility, attendants at an AA meeting usually conclude by joining, holding hands and saying the "Lord's Prayer". ACIM meetings could do the same:

Forgive us our illusions, Father, and help us to accept our true relationship with You, in which there are no illusions, and where none can ever enter. Our holiness is Yours. What can there be in us that needs forgiveness when Yours is perfect? The sleep of forgetfulness is only the unwillingness to remember Your forgiveness and Your love. Let us not wander into temptation, for the temptation of the Son of God is not Your will. And let us receive only

STEVE H.

what You have given, and accept but this into the minds which You created and which You love. Amen. (ACIM)

It is recommended that all ACIM meetings and discussions begin and end in humble prayer.

TRADITION 12:

Anonymity is a spiritual principle that excludes EGO. Members ought check their titles, histories, heroics, pocket books, etc., as well as their EGO at the door prior to an ACIM meetings and business or group discussions, ACIM service work or ACIM public relations. Spiritual principles take priority over personalities. Always ask HOLY SPIRIT for direction prior to speaking or acting for ACIM. (AA)

Spiritual Principles are a paradox to the world of EGO. To succeed with Spiritual Principles, EGO must be smashed (this is the only must that you will find in the Traditions - Beware of the scolding "Must Nazies"; they'll tell you that a suggestion is a subtle command; always reserve the right to decide with your personal understanding and relationship with HOLY SPIRIT for yourself). The Spiritual Principle of anonymity protects the individual member as well as the common welfare of ACIM. Anonymity prevents one member or group of members from bullying or browbeating another member or group and maintains equality. It prevents the sale of "guilt tickets" or a "superiority/ inferiority complex" during the meetings or discussions. It instills comradery and fellowship. The highest position you can ever achieve in ACIM is equal. In turn, members remember to check with HOLY SPIRIT before speaking or acting on behalf of ACIM and develop a restraint of pen and tongue (EGO). As we align ourselves with HOLY SPIRIT, the Will of the Father acts through us and we discover that we are receiving what we always wanted.

ACIM is not a secret society, but there are many ways where EGO can re-raise its ugly head. Take caution that EGO works best when we are no longer joined with each other or HOLY SPIRIT. In early sobriety, I once put an AA bumper sticker on the back of my car: "But, for the grace of God..." which represented a beautiful story about St. Francis of Assisi. I was late for mass and I was bullying my wife, and drove like a madman only to get out of my car and read the bumper sticker. Sometimes humiliation leads us to humility. I decided that from then on, I needed to put the bumper sticker inside my car on the dash, and not advertise my hypocrisy to the public.

I also thought it was best when I started my new job to proudly let my employer know that I was a member of Alcoholics Anonymous which might be a very valid reason that I was passed over for promotion 12 times in the past 18 years. Gossip, rumors and propaganda in the competitive world of EGO can be devastating. I've been openly (and I am sure many times behind my back) accused of drinking and I've been told by the Chief Engineer (unsolicited) that he had read the book ALCOHOLICS ANONYMOUS implying and later acting upon a very rigorous, prejudice and bias handling of my work and discipline. But had I not set the ball in motion.

On the other hand, sitting quietly in the corner, afraid and not sharing your experience, strength and hope with the fellow members is being introverted and perhaps too anonymous. We are not asking that you go from introvert to extravert, one extreme to the next, but slowly allow yourself time to fit in (it might take six months), but "Keep Coming Back". Live to learn and learn to live.

Also just as a word to the wise: anonymity in the restaurants and side functions is also recommended. We can often be quite spiritual at the meeting, but later when we let our hair down, we lose focus on who may be watching or judging our words and our behavior (which

STEVE H.

in turn could possibly be misconstrued by someone's EGO to reflect negatively upon ACIM). It's best not to use or advertise the ACIM name in our social activities outside of our meetings and service activities. Have fun, be your true SELF. Remember, God (HOLY SPIRIT) works anonymously; so should we.

CHAPTER 3 – MEETINGS TO TEACH AND CARRY THE ACIM MESSAGE

Bill Wilson believed strongly in democracy, whereas his Midwestern counter-part founders probably had much stronger roots with government by republic, where the elders decide what's best for the whole. Also the Midwesterners were much more strict, staunch and conservative with their religious dogma. The editor of this proposal sides with Bill, so most of the presentation of this AA information will be portrayed from a liberal, democratic equality point of view, however not all meetings in AA function democratically. And with the tradition of autonomy, that's just fine. There are meetings where members dress formally and it is pretty much rank and file, and I have been to some meetings that were even too liberal for me. The "Old Duffy's" group for instance has no rules per say. They welcome cross talk and if you got drunk feel free to share. There are the richest of the rich meetings and the poorest of the poor meetings, and all sorts of shades in between. There are men's stag meetings and women's stag (I thought it should be "doe") meetings. Birds of a feather fl ock together so there are meetings of predominately one race or ethnic group. There are professional meetings for attorney's, doctors, nurses, pilots, etc. There are gay meetings. There are large meetings with hundreds of people and others with just a handful. Some meetings form into groups and others just remain as meetings with little other organization involved. Each has established their ground rules. Although ACIM is nowhere near this stage of this type of development, who knows what could happen in a hundred years, especially if ACIM has the ability to get the 12 Steps out to those who are not alcoholic or addicts. With the remarkable and rapid healing ability of the Steps, many who ordinarily wouldn't be exposed to ACIM (or have any desire to be) now could be warmly introduced to its concept.

There are also many types of meetings in AA. There are speakers meetings where one person tells his drinking autobiography, (Aka. drunkalog) where they tell what they were like, what happened, and what they are like now (in ACIM we could tell what it was like with EGO, what happened, and what is it like with HOLY SPIRIT). The speaker's meeting usually lasts for about an hour including all the other functions of a meeting. And there are various spin-offs of this version. Also, there are book study meetings, where each attendee reads a paragraph from what they are studying and comments or comments later during a discussion period of the meeting. The book study meetings can be for the Steps, Steps and Traditions, the AA Text, etc. ACIM could easily include this type of meeting to study the ACIM text, workbook and teachers manual. In its democratic style it is very enlightening when everyone shares their perspective. There are also topic discussion meetings, where the chairman or a volunteer picks a topic (e.g. forgiveness) and everyone takes turns sharing their experience, strength and hope on that particular topic.

The meeting usually consists of:
1. <u>An opening group prayer</u> (AA uses the Serenity Prayer); Naturally ACIM members might have other prayers from ACIM text that they prefer. For example the ACIM text meetings could read the Introduction to ACIM:

This is a course in miracles. It is a required course. Only the time you take it is voluntary. Free will does not mean that you can establish the curriculum. It means only that you can elect

STEVE H.

what you want to take at a given time. The course does not aim at teaching the meaning of love, for that is beyond what can be taught. It does aim, however, at removing the blocks to the awareness of love's presence, which is your natural inheritance. The opposite of love is fear, but what is all encompassing can have no opposite. The course can therefore be summed up very simply in this way:

Nothing real can be threatened
Nothing unreal exists.
Herein lies the peace of God. (ACIM)

It has an amazing effect to hear the same concept repeated over and over, ritualistically at every meeting. Another good opener would be:

I am here only to be truly helpful.
I am here to represent Him who sent me.
I do not have to worry about what to say or what to do,
because He Who sent me will direct me.
I am content to be wherever He wishes,
knowing He goes there with me.
I will be healed as I let Him teach me to heal. (ACIM)

The ACIM texts says, "You can do much on behalf of your own healing and that of others if, in a situation calling for help, you think of it this way" (ACIM).

2. <u>Reading of the Preamble:</u> (changing the AA preamble to better suit ACIM; here goes:) ACIM is a fellowship of men and women who share their experience, strength and hope with each other that they may recover from EGO and return to HOLY SPIRIT and help others to do the same. The only requirement for membership is a desire to learn and live ACIM. There are no dues or fees for ACIM membership, we are self supporting through our own contributions. ACIM is not allied with any sect, denomination, politics, organization or institution; does not wish to engage in any controversy; neither endorses nor opposes any causes. Our primary purpose is to stay with HOLY SPIRIT (and experience miracles) and help others to achieve the atonement and holy relationships.

This opens the meeting to anyone from any denomination, sect, religion, culture, etc.

3. <u>Introductions:</u> The chairman asks if there is anyone new to the meeting and if they would like to introduce themselves. (AA conventionally applauds as a way to welcome the individuals.) The chairman also asks if there are any out of town visitors (again applause). Sometimes each participant introduces themselves (and at that time they can qualify by saying after their name that they have a desire to learn and live ACIM).

4. <u>Reading the ground rules and describing the type of meeting:</u> An example would be as follows:

This is a meeting of ACIM. This meeting will be an ACIM Text Study meeting. Each participant will read a line or two from Chapter _____, Section(s) _____ starting with my right and pass it on to the next until our reading is complete. Afterwards, the next person in line will share what they learned or understand from the reading and each participant will have an opportunity to share continuing in this circular motion to the right (time permitting). Each person is asked to say their name and that they have a desire to learn and live ACIM prior to reading or sharing, or they can choose to pass. It is also recommended that prior to speaking, take a moment to ask HOLY SPIRIT to guide your words so others shall be blessed. Please be respectful of the other members when they are reading or talking, not to disrupt or interrupt their participation. Due to time constraints, each person shall take only one opportunity to talk and limit their sharing to 5 minutes. About halfway through the meeting, we will pass a hat for ACIM support, respecting the seventh tradition which states to the effect that every ACIM meeting, group or service function ought to be fully and voluntarily self supporting by its own members. The meeting will end at _____.

There are as many formats as there are meetings. I chose the style that goes around the room and puts a restraint on the frequency and amount of time one can speak during a meeting. It is the most democratic, but there are many other types: e.g. (1) the chairman chooses who is to share, (2) one person starts and when finished calls upon another, (3) people just speak out when one person finishes, etc. Usually there is no cross talk; that is we do not have cross conversations or address one another, give advice, or speak directly to them as we share, and we do not interrupt while someone has the floor. However, some meetings prefer cross talk or are very lax with comments from the peanut gallery. Some meetings only let the elders speak; and naturally, if it is a speakers meeting only one person talks.

The meeting can be at someone's house or a rented hall. Once the meetings and groups begin to grow, clubs open up where you can come by most anytime to speak and hear ACIM or just relax. As stated in the Traditions, the clubs and halls should remain a separate entity from ACIM meetings. Some clubs have expanded into rather large complexes while others just provide a place for the meeting and lock the door afterwards. Some clubs have meetings around the clock and others might have one or two a day. This information is provided to give an idea of how and what direction ACIM could go using AA experience.

1   Self Supporting Collection: About halfway through the meeting, it is halted and the hat (or basket) is passed. Usually someone reads the 12 Traditions or just the 7th Tradition while this is happening. Then the discussion resumes. The chairman or treasurer counts the money, divides the rent money and other bills and tabulates the prudent reserve. For ACIM, the chairman or treasurer also forwards funds to the service functions formed (group, central district, geographic area, national, and world). The amounts are predetermined by the collective conscience ground rules of the particular convention of members providing the funds. Often business discussion meetings are held after the regular meeting if ground rules need to be changed or a collective conscience about any particular matter may be necessary.

2   Closing of the Meeting: Usually five minutes before the end of the meeting the chairman stops the discussion and asks for any ACIM announcements (those making the meeting ground rules can decide if they also want outside announcements). They can give a tally of the funds, if so desired, or explain the meeting schedule, letting everyone know when the next meeting will be held. In genuine humility, attendants at an AA meeting usually conclude by joining holding hands and saying the "Lord's Prayer". The ACIM version is:

Forgive us our illusions, Father, and help us to accept our true relationship with You, in which there are no illusions, and where none can ever enter. Our holiness is Yours. What can there be in us that needs forgiveness when Yours is perfect? The sleep of forgetfulness is only the unwillingness to remember Your forgiveness and Your love. Let us not wander into temptation, for the temptation of the Son of God is not Your will. And let us receive only what You have given, and accept but this into the minds which You created and which You

STEVE H.

love. Amen. (ACIM)

It is recommended that all ACIM meetings and discussions begin and end in humble prayer.

AA took a very long time to get off the ground. Some who tried to start meetings sat in empty rooms for quite awhile. Much of their initial plan was to find those like themselves that they could tell the story of their drinking life to and the miraculous recovery that they have experienced from the spiritual principles they were given. Outside publicity greatly helped AA in the beginning and naturally AA had a cause - a successful recovery plan for the disease of alcoholism. The effects of EGO may not be as readily accepted as an American Medical Society recognized disease. And obviously there may not be a large amount of present course students that will be interested in what is contained in this proposal. However, the author did feel a sense of responsibility since he did spend a large segment of his life studying these two text books, AA & ACIM, to make this particular perspective available in print for those who may want or need it. As it happens to turn out, the meetings provide the best way to help others. Just as we learned that our presence and word in speaking the Truth is very powerful in helping others, ACIM has a very healing effect in itself. The meeting has an indescribable effect on those who attend (similar to a good day in church). It fills the void that many carry inside with the nectar of spirituality. Its taste is so sweet and delicious, that we come back for more. Vigilance is a difficult task for many of us and alone with EGO we often fall into the pits of despair. But just by bringing the body to a meeting, within an hour a miracle occurs and we are back into the light of HOLY SPIRIT. Just by entering the room, we join with HOLY SPIRIT. It doesn't matter if you come late or walk in just for the last five minutes. The holy effect from joining is always the same. It's in the meeting that we get recharged and rejuvenated. And when our spiritual tank gets low, we come back in for a fill up.

When I was in a small town attending meetings, a gentleman shared that he had stayed away from meetings for awhile and had progressively felt depressed and angry. When he finally talked to his sponsor (teacher), his sponsor asked, "How did you feel when you went to meetings regularly?" in which he responded, "Great!" And his sponsor asked, "How do you feel now that you haven't gone to meetings for awhile?", and he responded, "Horrible!" His sponsor then asked, "Well, do you get it?" And he didn't get it (because he was too deep into EGO. After several meetings and rejoining with HOLY SPIRIT, you get it.) Unfortunately or fortunately (I don't know if it is good or bad), this became a standard joke for anyone who had stayed away for awhile and came back with many arrows in their behind. Everyone in the meeting would laugh except the person coming back. They didn't get it (but after awhile, I did). I am sometimes asked, do you have to go to those meetings the rest of your life and I reply that I want to go to those meetings for the rest of my life. Anything that can keep me out of the grips of EGO is well worth it. [An AA antidote is: I asked my sponsor (teacher) how long do I have to go to meetings and he responded, "Just until you want to go".] We also find another spiritual paradox from the meetings that as we help ourselves, we help others. True altruistic and humble service work happens by attending meetings.

We also celebrate our anniversaries in AA. We call them our "Birthdays". We usually announce it on the day of the anniversary, and sometimes we bring cake. At the end of the week or month, we also have larger anniversary celebrations and each celebrant is asked to share their experience, strength and hope. We celebrate the first 30 days, the first 3 months, the first 6 months and for each year after since we have been coming to meetings. Not only does it boost the morale of everyone attending, but it facilitates the new comers spotting and identifying with other new comers and spotting the old timers as well. A great deal of respect is given for longevity and now-a-days there are many persons with 30 and 40 years of continuous anniversary celebrations.

As the years go by not only do our shyness and quirks leave us, but we greatly improve our speaking skills. And so do our listening skills improve. When I started meetings, I often daydreamed and thought that an hour was much too long. I also tried to prepare what I was going to say. (I always remembered what I said in the meeting, but generally that was all.) As a result, I didn't listen much. I was having a lot of emotional problems and I talked to an old timer, who suggested that during the meetings I watch the mouth of each person who is talking and concentrate on my two ears. If I hadn't been so desperate, I probably would have ignored his advise; but his advise worked and I have been using it ever since. It's how I take my medicine.

In Carl Roger's book ON BECOMING A PERSON he shares his discovery that people usually solve their own problem if they have someone to listen. In college I took a communication and counseling class. Our only assignment was to come to class prepared to talk about ourselves with some one else or be prepared to listen to someone else talk. The rules were, as speakers, we were responsible for what we wanted to discuss and how much information we wanted to reveal; as listeners we were to keep eye contact and focus on what they were saying, being prepared to repeat back to them what they said at anytime they stopped talking. We were not to share a common experience or give advice or be empathetic to their feelings. Usually when they heard what they had said, they nodded and were stimulated to share more. It was a most rewarding experience to talk, but I found it very taxing to listen. (I had much less work to do with this class and I remember this class above everything else I spent great time and effort to cram in with the other classes I had.) I found that in meetings, the Carl Roger's method is what is being applied to everyone who shares. (Another paradox; because those who share, take; and that is why it is important to give everyone a chance to talk in the meetings.) They solve their own problems (and usually when everyone puts their problems on the table, we willingly take our own back, because we know best how to deal with them).

I used to listen to an old timer who would share that AA meetings weren't a social club, dating service or therapy session, but I found that it was all of those things and more. We had AA dances; we would socialize in restaurants after the meetings; and because of the nature of what we share, we often became intimate friends with each other in short order. And if we are looking for a partner or mate, isn't it a good idea to have a good sound spiritual foundation from the meetings first. (In AA they say: first we make the cake, and then we put on the icing.) Besides the meetings are so much fun. There are the many stories and antidotes (besides the slogans and clichés) from all around the nation.

1   In the jungle, the wildebeest stays with the herd, those that stray are usually the target of the lions (or EGO).
2   A wise man learns from others mistakes, a smart man learns from his own, and a fool learns from none.
3   Three blind men walked up to an elephant and tried to describe what they had encountered. The first said it was a tall tree, the second said it was a great wall and the third said it was a vine.
4   A man walked down a path and fell into a hole. It took him a great deal of time and effort to get out. Much later the man came down the path and fell into the hole again, but this time it

took less effort because he knew the way out. And again later, the man came down the path, but this time he decided to walk around the hole. Sometime later the man decided to no longer take that path…

5   An airplane gets to its destination by making minor (not major) adjustments to its route.

6   About six months later, the man pondered, "I wonder how that hole in the path is doing?"

The stories and antidotes go on and on; and they are eloquently told from the heart. And all forms of colloquial humor show up in the meetings. I don't think I ever been to a meeting where I didn't laugh. (And in an instant later, the next person is pouring their heart out.) No matter what was going on in my life, the meeting provided at least an hour's reprieve. If anything, the meetings are great entertainment (and at a good economic price) which cleanses the soul. And over time our patience and tolerance grow for a wide spectrum of different people from this planet.

It takes meetings and joining with each other (and HOLY SPIRIT) to battle EGO. Instead of listening to EGO and continuously going to war with one another, we now have an alternative: to join in ACIM meetings. EGO is like the wizard of Oz hiding behind the curtain making all sorts of noise; he has a hidden agenda: war. We war at work, on the highways, with other countries, outside the meetings and even at home with our loved ones. Some say that we must love EGO, but from the ACIM introduction, that would be difficult since we don't really know what love is. We really need the HOLY SPIRIT's help, but if it's just HOLY SPIRIT and I, chances are that I am going to be giving EGO equal time. This is quite a challenge to think that some day enough of us could smash EGO and stay connected with HOLY SPIRIT to reach critical mass (or the 100th monkey) and return at once to the Truth. Imagine critical mass in traffic or at work. It would definitely take a miracle. Since there is no order in the magnitude of miracles, we can best start accumulating miracles by starting and attending ACIM meetings. Who knows what a hundred years from now can hold, in fact this proposal of using AA methods to conduct meetings to study ACIM text, workbook and teacher manual could be a hundred year plan for world peace called: <u>The ACIM 12 Step Plan for World Peace</u>. As far as I know, there isn't any other plan for world peace in effect. And we don't have to have everyone, just critical mass. Seems like a worthy 100 year goal. The "100th monkey in 100 years"; that's a monkey a year.

CHAPTER 4 - AA IDEAS ON SPONSORSHIP FOR ACIM TEACHERS & STUDENTS

AA uses the term sponsor, most likely because Bill was a corporate man, or maybe it was from that era (a time before television and computers, when various fellowships were more common). The term is used only once in the AA "big book" and maybe twice in the AA "12 + 12" text. The word has evolved with out too many guidelines being written-down, therefore it can have a different meaning from town to town and group to group. Talk in meetings about sponsors is often greatly exaggerated, putting the sponsor on a pedestal and setting it as a standard for everyone to live up to. And rank and file is often established where my sponsor's-sponsor's advise about something he may have said (or may not have said) in the past becomes doctrine. And what the person says during the meeting about their sponsor is accepted as the truth, because everyone knows that we are honest and we don't lie (or exaggerate) in the meetings (tongue in cheek). Patronizing sponsors empowers the speaker and in the world of EGO, flattery will get you everything. However, from what I can get from the one place were sponsor is used in the AA text , is that Doctor Bob sat down with a newcomer one afternoon and they worked through some of the procedures involved with working the Steps (6 Steps at that time). So a sponsor is a teacher. They teach what they know and help the student through the process in order for them (both) to obtain the spiritual enlightenment (miracle) that comes by doing the process. For ACIM I suppose that it would be the person that points the way from EGO to HOLY SPIRIT. EGO must be removed from the formula for every act of sponsorship (teaching) and I suppose for every time someone explains what sponsorship (teaching) is or how they experienced it. Sponsoring (teaching) requires close involvement with HOLY SPIRIT, and usually the student is less adept in the process of contacting HOLY SPIRIT; so the teacher should start and finish each teaching action or session in prayer (and a short meditation is recommended).

Although AA tries to maintain the least amount of organization and does not wish to govern anyone, the General Service Office in New York provides many pamphlets providing members suggestions and guidance. Each pamphlet lists the books, booklets, pamphlets and videos available. The AA pamphlet QUESTIONS & ANSWERS ON SPONSORSHIP explains: "In AA, sponsor and sponsored meet as equals just as Bill and Dr. Bob did. Essentially, the process of sponsorship is this: An alcoholic who has made some progress in the recovery program shares that experience on a continuous, individual basis with another alcoholic who is attempting to attain or maintain sobriety through AA." It doesn't indicate that tenure prerequisites are necessary; you can have any amount of time in the program to help the next person. It does indicate that the relationship is based on seniority (such as with an apprenticeship), but it also says that they meet as equals. They share their experience with each other. However the direction they should be going is pointed out; spiritual progress and not spiritual regression and hopefully the lead person (and preferably both) observes that responsibility. The program is moral as well as spiritual. The pamphlet goes on to address the newcomer: "When we first begin to attend meetings, we may feel confused ... and apprehensive. Although people at meetings respond to our questions willingly, that alone isn't enough. Many other questions occur to us between meetings; we find that we need...close support. So we select a...member with whom we feel comfortable, someone with whom we can talk freely and confidentially..." (AA) This approach can prevent the new person from experiencing the "fire hose" effect one gets from asking questions during meetings.

What is shared by everyone during the meetings is group sponsorship. The AA pamphlet says, "Sponsorship can also mean the responsibility of the group as a whole has for helping the newcomer." (AA) It is only natural that we flock to our long established friends and the people we like, but as group sponsors, before or after the meeting we ought to seek out the newcomer, the visitor, or the person who looks like they are down on their luck. A brief introduction and generalized social conversation will suffice. (Leave the fire hose on the wall). Just let them know that they are welcome and maybe later they may ask you some questions. It often takes many months for some to develop courage and gain trust for friendships. Not everyone coming to meetings is extroverted or socially adept. Often the people that appear repulsive to us in their looks or behavior have something to offer us. At a recent meeting, I observed a friend of mine cringe every time this new comer talked, but as I remembered my friend's behavior was very similar when she began coming to meetings. (Our EGO often reacts with anger and disdain to what is said in the meetings as an attempt to keep us from not coming back). When I told my friend that the newcomer reminded me of her when she started meetings, she laughed and thought I was joking. We seem to block out the things that we don't like about ourselves and it upsets us when we see it coming out in others. When we approach that person in a kind way, usually a tremendous healing of that issue takes place in us. It doesn't always happen right away and can sometimes take months or years of working the spiritual principles with that person to obtain the healing. But if we ignore it, the defect stays with us in our character and usually it pops up again somewhere (It's like trying to hold a heavy duty spring down for an extended period of time).

AA also has a slogan, "When anyone, anywhere, reaches out for help, I want the hand of AA to always be there. And for that I am responsible". (AA) It is a suggestion and not a command. One time, on Christmas Eve, nonetheless, as I was leaving an evening meeting, a man that appeared to be a hobo asked me if I could help him. I had no desire to do so, but he said the magic words, "Will you help me?" I asked him what he specifically wanted and he said that he wanted someone to take him to the hospital to detox. The emergency room was very busy and we spent about three hours talking about what I had learned in AA. After midnight I apologized and said that I couldn't be of much more help. The next day he came to a meeting and told me that the hospital had provided him a motel room for the night. He kept coming to meetings and we would talk briefly before and after the meeting. One night he called me and asked if I would tell his friend about AA and I said, "No, that's your job". Tell him what you learned this last week and try to get him to come to meetings. That will keep you sober. (Another 12 Step fellowship uses the slogan "Each one, Teach one.") Well sure maybe that was a cop out, but would it have been wise for me to go downtown alone in an unfamiliar area by myself to carry the message. It is best if I do most of my sponsorship at or near the meetings, (and before and after) which is a safe location and the people that come want to hear the message. About a month later my hobo friend indicated that he had contacted some family members and was moving there (and I kept it a happy ending in my memory ever since). Also if I want someone to sponsor (teach) me, I usually go to the meetings they go to, knowing that what they are saying during the meeting is perhaps a bit more connected to HOLY SPIRIT than what we may discuss outside in the parking lot.

Beware that sponsoring (teaching) someone may be EGO intoxicating, if done without HOLY SPIRIT, and it takes quite a while to develop the discipline necessary to stay close to HOLY SPIRIT. Therefore you are going to make some mistakes. It is easy to be played a fool. Sponsorship (teaching) does not require that you carry the person on your back, build them a new home or any other kind of heroics. Just provide them the information similar to the adage "If you give a man a fish you feed him for a day, if you teach him to fish, you feed him for a lifetime". We can learn from our own mistakes or we can learn from others sharing in meetings (or we can continue to make the same mistake over and over again, too.) Confidentiality is easier said than done and there can often be things brought up that are very difficult not to pass judgment upon. Leave that job for priests and attorneys. As a sponsor (teacher) it would be best to discuss confidentiality right up front and find a territory that you are both comfortable with. Always use the sense of enlightenment as a guide to let you know if you are sponsoring (teaching) correctly. For either sponsor or sponsee, if it is effortful, burdensome, painful, or unrewarding, you are probably doing it with EGO and not HOLY SPIRIT. Remember, easy does it.

AA also relies on its literature to sponsor (teach) people. Bill Wilson wrote the AA text with that intent. From the book AA COMES OF AGE, Bill wrote (the editor has copied with a few minor changes almost the entire section into the following; although some of it does not pertain to sponsorship, it is very useful and significantly informative): "The problem that had secretly worried the life out of me was I had never written anything before and neither had any other member of the New York group. Progress on the book had been too slow for several of the stock subscribers and they had slacked off on their contributions. The hassling over the four chapters already finished had really been terrific. I was exhausted. On many a day I felt like throwing the book out the window. I was in this anything-but-spiritual mood on the night when the Twelve Steps of Alcoholics Anonymous were written. I was sore and tired clear through. I lay in bed at 182 Clinton Street with pencil in hand and with a tablet of scratch paper on my knee. I could not get my mind on the job, much less put my heart in it. But here was one of those things that had to be done. Slowly my mind came into focus. Since Ebby's visit to me in the fall of 1934 we had gradually evolved what we called "the word of mouth program". Most of the basic ideas had come from the Oxford Groups, William James, and Dr. Silkworth. Though subject to considerable variation, it all boiled down into a pretty consistent procedure which comprised six steps. These were approximately as follows:

1	We admitted that we were licked, that we were powerless over alcohol.
2	We made a moral inventory of our defects or sins.
3	We confessed or shared our shortcomings with another person in confidence.
4	We made restitution to all those we harmed by drinking.
5	We tried to help other alcoholics with no thought of reward in money or prestige.
6	We prayed to whatever God we thought there was for power to practice these precepts.

This was the substance of what, by the fall of 1938, we were telling newcomers. Several of the Oxford Groups' other ideas and attitudes had been definitely rejected, including any which could involve us in theological controversy. In important matters there was still considerable disagreement between the Eastern and the Midwestern viewpoints. Our people out there were still active Oxford Group members, while we in New York had withdrawn a year before. In Akron and vicinity they still talked about the Oxford Groups' absolutes: absolute honesty,

STEVEH.

absolute purity, absolute unselfi shness, and absolute love. This dose was found to be too rich for New Yorkers, and we had abandoned the expressions...By now we knew from experience that the new prospect had to accept Step One or get no place. This particular evening, as my mind ran over these developments, it seemed to me that the program was still not definite enough. It might be a long time before a reader of the book in distant places and lands could be personally contacted. Therefore our literature would have to be more explicit. There must not be a single loophole through which the rationalizing alcoholic could wiggle out. Maybe our six chunks of truth should be broken up into smaller pieces. Thus we could better get the distant reader over the barrel, and at the same time we might be able to broaden and deepen the spiritual implications of our whole presentation. So far as I can remember this was all I had in mind when the writing began. Finally I started to write. I set out to draft more than six steps: how many more I did not know. I relaxed and asked for guidance. With a speed that was astonishing, considering my jangling emotions, I completed the first draft. It took perhaps a half an hour. The words kept right on coming. When I reached a stopping point, I numbered the new steps. They added up to twelve. Somehow this number seemed significant. Without any special rhyme or reason I connected them with the twelve apostles. Feeling greatly relieved now, I commenced to reread the draft." (AA) (The section above is very sentimental to the editor and many other AA's who are grateful for the Steps).

The ACIM Manual for Teachers is much more specific about teaching, and because the information is presented after two very extensive works, the ACIM text and workbook (that may take several years to get through) excerpts from the beginning of the manual will be put down in the following text for the benefit of the reader. First of all the manual says that "This is a manual for the teachers of God (HOLY SPIRIT). They are not perfect, or they would not be here. Yet it is their mission to become perfect here, and so they teach perfection over and over, in many ways, until they have learned it. And then they are seen no more, although their thoughts remain a source of strength and truth forever. Who are they? How are they chosen? What do they do? How can they work out their own salvation and the salvation of the world? This manual attempts to answer these questions." (ACIM) From this manual, the entire text from the Introduction and the first chapter and parts of Chapters 2,3 & 4 will be provided for the reader (except that the word HOLY SPIRIT will be put next to the word God in order to remain consistent with the previous writings in this text; the words are basically the same, except in the ACIM philosophy HOLY SPIRIT is specific for this world and understands the workings of EGO, whereas God is absolute perfection). The manual starts with:

    INTRODUCTION
1   WHO ARE GOD'S (HOLY SPIRIT'S) TEACHERS?
2   WHO ARE THEIR PUPILS?
3   WHAT ARE THE LEVELS OF TEACHING?
4   WHAT ARE THE CHARACTERISTICS OF GOD'S (HOLY SPIRIT'S) TEACHERS?

      I. Trust
      II. Honesty
      III. Tolerance
    IV. Gentleness
    V. Joy

      VI. Defenselessness
     VII. Generosity
    VIII. Patience
   IX. Faithfulness
  X. Open-Mindedness (ACIM)

From the INTRODUCTION it explains what is teaching. "The role of teaching and learning is actually reversed in the thinking of the world. The reversal is characteristic. It seems as if the teacher and the learner are separated, the teacher giving something to the learner rather than himself. Further, the act of teaching is regarded as a special activity, in which one engages only a relatively small proportion of one's time. The course, on the other hand, emphasizes that to teach is to learn, so that teaching and learning are the same. It also emphasizes that teaching is a constant process; it goes on every moment of the day and continues into sleeping thoughts as well." "To teach is to demonstrate. There are only two thought systems, and you demonstrate that you believe one or the other is true all the time. From your demonstration others learn, and so do you. The question is not whether you will teach, for in that there is no choice. The purpose of the course might be said to provide you with a means of choosing what you want to teach on the basis of what you want to learn. You cannot give to someone else, but only to yourself, and this you learn through teaching. Teaching is but a call to witness; to attest to what you believe. It is a method of conversion. This is not done by words alone. Any situation must be to you a chance to teach others what you are, and what they are to you. No more than that, but also never less." "The curriculum you set up is therefore determined exclusively by what you think you are, and what you believe the relationship of others is to you. In the formal teaching situation, these questions may be totally unrelated to what you think you are teaching. Yet it is impossible not to use the contents of any situation on behalf of what you really teach, and therefore really learn. To this the verbal content of your teaching is quite irrelevant. It may coincide with it or it may not. It is the teaching underlying what you say that teaches you. Teaching but reinforces what you believe about yourself. Its fundamental purpose is to diminish self-doubt. This does not mean the self your are trying to protect is real. But it does mean that the self you think is real is what you teach." "This is inevitable. There is no escape from it. How could it be otherwise? Everyone who follows the world's curriculum, and everyone here does follow it until he changes his mind, teaches solely to convince himself that he is what he is not. Herein is the purpose of the world. What else, then, would its curriculum be? Into this hopeless and closed learning situation, which teaches nothing but despair and death, God (HOLY SPIRIT) sends His teachers. And as they teach His lessons of joy and hope, their learning fi nally becomes complete." "Except for God's (HOLY SPIRIT's) teachers there would be little hope of salvation, for the world of sin would seem forever real. The self deceiving must deceive, for they must teach deception. And what else is hell?" (ACIM) In AA they claim that their program may not open the gates of heaven and let you in, but it will open the gates of hell and let you out. ACIM goes one step further and opens the gates of Heaven to let us in. After being spiritually awakened, ACIM helps you stay awake with HOLY SPIRIT and nurtures your spiritual growth. To be a Teacher of God (HOLY SPIRIT) is the Thirteenth Step.

WHO ARE GODS (HOLY SPIRIT'S) TEACHERS? "A teacher of God (HOLY SPIRIT) is anyone who chooses to be one. His qualifications consist solely in this: somehow, somewhere he has made a deliberate choice in which he did not see his interests as apart from someone else's. Once he has done that, his road is established and his direction is sure. A light has entered the darkness. It may be a single light, but that is enough. He has entered an agreement with God (HOLY SPIRIT) even if he does not yet believe in Him. He has become a bringer of salvation. He has become a teacher of God (HOLY SPIRIT)." "They come from all over the world. They come from all religions and from no religion. They are the ones who have answered. The Call is universal. It goes on all the time everywhere. It calls for teachers to speak for It and redeem the world. Many hear It, but few will answer. Yet it is all a matter of time. Everyone will answer in the end, but the end can be a long, long way off. It is because of this that the plan of the teachers was established. Their function is to save time. Each one begins as a single light, but with the Call at its center it is a light that cannot be limited. And each one saves a thousand years of time as the world judges it. To call Itself time has no meaning." "There is a course for every teacher of God. The form of the course varies greatly. So do the particular teaching aids involved. But the content of the course never changes. Its central theme is always, **God's Son is guiltless, and in his innocence is his salvation.** It can be taught by actions or thoughts; in words or soundlessly; in any language or in no language; in any place or time or manner. It does not matter who the teacher was before he heard the Call. He has become a savior by his answering. He has seen someone else as himself. He has therefore found his own salvation and the salvation of the world. In his rebirth is the world reborn." "This is a manual for a special curriculum, intended for teachers of a special form of the universal course. There are many thousands of other forms, all with the same outcome. They merely save time. Yet it is time alone that winds on wearily, and the world is very tired now. It is old and worn and without hope. There was never a question of outcome, for what can change the Will of God? But time, with its illusions of change and death, wears out the world and all things in it. Yet time has an ending and it is this that the teachers of God (HOLY SPIRIT) are appointed to bring about. For time is in their hands. Such was their choice and it is given them." (ACIM)

Can you see why EGO raises a ruckus about this issue. It is the end of EGO's world and all that is attached to EGO. I am writing this book so maybe I can gain some royalties that will make my retirement more comfortable (humbly said -- with many other greedy fantasies kept in the background of my EGO mind). The actual realization of what HOLY SPIRIT is asking, to give up the world as we know it, our family, the beauty of nature, etc., is frightening. Can you see how using promotion instead of attraction could create havoc (in the world of EGO). Teaching must be wisely done with the help of HOLY SPIRIT each step of the way. EGO is a jealous God and a subtle foe. EGO demands that we praise Him, worship Him and make sacrifices for Him. I don't think that he is going to be very tolerant of the teachers of God (HOLY SPIRIT) and their mission to end His world. Becoming a teacher in this sense is a very important decision and may be irreversible. Look before you leap. (Without the strength I gain from attending daily meetings and knowing that there are many others trying to do the same, I would not have been able to not drink alcohol for 25 years, for I continually find that alone I lose my courage and fold on my principles; its strictly a daily reprieve from EGO by joining with others and practicing spiritual principles to some degree).

(I have always had a tough time with hypocrisy. I would listen to the old timers in the AA meeting and put them on pedestals, but their language and perceptions changed greatly in the parking lot and the restaurants. I was very disappointed and resentful. I would often confront them with their shortcomings in a caring heart which only produced anger, resentment and retaliation. It was my defense mechanism for an inferiority complex; it would allow me to feel superior to you. When I was in the military service, I took a night class for Psychology 101. When we got to the part on abnormal psychology, I analyzed all my friends, first; but when I got around to looking at myself it frightened me. In AA I took everyone else's inventory first and found them all wanting; there were no spiritual awakenings, drastic psychic changes and no avatars. There was a lot of talk, bragging, and heroics (EGO), but very few demonstrations (please note that my perception was incorrect then and it still is now). What I did discover was that I was as much of a hypocrite as the rest of them. In early sobriety, I would pray to be honest before doing my income taxes and then spend hours doing every math calculation in order to find any loop hole. Today, I still spend a great deal of my waking hours thinking in resentment and condemnation of others and a small portion of the time I pray for the ability to forgive them. I have found that persistent discipline (something that I will need a great deal more work at) is necessary in order to be an effective Teacher of God. I do discover that when I go through the process of the Steps, I experience temporary sanity.

In the last paragraph from <u>WHO ARE THEIR PUPILS?</u> it states: "When pupil and teacher come together, a teaching-learning situation begins. For the teacher is not really the one who does the teaching. God's (HOLY SPIRIT's) teacher speaks to any two who join together for learning purposes. The relationship is holy because of that purpose, and God has promised to send His Spirit into any holy relationship. In the teaching-learning situation, each one learns that giving and receiving are the same. The demarcations they have drawn between their roles, their minds, their bodies, their needs, their interests, and all the differences they thought separated them from one another fade and grow dim and disappear. Those who learn the same course share one interest and one goal. And thus he who was the learner becomes a teacher of God (HOLY SPIRIT) himself, for he has made the one decision that gave his teacher to him. He has seen in another person the same interests as his own." The text also explains that time is an illusion and gets pretty deep into the explanation. "His pupils have been waiting for him…it is only a matter of time. Once he has chosen to fulfill his role, they are ready to fulfill theirs. Time waits on his choice, but not on whom he will serve. When he is ready to learn, the opportunities to teach will be provided him."… "The world of time is an illusion. What happened long ago seems to be happening now. .. as the course emphasizes, you are not free to choose the curriculum, or even the form in which you will learn it. You are free, however, to decide when you want to learn it. And as you accept it, it is already learned. Time really, then goes backwards to an instant so ancient that is beyond all memory and past even the possibility of remembering." "Atonement corrects illusions, not truth. Therefore it corrects what never was." (ACIM)

It also points out in <u>WHAT ARE THE LEVELS OF TEACHING</u> that there are no levels of teaching. "It is difficult to understand that levels of teaching the universal course is a concept as meaningless in reality as is time. The illusion of one permits the illusion of the other. In time, the teacher … seems to begin to change his mind about the world with a single decision, and then learns more and more about the new direction as he teaches it. We have covered the illusion of time already, but the illusion of levels of teaching seems to be something different. Perhaps the best way to demonstrate that these levels cannot exist is simply to say that any level of the teaching learning situation is part of God's plan for Atonement, and His plan can have no levels, being the reflection of His Will. Salvation is always ready and always there. God's

STEVE H.

(HOLY SPIRIT'S) teachers work at different levels..." (ACIM) So therefore in the world of EGO as we know it, we perform as teachers ... in levels (that do not really exist in the world in which we belong, God's world). We don't even remember what it was like in God's world. Talk about a leap of faith. Its like jumping off a cliff and being told that God will catch you.

But from the perspective of HOLY SPIRIT "the ultimate goal is the same; to make the relationship a holy relationship, in which both can look upon the Son of God as sinless." Now that doesn't seem too difficult, especially if we are connected with a group that is doing the same as we are. "The simplest level of teaching appears to be quite superficial. It consists of what seems to be very casual encounters; a "chance" meeting of two apparent strangers in an elevator, a child who is not looking where he is going running into an adult "by chance", two students "happening" to walk home together. These are not chance encounters. Each of them has the potential for becoming a teaching-learning situation. Perhaps the seeming strangers in the elevator will smile to one another; perhaps the adult will not scold the child for bumping into him; perhaps the students will become friends. Even at the level of the most casual encounter, it is possible for two to lose sight of separate interests, if only for a moment. That moment will be enough. Salvation has come." ... "The second level of teaching is a more sustained relationship, in which, for a time, two people enter into a fairly intense teaching, learning situation and then appear to separate. As with the first level, these meetings are not accidental, nor is what appears to be the end of the relationship a real end. Again, each has learned the most he can at the time..." "The third level of teaching occurs in relationships which, once they are formed, are lifelong. These are teaching-learning situations in which each person is given a chosen learning partner who presents him with unlimited opportunities for learning. These relationships are generally few, because their existence implies that those involved have reached a stage simultaneously in which the teaching-learning balance is actually perfect." (ACIM) Now get this, here's the kicker: "This does not mean that they necessarily recognize this; in fact, they generally do not. They may even be quite hostile to each other for some time, and perhaps life. Yet, should they decide to learn it, the perfect lesson is before them and can be learned. And if they decide to learn that lesson, they become the saviors of the teachers who falter and may even seem to fail. No teacher of God (HOLY SPIRIT) can fail to find the Help he needs." (ACIM) [I put the above information in, but I am not really sure what that means. I'd ask HOLY SPIRIT but I don't get too clear of a signal all of the time. If you need a better understanding of ACIM I would recommend going online and contacting someone such as Robert Perry, Circle of Atonement, Sedona, Arizona-[robert@circleofa.org] and his students to find out. It is one source that I am familiar with (out of many more in other geographic locations); the Circle of Atonement is a group of highly advanced and extremely knowledgeable ACIM students and teachers. Jon Mundy also provides ACIM publications (e.g. Miracles Magazine) that provides many other sources for ACIM information. I thought that I was understanding the above quotes from the ACIM Manual for Teachers, but this last part threw me off. I have had and still have plenty of hostile relationships especially driving. At work, I know that my function is to forgive them and form holy relationships, but I haven't quite got their cooperation and after they kick my butt around I get defensive. But then again, I am still trying to serve two masters] There is obviously a process one must go through to become an advanced teacher of God (HOLY SPIRIT), similar to what is in the book THE PEACEFUL WARRIOR or what John was trying to tell us in his language of the BOOK OF REVELATIONS, or as Paramahansa Yogananda discusses in his comments of the Bhagavan Gita "as a rununciant, one strives for inner desirelessness and nonattachment: and as a yogi, one envelopes himself in the meditative bliss of Divine Presence and then offers his actions in selfless service to share that Presence with other seeking souls" (SRF), but it is something that I have not experienced, mostly because of cowardice and fear (which isn't a fun place). I have only taken in this metaphysical information as an avocation so far.

"First, the Teacher of God (HOLY SPIRIT) must go through what might be called "a period of undoing." This need not be painful, but it usually is so experienced. It seems as if things are being taken away, and it is rarely understood initially that their lack of value is merely being recognized. How can lack of value be perceived unless the perceiver is in a position where he must see things in a different light? He is not yet at a point at which he can make the shift entirely internally. And so the plan will sometimes call for changes in what seem to be external circumstances. These changes are always helpful. When the teacher of God (HOLY SPIRIT) has learned that much, he goes on to the second stage." "Next, the teacher of God must go through a period of sorting out. This is always somewhat difficult because, having learned that the changes in his life are always helpful, he must now decide all things on the basis of whether they increase the helpfulness or hamper it. He will find that many, if not most of the things he valued before will merely hinder his ability to transfer what he has learned to new situations as they arise. Because he has valued what is really valueless, he will not generalize the lesson for fear of loss and sacrifice. It takes great learning to understand that all things, events, encounters and circumstances are helpful. It is only to the extent to which they are helpful that any degree of reality should be accorded them in this world of illusion. The word value can apply to nothing else." "The third stage through which the teacher of God (HOLY SPIRIT) must go can be called a period of relinquishment. If this is interpreted as giving up the desirable, it will engender enormous conflict. Few teachers of God (HOLY SPIRIT) escape this distress entirely. There is, however, no point in sorting out the valuable from the valueless unless the next obvious step is taken. Therefore the period of overlap is apt to be one in which the teacher of God (HOLY SPIRIT) feels called upon to sacrifice his own best interests on behalf of truth. He has not realized as yet how wholly impossible such a demand would be. He can learn this only as he actually does give up the valueless. Through this, he learns that where he anticipated grief, he finds a happy lightheartedness instead; where he thought something was asked of him, he finds a gift bestowed on him." "Now comes a period of settling down. This is a quiet time, in which the teacher of God (HOLY SPIRIT) rests a while in reasonable peace. Now he consolidates his learning. Now he begins to see the transfer value of what he has learned. Its potential is literally staggering; and the teacher of God (HOLY SPIRIT) is now at the point in his progress at which he sees in it his whole way out. Give up what you do not want and keep what you do. How simple is the obvious! And how easy to do! The teacher of God (HOLY SPIRIT) needs a period of respite. He has not yet come as far as he thinks. Yet when he is ready to go on, he goes with mighty companions beside him. Now he rests a while, and gathers them before going on. He will not go on from here alone." "The next stage is indeed a period of unsettling. Now must the teacher of God understand that he did not really know what was valuable and what was valueless. All that he really learned so far was that he did not want the valueless, and that he did want the valuable. Yet his own sorting out was meaningless in teaching him the difference. The idea of sacrifice, so central to his own thought system, had made it impossible for him to judge. He thought he learned willingness, but now he sees that he does not know what the willingness is for. And now he must attain a state that may remain impossible to reach for a long, long time.

STEVEH.

He must learn to lay all judgment aside, and ask only what he really wants in every circumstance. Were not each step in this direction so heavily reinforced, it would be hard indeed!" "And finally, there is a period of achievement. It is here that learning is consolidated. Now what was seen as merely shadows before become solid gains, to be counted on in all emergencies as well as tranquil times. Indeed, the tranquility is their result; the outcome of honest learning, consistency of thought and full transfer. This is the stage of real peace, for here is Heaven's state fully reflected. From here, the way to Heaven is open and easy. In fact, it is here. Who would go anywhere, if peace of mind is already complete? And who would seek to change tranquility for something more desirable? What could be more desirable than this?" (ACIM)

I think he lost me somewhere along the way. But I would think it only fair that you know what you are getting yourself into before you make a decision to do it (which generally isn't the case in this world of EGO). Ultimately it is the only way to go. (I just thought that it would be in a effortless instant.) Also if you are this far along in the reading, it should be made clear that the author of ACIM is Jesus Christ. It was not intended by the editor to milk you along and then land this big Christian conversion trip on you. Although many of us will not get quite this far along in ability in this lifetime as which Jesus describes in the ACIM text, maybe the next generation will get a little further down the road, or maybe when our generation returns (that is if you buy the reincarnation stuff) they will be teaching these ideas in the schools.

WHAT ARE THE CHARACTERISTICS OF GOD'S (HOLY SPIRIT'S) TEACHERS? IT SAYS "...THE ADVANCED TEACHERS OF GOD HAVE THE FOLLOWING CHARACTERISTICS:

1. <u>Trust:</u> ...The teachers of God (HOLY SPIRIT) have trust in the world, because they have learned it is not governed by the law the world made up. It is governed by a Power that is in them but not of them. It is this Power That keeps all things safe. It is through this Power that the teachers of God (HOLY SPIRIT) look on a forgiven world. When this Power has once been experienced, it is impossible to trust one's own petty strength again...who would place his faith in the shabby offerings of the EGO when the gifts of God (HOLY SPIRIT) are laid before him? (ACIM)

2. <u>Honesty:</u> All other traits of God's (HOLY SPIRIT's) teachers rest on trust. Once that has been achieved, the others cannot fail to follow. Only the trusting can afford honesty, for only they can see its value. Honesty does not apply only to what you say. The term actually means consistency. There is nothing you say that contradicts what you think or do: no thought opposes any other thought; no act belies your word; and no word lacks agreement with another. Such are the truly honest. At no level are they in conflict with themselves. Therefore it is impossible for them to be in conflict with anyone else or anything...The peace of mind which the advance teachers of God (HOLY SPIRIT) experience is largely due to their perfect honesty. It is only the wish to deceive that makes for war. No one at one with himself can even conceive of conflict. Conflict is the inevitable result of self deception and self deception is dishonesty. There is no challenge to a teacher of God (HOLY SPIRIT). Challenge implies doubt, and the trust on which God's (HOLY SPIRIT's) teachers rest secure makes doubt impossible. Therefore they can only succeed, because they never do their will alone... (ACIM)

3. <u>Tolerance:</u> God's (HOLY SPIRIT'S) teachers do not judge. To judge is to be dishonest, for to judge is to assume a position you do not have. Judgment without self-deception is impossible. Judgment implies that you have been deceived in your brothers. How, then, could you not have been deceived in yourself? Judgment implies a lack of trust, and trust remains the bedrock of the teacher of God's (HOLY SPIRIT'S) whole thought system. Let this be lost, and all his learning goes. Without judgment are all things equally acceptable, for who could judge otherwise? Without judgment are all men brothers, for who is there who stands apart? Judgment destroys honesty and shatters trust. No teacher of God (HOLY SPIRIT) can judge and hope to learn. (ACIM)

4. <u>Gentleness:</u> Harm is impossible for God's (HOLY SPIRIT's) teachers. They can neither harm nor be harmed. Harm is the outcome of judgment. It is the dishonest act that follows a dishonest thought. It is a verdict of guilt upon a brother, and therefore on oneself. It is the end of peace and the denial of learning. It demonstrates the absence of God's (HOLY SPIRIT's) curriculum, and its replacement by insanity. No teacher of God (HOLY SPIRIT) but must learn, --and fairly early in his training,--that harmfulness completely obliterates his function from his awareness. It will make him confused, fearful, angry, and suspicious. It will make the HOLY SPIRIT's lessons impossible to learn. Nor can God's teacher (HOLY SPIRIT) be heard at all, except by those who realize that harm can actually achieve nothing. No gain can come from it... therefore, God's (HOLY SPIRIT'S) teachers are wholly gentle. They need the strength of gentleness, for it is in this that the function of salvation becomes easy... The might of God's

(HOLY SPIRIT's) teachers lies in their gentleness, for they have understood their evil thoughts came neither from God's Son nor his Creator. (ACIM)

33

5 <u>Joy:</u> Joy is the inevitable result of gentleness. Gentleness means that fear is now impossible, and what could come to interfere with joy? The open hands of gentleness are always filled. The gentle have no pain. They cannot suffer. Why would they not be joyous? They are sure they are beloved and must be safe. Joy goes with gentleness as surely as grief attends attack. God's (HOLY SPIRIT's) teachers trust Him. And they are sure His Teacher goes before them, making sure no harm can come to them. They hold His gifts and follow in His way, because God's Voice directs them in all things. Joy is their song of thanks. And Christ looks down on them in thanks as well. His need of them is just as great as theirs is of Him. How joyous it is to share the purpose of salvation. (ACIM)

6 <u>Defenselessness:</u> God's (HOLY SPIRIT's) teachers have learned how to be simple. They have no dreams that need defense against the truth. They do not try to defend themselves. Their joy comes from their understanding Who created them. And does what God created need defense? No one can become an advanced teacher of God (HOLY SPIRIT) until he fully understands that defenses are but foolish guardians of mad illusions. The more grotesque the dream, the fiercer and more powerful its defenses seem to be. Yet when the teacher of God (HOLY SPIRIT) finally agrees to look past them, he finds that nothing was there. Slowly at first he lets himself be undeceived. But he learns faster as his trust increases. It is not danger that comes when defenses are laid down. It is safety. It is peace. It is joy. And it is God. (ACIM)

7 <u>Generosity:</u> The term generosity has a special meaning to the teacher of God (HOLY SPIRIT). It is not the usual meaning of the word: in fact, it is a meaning that must be learned and learned very carefully. Like all the other attributes of God's (HOLY SPIRIT'S) teachers this one rests ultimately on trust, for without trust no one can be generous in the true sense. To the world, generosity means giving away in the sense of giving up. To the teachers of God (HOLY SPIRIT), it means giving away in order to keep. This has been emphasized throughout the text and workbook, but it is perhaps more alien to the thinking of the world than many other ideas in our curriculum. Its greater strangeness lies merely in the obviousness of its reversal of the world's thinking. In the clearest way possible, and at the simplest of levels, the word means the exact opposite to the teachers of God (HOLY SPIRIT) than to the world. (ACIM)

8 <u>Patience:</u> Those who are certain of the outcome can afford to wait and wait without anxiety. Patience is natural to the teacher of God (HOLY SPIRIT). All he sees is certain outcome, at a time perhaps unknown to him as yet, but not in doubt. The time will be as right as is the future. The past as well held no mistakes; nothing that did not serve to benefit the world, as well as him to who it seemed to happen. Perhaps it was not understood at the time. Even so, the teacher of God (HOLY SPIRIT) is willing to reconsider all his past decisions, if they are causing pain to anyone. Patience is natural to those who trust. Sure of the ultimate interpretation of all things in time, no outcome already seen or yet to come can cause them fear. (ACIM)

9 <u>Faithfulness:</u> The extent of the teacher of God's (HOLY SPIRIT's) faithfulness is the measure of his advancement in the curriculum... Faithfulness is the teachers of God's (HOLY SPIRIT's) trust in the Word of God to set all things right; not some, but all...To give up all problems to the one Answer is to reverse the thinking of the world entirely. And that alone is faithfulness...Yet each

degree however small, is worth achieving…True faithfulness, however does not deviate. Being consistent, it is wholly honest. Being unswerving, it is full of trust. Being based on fearlessness, it is gentle. Being certain, it is joyous. And being confident, it is tolerant. Faithfulness, then, combines in itself the other attributes of God's (HOLY SPIRIT's) teachers… (ACIM)

10 <u>Open-Mindedness:</u> The centrality of open-mindedness, perhaps the last of the attributes the teacher of God (HOLY SPIRIT) acquires, is easily understood when its relation to forgiveness is recognized. Open-mindedness comes with lack of judgment. As judgment shuts the mind against God's Teacher, so open-mindedness invites Him to come in. As condemnation judges the Son of God as evil, so open-mindedness permits him to be judged by the Voice of God on His behalf. As the projection of guilt upon him would send him to hell, so open-mindedness lets Christ's image be extended to him. Only the open-minded can be at peace, for they alone see reason for it. How do the open-minded forgive? They have let go all things that would prevent forgiveness. They have in truth abandoned the world, and let it be restored to them in newness and in joy so glorious they could never have conceived of such a change…Now the goal is achieved. Forgiveness is the final goal of the curriculum. It paves the way for what goes far beyond all learning. The curriculum makes no effort to exceed its legitimate goal. Forgiveness is its single aim, at which all learning intimately converges. It is indeed enough. (ACIM)

Although I may have gone quite overboard providing all of this text from ACIM, it should give the reader a good idea what the final goal really is and how to go about it. Many are not quite ready to go to such great lengths. We are content to do just enough to keep us in a happy dream instead of a miserable one. I don't really think that Hedonism works. The truth in this book is the same truth as in other spiritual books. The BHAGAVAD GITA says it like this: "The physical ego, the active consciousness in man, should uplift its body-identified self into unity with soul, its true nature; it should not allow itself to remain mired in the lowly delusive strata of the senses and material entanglement. The ego acts as its own best friend when by meditation and the exercise of its innate qualities it spiritualizes itself and ultimately restores it own true soul nature. Conversely, the physical ego (the active consciousness) serves as its own worst enemy when by illusive material behavior it eclipses its true nature as the ever blessed soul." "When the physical ego has become spiritualized and united to the soul, it is able to keep the intelligence, mind and senses under control, guided by the discriminative wisdom of the soul-- i.e., the self (EGO) has been conquered by the Self (soul). -- then the soul is the friend, the guide and benefactor, of the active physical consciousness. But if the lower ego-self has not been thus controlled and persists in keeping the consciousness matter-bent, then the soul is the enemy of the ego. This follows the Gita allegory described in chapter one: Krishna (the soul) is the friend and guide of the spiritual endeavors of the devotee Arjuna, along with the Pandava army of divine qualities; Krishna (the soul) is therefore an enemy (an oppose) of Duryohana's Kauarava army of materialistic inclinations, which is under the guidance of EGO." "the soul, imical to EGO, withholds its blessings of peace and lasting happiness while the EGO, behaving ignorantly as its own enemy, sets in motion the misery-making karmic forces of Nature. Without the benefit of the soul's (HOLT SPIRIT's) protection in the world of EGO, the EGO finds to its regret that its own actions against its true soul nature turn back on itself, like boomerangs, destroying each new illusion of happiness and attainment". (SRF)

ACIM says, "When you unite with me (Jesus Christ) you are uniting without the EGO, because

STEVE H.

I have renounced the EGO in myself and therefore cannot unite with yours. Our union is therefore the way to renounce the EGO in you...Very simply, the resurrection is the overcoming or surmounting of death. It is an awakening or a rebirth; a change of mind about the meaning of the world...Here the curriculum ends. From here on, no directions are needed. Vision is wholly corrected and all mistakes undone. Attack is meaningless and peace has come. The goal of the curriculum has been achieved. Thoughts turn to Heaven and away from hell. All longings are satisfied, for what remains unanswered or incomplete?...This is God's final Judgment: **You are still My holy Son, forever innocent, forever loving and forever loved, as limitless as your Creator, and completely changeless and forever pure. Therefore awaken and return to Me. I am your Father and you are My Son.** (ACIM).

CHAPTER 5 – THE 12 CONCEPTS AND 12 WARRANTIES OF A VENERABLE DEMOCRATIC CORPORATE FELLOWSHIP

ACIM fellowship is no way close to needing most of the ideas presented in the AA concepts and warranties, however if and when ACIM meeings were to grow exponentially, the AA inverted pyramid style of management supported by the use of spiritual principles in all policy making decisions could greatly benefit ACIM groups as a whole. Unfortunately the author has very little experience with the AA concepts or warranties and has not participated in any of the AA activities at group or above levels. The concepts and warranties are found in the AA book THE AA SERVICE MANUAL / TWELVE CONCEPTS FOR WORLD SERVICE. It is highly recommended that every trusted servant read them. There is a condensed version and a pamphlet available from the AA General Service Office, Box 459, Grand Central Station, New York, New York 10115 (www.aa.org); it is recommended that you contact them for more and accurate information. Nevertheless, in this chapter the editor will attempt to revise some of the information and try to present it from an ACIM perspective. The information presented will be highly speculative for ACIM, and not intended to be a rule. Many of the words such as "group, assembly, conference, and convention" will have there own specific meaning, however some ambiguity may have been missed and remain in the material presented. The editor is also grossly inexperienced with the legalities of Foundations, Charters, Boards, Bylaws, etc. Hopefully the information will be presented in a manner that can be usable if and when the need arises.

It must be noted that the formation of these concepts occurred over a period of time in a progressive manner. The founders of AA had no idea what was to happen next, but when they recognized their own mortality, they actualized a system of spiritual democracy in order to perpetuate the fellowship of AA. Occupationally, Bill Wilson was a stockbroker who studied corporations -- especially their management and efficiency in order to make recommendations and referrals on their marketable value. In the process, Bill developed many ideas on how to run an organization effectively. Bill's experience is reflected in the success and longevity of AA. It also appears that Bill was a democratic idealist (not intended as criticism) who greatly respected individual rights. With Bill's revelation of the importance of having God first in your life (seek first the Kingdom of God), he was able to fi nd the mortar that would hold all his ideas soundly together. In 1955, Bill succeeded in passing on the vital role of leadership back to the membership and his concepts have triumphantly lasted throughout the following years.

Unless your are just starting this book with this chapter and have no AA or ACIM experience, by now the reader should have a better understanding of just what is meant by the word EGO. It's the antithesis of creation. The 12 Concepts are the spiritual structure of AA, but EGO has the ability to undermine the foundation. In Chapter One, it discussed creating a debit and credit list. To better define EGO, it would be beneficial to create an EGO and HOLY SPIRIT list:

EGO	HOLY SPIRIT
Competitive	Surrendering
Dominating	Cooperative
Overbearing	Easy going

STEVE H.

        Loud mouthed   Quiet voiced

Whereas as EGO and HOLY SPIRIT would be opposites in this world, in God's world there is only one truth and no opposites. The reason I bring up this issue is because there is another form of the "two step", where we join the fellowship and then we want to run it. EGO provides a lot of untested "bright ideas", but when put into operation they do exactly what they are designed to do -- fail. For example, I had all sorts of "bright ideas" about parenting; I wasn't going to do the mistakes my parents made. I had a better way. However that was before having to do the job. When we are finished with that job, we see things from a different aspect and hopefully, we are able to laugh at our "bright ideas" and then at what actually happened. The same was true with divorce. In my first marriage, I would say, "I don't know why people get divorced, but it will never happen to me". But after going through the experience and through the emotional reactions to divorce, I developed a little more compassion for those who followed me, and because of the experience I was able to be helpful and comforting to others because I knew how it felt from my own experience. In my second marriage, I was prepared with "bright ideas" so that I would not make the same mistakes and behold – Deja-vu. The point I am trying to make is for those wanting to participate in the steering of the fellowship; it might be best to establish some guidelines to weed out EGO from the process. I have been a Health Inspector as an occupation most of my life. Quality control is very beneficial to a society. It is apparent that although government may be very confusing and bureaucratic, the advantages and desirability of living in the U.S. are obvious when compared to countries that do not have inspections and quality controls in their society. As an inspector, EGO always wants to participate with power, domination, vanity, etc. There is sometimes a subtle difference between zealous and enthusiastic. In Germany, the inspectors come from the retired class of experienced professionals rather than young fresh college graduates. The advantage is that there is less EGO involved (not that older people don't have the same issues with EGO). I use the above only as an example prior to describing the Concepts and Warranties as a forewarning. If you are still speaking through your mouth and listening with your ears (and you have a body), you most likely are still living in the world of EGO. We need HOLY SPIRIT to lead us out. It might be best to develop the skills of staying with HOLY SPIRIT in your personal life and decision making before you start participating in making decisions for other members. As we practice spiritual principles in our personal lives, as we progress and purify, miracles and spiritual experiences become common place; we discover that the real proof of our spiritual progress is that we have become more loving, understanding, peaceful and forgiving; we see the folly of our EGO; our ability to serve others improves immensely; and service work becomes effortless and joyous. Intuitive skills and the ability to join and follow the Collective Conscience are necessary at this level of service to others.

CONCEPT I:

The final responsibility and the ultimate authority for ACIM world services should always reside in the collective conscience of the entire membership. However, economics must always be considered in planning and decision making, realizing that we are self supporting through our own contributions. Therefore it is recommended, when practical, that the hat or basket be passed during all official conventions of members (e.g. meetings, business discussions, assemblies, conferences, offi cial office and board meetings with members, etc.) for voluntary contributions. (The Spiritual Principle is that giving and receiving are equal). Paid employees are asked not to contribute if they choose. (AA) As bodies, we are perishable. As bodies, EGO presides in much of our thought and activities. As long as we are experiencing an individual conscious mind, we are separate from the mind of God. Somehow we must not only try to get back to the one mind, we must develop the desire to do so. Without the experience of joining with others in a collective consciousness, we would not know the joy and reward of doing so. We would remain in ignorance having contempt prior to investigation. With the spiritual integrity we gain from ACIM Text, Workbook and Teacher's Manual and practicing the Steps and Traditions, we become a joined spiritualized society, characterized by enough enlightenment; enough responsibility and enough love to insure that management by collective consciousness will work under all conditions. Bill stated, "Throughout the entire world, we are witnessing the breakdown of group conscience. It has always been the hope of democratic nations that their citizens would always be enlightened enough, moral enough, and responsible enough to manage their own affairs through chosen representatives. But in many self governing countries we are now seeing the inroads of ignorance, apathy, and power-seeking upon democratic systems. Their spiritual resources of right purpose and collective intelligence are waning...Happily for us, there seems little prospect of such a calamity in AA. The life of each individual and of each group is built around our Twelve Steps and Twelve Traditions. We very well know ... the penalty for extensive disobedience to these principles....and an even greater force for AA's unity is the compelling love that we have for our fellow members and for the principles upon which our lives today are founded." (AA)

As AA grew from 100 to 100,000, national and world services became necessary. Public relations, assisting members starting new groups, standardizing the literature, etc. began to play a vital role of keeping the fellowship intact. In order to maintain unity and prevent separation, AA developed a General Service Conference of delegates, trustees, and service workers to steer and guide in making the necessary decisions to provide national and world service, based on spiritual principles and democracy. For ACIM, such a conference would allow HOLY SPIRIT to be at the helm. Categories of representative conventions of members and service functions could be:

1 Meetings & Business Discussions
2 Groups (Office optional)
3 Central District Service Assembly & Office
4 Geographic Area Service Assembly & Office
5 National Service Conference & Board (& subsidary operations)
6. World Service Conference & Board (& subsidary operations)

Representatives and leaders are to be entrusted with the responsibilities delegated from the membership. The ACIM member's (and employees) collective conscience is always to be the final authority. All services and decisions are to support the ACIM membership and message. The members have the ultimate power to criticize and alter the service structure by business discussion and collective conscience voting. This concept puts the power in the hands of the membership for reorganization, re-election, reproach, disapproval, admonition, and reprehension for bad performance of service or out of line servants. They have the ultimate authority to correct inefficiency, ineffectiveness and abuse. The membership and their representatives, delegates, directors, committees, trustees should always be financially responsible in their activities and decisions. (AA) Once again, we are self supporting through our own contributions, therefore it is recommended, when practical, that the hat or basket be passed during all official conventions of members (e.g. meetings, business discussions, assemblies, conferences, offi cial office and board meeting with members, etc.) for voluntary contributions. (The Spiritual Principle is that giving and receiving are equal). Paid employees are asked not to contribute if they choose.

CONCEPT II:

At the time when such Service Functions and Offices are formed (or dissolved), the action must be ratified (by a substantial majority or unanimity of the collective conscience of the elected representatives from the originating convention of members). Once ratified, the new Service Function (Convention, Office, Board,. etc.) is delegated the authority for decision, management and maintenance of service for the ACIM members and the ACIM message (except when to do so would cause substantial harm or damage to ACIM members or ACIM as a whole). (AA)

The need for services grows proportionally to the membership growth. As the number and frequency of meetings grow, they can form groups to be more efficient and economize responsibilities. (However, a meeting or a series of meetings does not have to grow and become a group. It can remain solely a meeting, without any other affiliation.) If a group is formed, the representatives from the meetings should be equally represented and can rotate their volunteer work or let one or several dedicated persons carry out the functions for any period of accepted time. There are many ways the needed tasks can be accomplished and sometimes new members want to change to another way. This document is not intended to hold any set and fast rule to the process. Terms of service can be established, if desired, by the forming convention of members. If deemed necessary, professional services (e.g. janitorial, maintenance, consultants, secretaries, etc.) can be obtained or a permanent office with staff can be created. When groups see that further organization may be wise or beneficial, a central service assembly and office can be created using the same concepts to form, dissolve, and manage the service operations. Again, no one set rule applies. Economy, expedience and practicality should always be considered, attempting to keep organization limited to within reason. And if or when ACIM grows, central district, geographic area, national and world conventions, service offices and boards can be developed. (Most of these ideas presented for what ACIM could do are highly speculative and are intended only to provide some plans and blueprints from what AA has done.)

Once a service function is created, then the convention of member delegates and the office and board staff must have the authority to act on behalf of ACIM as the voice and effective conscience. The convention of representatives must have the authority to provide the guidance and the office and board staff must have the authority to carry out those functions. In order to perform, they must be trusted to be competent and be provided sufficient authority to carry out their duties efficiently and effectively. Likewise communication must be two ways. When crucial difficulties or problems arise, staff and representatives must have the capability and should inform the originating convention of members. (AA) As of this writing, these ideas are mostly theory and in the world of EGO, things don't always function in the way that they were planned. Flexibility and adaptability are necessary. We do this work joined in HOLY SPIRIT and not alone with EGO. We must be aware of the quick mental twist of EGO. Instead of being the servant to HOLY SPIRIT, we suddenly begin complaining, judging and start bossing HOLY SPIRIT (and others) around. We begin to demand service from HOLY SPIRIT. We only think we are humble, but inside EGO is screaming for praise and adulation; "Look what I have done for others". The enemy, rationalization, comes forth with questions like "Isn't competition a good thing?" as an excuse for petty rivalries. The loud questions of EGO, "What's to become of us if we just trust, aren't we supposed to take care of ourselves first?" In the world of EGO, words pride and control are valued, but not so in the world of HOLY SPIRIT. Capitalism and the society we live in are not necessarily based on spiritual principles. Without the support of our basic meetings and groups, our service work can be easily distorted and become burdensome. It is important for persons performing service work not to become so busy and important that they cannot continue to go regularly to meetings. Trusting HOLY SPIRIT can be a tall order and we often balk. See to it that your own house is in order first. Working for the HOLY SPIRIT is a joyous and effortless experience. Groups of people such as mobs and vigilantes do not always behave in a positive way and groups can easily justify their actions (just as we do as individuals, but now we have support and back up of our actions from other like minds). We, as a group are still often like the play director trying to arrange the lights and show to satisfy us, when in fact we should consider all members, including the minority opinion. That is primarily what "substantial majority or unanimity" is about. Therefore before carrying out any decisions by a convention of members (e.g. discussion, meeting, group, assembly or conference), the action should be evaluated as to the effect on ACIM individual members and ACIM as a whole. For instance: if meetings are to become no smoking, then provisions for smoking meetings should also be included. No staff or convention of members should have the authority to punish, exclude, dominate or govern others. Not only is there the spiritual principle of equality between members, but like wise between the different levels of member conventions (e.g. meetings, groups, assemblies, conferences, discussions, service offices, boards, etc.) Each has a specific job to do and one is not more important or superior to another.

CONCEPT III:

As a traditional means of creating and maintaining clearly defined working relationships and communication between the members, meetings, groups, assemblies, conferences, service offices, boards, representatives, trustees, staff, committees, executives, etc, it is suggested that each position be endowed with the "Right of Decision". (AA)

Although I referred to Bill as an idealist previously, he also was very practical in understanding that operations in this world don't always function as planned. He obviously had a good understanding and working knowledge of how principles can get in the way of accomplishment. This concept may seem redundant, but it is part of a system of checks and balances that provides common sense approaches for performing spiritual work. Kind of like what someone said in a meeting about "sitting along side his bed for three days, praying for God to put his pants on." For service to function, it is not advisable to go to any extreme of having members dominating staff or staff dominating members. So you may say this shouldn't happen if we live by spiritual principles. Beware that EGO is a subtle foe. It has been the experience in AA that with the smallest of business meetings to the trustees themselves, EGO has snuck in to orchestrate the show. AA uses a slogan from its 12th tradition (which the editor did not include with his rendition of the traditions because the slogan can sometimes be misinterpreted and misused), "Principles before Personalities". It would be best to respect both. Trusted servants must be trusted to do their best. They have access to HOLY SPIRIT as well as anyone or any group.

The AA pamphlets discusses the Charters and Bylaws that are necessary and provide specific instructions, however the day to day issues could not be performed if no one had the authority to decide which problems they will dispose of themselves and which matters they will report, consult or ask specific questions. "This is the essence of the Right of Decision". At all levels, members performing service work must have mutual trust and the right to decide how they will interpret and apply their own authority and responsibility to each particular situation as it arises. As we trust HOLY SPIRIT, we also trust each other. However Bill also warns the members against using the Right of Decision as an excuse for failure to make the proper reports of actions taken; or for exceeding a clearly defined authority; or for failing to consult the proper people before making an important decision. (AA) From the editor's interpretation of what Bill Wilson was trying to do with this concept was to establish as a balance between delegated responsibility and the ultimate authority of charters and bylaws. He realized that the fellowship could neither throw out the corporate charters, bylaws, job definitions, etc. nor could they refuse to give the leaders discretion to perform their responsibilities by establishing extensive lists of rules and regulations. Bill believed that the Right of Decision was an indispensable privilege to be granted to every level of service. He knew people. He knew they were not machines and they had to have esteem in performance of service. He understood that spiritual principles were to bring joy and not strife. Service work incorporates spiritual principles of honesty, humility, equality, etc. and the people doing those jobs have those qualities. He also understood the need for charity and forgiveness for errors, mistakes and oversights. He also wanted to make it clear that the delegates and representatives receive an education and more information on issues as they affect the whole when they attend the discussion, assembly or conference. They should not be held to hard and fast rules from the members they are representing and be entitled to make decisions and cast votes "according to the best dictates of their own judgment and conscience at that time". (AA) Trust must be the

STEVEH.

watchword or otherwise there would be no reputable leaders.

CONCEPT IV:

We ought to maintain the "Right of Participation" at all levels of service taking care that all members and nonmembers that have duties that are pertinent to the discussion be allowed to participate in convention discussions and be allowed voting representation for issues that will require a collective conscience of substantial majority or unanimity. (AA)

At first the concept may appear to be in contradiction with Traditions 2 & 3, however as a population of an organization grows to large proportions, true democracy is sometimes no longer feasible. For meeting, group and business discussions, members only ought to participate and only members present for the discussion should be allowed to vote in the collective conscience. At levels above the group level, concern for individual's (staff, trustee, consultant, etc.) esteem and overall operational efficiency took precedence over membership restrictions. Bill writes, "There is another good reason for participation and this one has to do with our spiritual needs. All of us deeply desire to belong. We want a ... relation of brotherly partnership. It is our shining ideal that the spiritual corporation ... should never include any members who are regarded as second class." Deep down, I think this is what we have been struggling to achieve in our world service structure. Here is perhaps the principal reason why we should continue to ensure participation at every ... level. Just as there are no second class...members, neither should there be any second class...service workers. Professional positions are needed for tasks such as office management, reception, administration, publishing, etc. where people are hired for their skills and not their belief system. It may not be feasible or possible to always obtain someone who has any ACIM or Steps/Traditions experience, too. However, they should not be excluded from participating in discussions that require their advice and will effect service operations. Nor should they be denied a vote in the collective conscience deciding the outcome. (AA)

Bill writes, "Perhaps someone will object that, on close votes ... the combined Trustees and service worker ballots may decide a particular question; But why not? Certainly our Trustees or service workers are no less conscientious, experienced and wiser than the Delegates. Is there any good reason why their votes are undesirable? Clearly there is none. Hence we ought to be wary of any future tendency to deny either our service people or Trustees their ... votes, except on special situations that involve past performances, job qualifications, or money compensation, or in the case of a sweeping reorganization ... occasioned by misfunction. The Conference is far more concerned with policies, plans and actions which are to take effect in the future. To take away the votes of Trustees and service workers on such questions would obviously be unwise. Why should our conference be deprived of the votes of such knowledgeable people as these?" (AA) And the AA Charter specifies the Trustees, the Directors and their respective executive staff as voting members.

At meeting and group levels some collective conscience votes occur during the meeting and some afterwards in what is called a "Business Discussion". Someone walking off the street that has no affiliation with ACIM or desire to be affiliated with ACIM should not be allowed to participate in the voting or misuse the system for less than desirable reasons. But in order to provide equality, anyone who has stated that they have a desire to learn and live ACIM becomes a member and is allowed to participate. (It is the editor's hope that no one or group of persons with less than desirable intentions ever misuses this spiritual ideology of equality to harm or damage ACIM.)   Also what is considered substantial unanimity and the idea of "no decision" can be very effective for weeding out nonsense issues in the smaller conventions, whereas it could cause paralysis with larger operations. At the smaller levels of voting, it is recommended to include abstention from voting as part of the count for substantial unanimity and use "No decision" and "Hat Decision" more frequently.   This method should effectively screen only the pertinent issues to receive administrative action.

Above the level of group, there are complex issues such as office staffing, office managers, directors, trustees requiring specific skills and assemblies, conference, and boards requiring communication and administration. Bill states, "It was years before we saw that we could never put all authority in one group and virtually all responsibility in another and then expect efficiency of operation, let alone real harmony. Of course, no one is against the idea of final authority. We are only against its misapplication or misuse. Participation can usually stop this sort of demoralizing nonsense before it starts." (AA) The concept of "No decision" remains for close votes that may cause turmoil if a decision where made either way, but the conditions for approval at assembly and conference levels should be relaxed to 2/3 substantial majority for Yes - No votes and for more than two alternatives subject to a collective conscience vote, a succession of votes should occur to weed out the lower ranking options. In the case of elections (e.g. delegates, representatives, etc.) this method is also applied to establish a two person final election, with a substantial (67%) majority (not counting abstentions) to be elected. Also the rules on abstention would be reversed from the meeting and group level decision making policies, where those who choose not to vote would not be counted as part of the majority calculation. Again, anyone not present for the discussion prior to the collective conscience vote should not participate in the vote. This recommendation should not apply to large elections because there is no discussion requiring a decision involved. (Further ground rules or bylaws for nomination procedures could be developed for the larger assembly and conference actions.) In order to weed out EGO, all discussions and elections open and end in prayer and after discussion (or announcement of the candidates); a five minute period of meditation for the members to individually consult with HOLY SPIRIT should be required prior to voting. If substantial majority is not reached, then all majority and minority candidate's names are placed into a "hat" and one name is randomly pulled to fill the position. (This sounds bizarre to me, but supposedly works well in keeping the peace between majority and minority factions that rapidly develop and disperse.)

Again, let the reader be informed that because of the inexperience of the editor in dealing with these levels of organization, this transcription may not do justice to the original writing and some key issues may be lost. Bill Wilson wrote these concepts after having the actual experience. The editor will attempt to identify the concept, and it's reasoning if in the event ACIM has grown to the extent where it might be interested in adopting some of these ideas for its own use. The concepts are a mixture of spiritual principles applied to corporate management that have been successful for over fifty years in AA. As AA grew up, it attempted to incorporate these spiritual principles of equality and democracy in all areas of corporate development. All positions in the corporation are chosen by a collective conscience vote (in one form or another--whether it be two persons deciding or 1,000) and all positions are then provided the authority to perform their responsibilities and the right to participate in all discussions, votes and elections pertinent to their position. Naturally the system is set up so that the membership can amend, revise or reorganize as the contingencies arise (EGO) or the case may warrant (HOLY SPIRIT).

CONCEPT V:

Throughout the service structure, a "Right of Appeal and Petition" ought to prevail, thus assuring that minority opinion will be heard and that petitions for the redress of grievances will be carefully considered. (AA)

Both the AA pamphlet and the service manual's long version of the concept are so well written and pertain to such intricate and consequential matters, the editor has opted to provide the information word for word:

From the AA Pamphlet: "Newcomers to AA's General Service Conference are often surprised at the pains taken by the presiding officer to make sure the minority has a second opportunity to present its views. Even after extensive debate on an issue, followed by a vote in which a substantial unanimity (or majority) is reached, those opposed are polled individually to see if they wish to speak further to their minority view. In fact, numerous instances can be cited in which this minority view is so compelling the Conference has reversed itself. This is AA's Right of Appeal in action and Bill says the same principle should apply to meetings (assemblies) of our area committees, trustee committees and boards. On an issue of grave importance, the minority has the actual duty of presenting its views. The right of Appeal recognizes that minorities frequently can be right; that even when they are in error they still perform a most valuable service when they compel a thoroughgoing debate on important issues. The well heard minority, therefore, is our chief protection against an uninformed, misinformed, hasty or angry majority. "Trusted servants", according to Bill, "do for the groups what the groups cannot or should not do for themselves." And in exercising their Right of Decision, trusted servants are almost always a small but truly qualified minority -- whether in the form of area committees, staffs, boards or even the General Service Conference itself. It is incumbent upon them, therefore, in their own meetings, to pay special deference to the minority voice. This concept also warns us of the tyranny of the majority and points out...that a simple majority is seldom sufficient basis for a decision. That's why we usually require at least two-thirds majority. Lacking this, it is preferable to delay the decision; or in the case of an election following the "Third Legacy Procedure" of going to the hat (explained below). The Right of Appeal also permits any person in the service structure, whether paid or volunteer, to petition for redress of personal grievance. He or she can complain directly to the General Service Board without prejudice or fear of reprisal. " (AA) **From the AA Service Manual - Twelve Concepts for World Service**: "In the light of the principle of the Right of Appeal, all minorities--whether in our staffs, committees, corporate boards, or among trustees -- should be encouraged to file minority report whenever they feel a majority to be in considerable error. And when a minority considers an issue to be such a grave one that a mistaken decision could seriously affect AA as a whole, it should then charge itself with the actual duty of presenting a minority report to the Conference. In granting this traditional Right of Appeal, we recognize that minorities frequently can be right; that even when they are partly or wholly in error they still perform a most valuable service when, by asserting their Right of Appeal, they compel a thorough - going debate on important issues...The traditional Right of Appeal should also permit any person in our service structure whether paid or unpaid" (member or nonmember)", to petition for redress of a personal grievance, carrying their complaint, if they so desire, directly to the General Service Board. He or she should be able to do this without fear of reprisal or prejudice. Though in practice this will be a seldom exercised right, its very existence will always tend to restrain those in authority from unjust uses of their power. Surely our workers should cheerfully accept the necessary direction and disciplines that go with their jobs, but all of them should nevertheless feel that they need not silently endure unnecessary and unfair personal domination. Concerning both Appeal and Petition, I am glad to say that in AA world services these valuable practices and rights have always been put to good use. Therefore I am committing them to writing only by way of helping confirm and enlarge their future applications. The Rights of Appeal and Petition of course aim at the total problem of protecting and making the best possible use of minority feeling and opinion. This has always been and still is a central problem of all free governments and democratic societies. In AA, individual freedom is of enormous importance. For instance, any alcoholic is a member of AA the moment he says so; we cannot take away his right to belong. Neither can we force our members to believe anything or pay anything. Ours is indeed a large charter of minority privileges and liberties. When we look at our world services, we find that here we have also gone to great lengths in our trust of minority groups. Under Tradition Two, the group conscience is the final authority for AA world service and it will always remain so respecting all the larger issues that confront us. Nevertheless the AA groups have recognized that for world service purposes the group conscience of AA as a totality has certain limitations. It cannot act directly in many service matters, because it cannot be sufficiently informed about the problems at hand. It is also true that during a time of great disturbance the group conscience is not always the best possible guide because, temporarily such an upset may prevent it from functioning efficiently or wisely. When, therefore, the group conscience cannot or should not act directly, who does act for it? The second part of Tradition Two provides us with the answer when it describes AA leaders as trusted servants. These servants must always be in readiness to do for the groups what the groups obviously cannot or should not do for themselves. Consequently the servants are bound to use their own information and judgment, sometimes to the point of disagreeing with uniformed or biased group opinion. Thus it will be seen that in world service operations AA often trust a small but truly qualified minority-- the hundred-odd members of its General Service Conference -- to act as AA group conscience in most of our service affairs. Like other free societies, we have to trust our servants, knowing that in the unusual event that they should fail their responsibilities, we shall have ample opportunity to recall or replace them. The foregoing observations illustrate, in a general way, AA's concern for the freedom and protection of individual members and the whole membership's willingness to trust able and conscientious servants to function in their several capacities, for us all. As the longtime recipients of this kind of trust, I am sure that many of AA's old-timers would like me to record their gratitude along with my own. By 1951, when the General Service Conference was put into experimental operation, these attitudes of trust already are an essential part of AA life. In drafting the Charter for our Conference, therefore, we naturally infused the documents with provisions which would insure protection and respect for minorities. This is exemplified, for instance, in our "Third Legacy" method of selecting Delegates. Unless the majority candidate can poll a two-thirds vote of his State or Provincial Assembly, he must place his name in a hat with one or more of the choices of the Assembly minority. By thus drawing lots, the minority candidates have an equal chance with the majority choice. Strictly speaking, a democracy operates on the will of the majority, no matter how slim that majority may be. So when making special concessions to the feeling and the often-demonstrated wisdom of minorities, we occasionally may deny democracy's cherished principle of final decision by a simple majority vote. Nevertheless we actually have found that our Third Legacy method of electing Delegates has much strengthened the spirit of democracy among us. Unity has been cemented, cooperation has been increased, and the Delegate is finally chosen, no discontented minority can trail in his wake. To increase the actual spirit of democracy by special deference to minority opinion is, we think, better than

to follow blindly the rule which always insists on an unqualified dominance by a slight majority vote. Consider another example: our respect for the minority position, plus a desire for unity and certainty, often prompts AA's General Service Conference to debate at length on important questions of policy, provided there is no need for an immediate or early decision. On many occasions the conference has insisted on a continuing discussion even in certain cases when a two-thirds majority easily could have been obtained. Such a traditional voluntary practice is evidence of real prudence and courteous deference to minority views. Unless it has been absolutely unavoidable, the Conference has usually refused to take important decisions on anything less than a two-thirds vote. This same kind of consideration for the minority position can be found in the Charter provision that no Conference vote can be considered binding on the Trustees of the General Service Board unless it equals two-thirds of a Conference quorum. This gives the Trustees a power of veto in cases where the majority is not great. By reason of this provision the Trustees, if they wish, can insist on further debate and so check any tendency to haste or emotionalism. In practice the Trustees seldom exercise this option. More often they go along with a simple majority of the Delegates, especially when prompt action on less critical matters is clearly needed. But the choice is always theirs, whether to veto a simple majority or to act with it. Here again is a recognition of the constructive value of a trusted minority. If to such a generous recognition of minority privileges we now add the traditional Rights of Appeal and Petition, I believe we shall have granted to all minorities, whether of groups or individuals, the means of discharging their world service duties confidently, harmoniously, and well. More than a century ago a young French nobleman named De Tocqueville came to America to look at the new Republic. Though many of his friends had lost their lives and fortunes in the French Revolution, De Tocqueville was a worshipful admirer of democracy. His writings on government by the people and for the people are classics, never more carefully studied than at the present time. Throughout his political speculation De Tocqueville insisted that the greatest danger to democracy would always be the tyranny of apathetic, self seeking, uninformed, or angry majorities. Only a truly dedicated citizenry, quite willing to protect and conserve minority rights and opinions, could, he thought, guarantee the existence of a free and democratic society. All around us in the world today we are witnessing the tyranny of majorities and the even worse tyranny of very small minorities invested with absolute power. De Tocqueville would have neither, and we AA's can heartily agree with him. We believe that the spirit of democracy in our Fellowship and in our world service structure will always survive, despite the counter forces which will no doubt continue to beat upon us. Fortunately we are not obliged to maintain a government that enforces conformity by inflicting punishments. We need to maintain only a structure of service that holds aloft our Traditions, that forms and executes our policies there under, and so steadily carries our message to those who suffer. Hence we believe that we shall never be subjected to the tyranny of either the majority or the minority, provided we carefully define the relations between them and forthwith tread the path of world service in the spirit of our Twelve Steps, our Twelve Traditions, and our Conference Charter -- in which I trust that we shall
one day inscribe these traditions of Rights of Appeal and Petition." (AA)

As the editor, this is actually my first look at this material and I am in awe at the amount of compassion and forethought that it takes to create standards for a fair society in order to make it last. Although, such forethought took place in the development of the United States government, the same is not always guaranteed in our employment. I have had the benefit of working in such a situation where human rights have deteriorated to the effect, as Bill put it, "you either resign or stay and rot". The experience helps me to appreciate all the more how wonderful it is to participate in a society of people that has provided these rights and protected the individual. I have been exposed to De Tocqueville's ideas previously in my participation in other professional societies and have been greatly impressed by his ideas. I have also respected the founders of this country's Constitution and Bill of Rights; people, such as Thomas Jefferson and Benjamin Franklin who have brought spiritual concepts from other successful societies, such as the great Seneca nations, into our government for the well being of all. Men, who have been infl uenced by EGO in their lives but then to ultimately, choose HOLY SPIRIT is a great significance in the development of protected societies. This is the work of Bill Wilson, which could definitely be adapted to other uses in our organizations, societies and government. This is the proposal I provide to ACIM.

CONCEPT VI:

The Trustee members of the Conference act as the Board taking the chief initiative and active responsibility in most national and world services. The Conference retains the authority for final decision on all large matters of general policy and finance. Likewise, as with the national and world service systems (conference and board), this concept, as well as all others, apply to the central district and geographic area service assembly and their respective offices. It is also recommended that meetings and groups attempt to align with the concepts whenever possible or unless it is in contradiction to already established procedures or ground rules. It is also recommended that prior to all major and important actions and decisions, joining, prayer and a five minute meditation with HOLY SPIRIT occur. (AA)

It is helpful to be familiar with the Conference or Assembly Charter and the Office or Board Bylaws to understand the relationship and the freedom of action that service workers (paid and unpaid) should have. There are legal and practical responsibilities that must be performed when the assembly or conference cannot be consulted. There are cash flows, payrolls, banking, and investing the prudent reserves. There are public information, reception, recruitment and publication activities. Just as meetings develop group operations to handle things more efficiently, and the designated representatives are delegated a certain amount of authority to act freely on behalf of the individual members, this process continues to develop as growth of ACIM occurs. The groups create a central office and assembly to handle things that ordinary group functioning cannot do effectively or economically. Not all meetings form groups and not all groups participate with the central district office. This is not recommended, but because of our great respect for autonomy and minorities, this should be tolerated. The process should always be voluntary and never coercive. There will always be enough persons willing to participate in these leadership activities. Just as the membership delegates authority to their assembly and conference representatives, the assemblies and conferences should delegate a liberal administrative authority to the office and board members so they may act freely in the absence of assembly or conference. They are the guardians and responsible for carrying the ACIM message. (AA) The whole AA service structure resembles that of a large corporation. The corporate form was deliberately chosen rather than institutional or governmental models, because the corporate structure is a better vehicle when it comes to the administration of policy and business. Although the AA objective is a spiritual one, the service structure acts like a large business. The groups are as stockholders; the delegates are their proxies; trustees act as company directors; the boards have subsidiaries and the offices have contracts, leases, etc. This analogy makes it clear that like any other corporate operation the office managers and directors must be given certain powers if they are to effectively run service operations. The process is one of balance, knowledge, and experience. The charter, bylaws, traditions and concepts spell out there boundaries and limitations of power, but as a society experiences growth it is not advisable to bind their hands and feet to the old ways and not be given the power to adapt to changing conditions. Relations should not be frozen into a rigid pattern. However satisfactory and right the present situation and arrangements seem, the future may reveal flaws that we do not envision. However, hasty and unwise changes and amendments are not recommended, but can occur. (EGO is patient.) These articles for arrangement of service activities allow for mistakes and safe return to HOLY SPIRIT.

CONCEPT VII:

The assemblies and conference recognize that the bylaws of the offices and boards are legal instruments providing the legal power to manage and conduct ACIM service and business; whereas the assemblies and conference obtain their power through the purse strings and tradition. (AA)

You might say that this is all redundant and a bit overboard and ask, "Why do we need all of this?" Remember that EGO is a subtle foe and would enjoy nothing better than to have the boards and conventions stuck in an adversarial role, attacking one another; locked in a stale mate where no one wins. With all the blessings of peace, it is easy to fall into spiritual sleep. The stories we tell of our experiences with EGO keep us awake and alert to the dangers. One story after another of the secret lives of sex addicts that hold prominent positions in our society, airline pilots hooked on cocaine for years, managers abusing their powers to hide their drinking, etc. let us know that the human mind and body are very capable of the Jekyll and Hyde existence. I was very close to someone who had great responsibilities in AA and with her occupation; could speak to and motivate several hundred people at a time, yet had never actually stopped drinking or abusing prescription drugs. Another whose father was a superintendent of the high schools system in New York City and mother an opera star, whose alcoholic lives behind the scenes created untold havoc in her life. I have personal friends who have been practicing spiritual principles in AA for years with very serious gambling or shopping problems. I have personally witnessed the retirement of a CEO and his staff who provided a very high esteem work place, to be secretly taken over by a regime (mostly from the Human Resource staff) which has placed very autocratic personalities in key positions and removed all rights of grievance from the contract language without consulting anyone. Almost overnight it has become a dictatorship with many clandestine activities. It has been very long and hard battles by the Union to try to get just of few of these rights back. So you say this couldn't happen in a spiritual organization, but it does. Treasurer's dip into the funds; chairmen lose their tempers; some only feign spirituality. The checks and balances are extremely important for harmony and longevity. It creates mutual respect, deters strife, and builds esteem. To make the assemblies and conference charters legal would require too much red tape, but nevertheless they retain the ultimate power with the ability to deny monies to the offices and the boards to operate. Likewise the offices and boards have the legal budgeting rights to limit expenditures to the assemblies and conferences making it very difficult to meet with a quorum. In either case it would always be a no win situation, thereby always requiring cooperation rather than antagonism. Assemblies and conventions can reorganize and offices and boards can veto, but no one benefits from war. The victor of a battle only seems to win. As with ACIM teaching, ACIM service requires trust. It is too much to ask the assemblies and conferences to do the hiring of office and board staff, so we trust their judgment to maintain and replace themselves. However the assemblies do retain the right through a collective conscience vote to dismiss office and board staff for gross negligence or misconduct. However, the assemblies and conferences have no legal right to require the offices and boards to follow most of their recommendations, but it wouldn't be wise to defy common sense requests and direction. Although the checks and balances may never need to be used, they serve as the corner policeman keeping the peace in the neighborhood. (AA)

CONCEPT VIII:

ACIM National and World Board Trustees are the principle planners, managers and executives for overall policy, finance, membership and public relations and other critical administrative matters in ACIM service. In turn they can provide custodial oversight for a full time national and world office and/or other constantly active services (e.g. publications, geographic area offi ces) by hiring full time directors or office managers. The directors in turn choose their staff according to the dictates of the convention of members they represent, directives from the board trustees and superior directors and managers, bylaws and available funds. Each subsidiary is separately incorporated and should possess its own bylaws, its own capital, its own expenses, its own offices and equipment, etc. The world service board chooses the director of the world service offi ce, the national service boards chooses the directors of the national service offices, the national director chooses his immediate staff and the managers of the geographic area service office (an alternate nominee list of at least five persons available to perform as manager for each geographic service office is provided by the geographic area service assembly and maintained by national service office); the geographic area service director chooses his immediate staff and the managers of the central district service office (a list of at least five alternative nominees available to perform the job of office manager for each central district service office is provided by each central district service assembly and maintained by the geographic area service office). Individual members, meetings and groups are autonomous and independent, unless their actions would cause damage or harm to the ACIM fellowship as a whole. They answer to no one but their own individual and/or collective conscience, however the traditions may warrant. (AA)

AA has a slogan "Keep it simple"; however there is a difference between being a simpleton and keeping it simple. There is also a difference between complicated and complex. Complexity is the systematic foundation of one simple idea on top of another. This concept is complex but simple and is ultimately necessary when dealing with exponential demographics. Communication involves not only the sender and a receiver, but feedback acknowledging agreement or disagreement. Communication must flow easily in all directions for effective action to take place. This concept not only delineates certain common responsibilities, but indirectly outlines the channels of communication. The membership has a channel to voice their wants and needs all the way to the board and the board provides service back down through the service offices. Also lateral communication between local offices and assemblies can occur for pertinent local matters and issues. By "keeping it simple" each operation does not have to be distracted with details or endless questions of issues in which they have no authority or responsibility for and can focus on routine service operations. Questions can be referred to the appropriate office that can handle the issue. This system also establishes a method of surveillance of one another to insure that large accumulations of wealth, power or misappropriation do not occur. And if one section does fail or have critical difficulties, by having each office or operation a separate entity, the system is like a submarine that can isolate the damage to one particular area without the entire ship going down. The system is obviously built for longevity. The system of checks and balances works upwards, downwards and laterally reminding everyone of the dangers of EGO and keeping us joined with HOLY SPIRIT in our service endeavors.

CONCEPT IX:

Good leadership is essential and indispensable for the longevity and posterity of ACIM. Reliable, sensible, and ethical methods of choosing leadership is also integral for its righteous functioning and existence. (AA)

Some Native American customs believe that their children are closer to God and the children came to assist their parents with their journey. Sometimes the ones most spiritual in the meetings are the ones just beginning. They are more motivated by the pain of EGO and quickly learn the spiritual basics to survive. They come to the meetings to help the old timers remember the basics. For the moment, they are the teachers. A wise leader knows how to listen as well as talk, and knows to listen intently to the newcomer. We can often get pretty far away from HOLY SPIRIT during our journey; where longevity and seniority don't always equate to spiritual progression. The success of the survival of a society is dependent upon the transference of the original leadership to its successors. It is critical that the society have an abundance of potential leaders whose dedication, stability, vision and skills will allow them to face every possible service requirement. The leader is someone who can personally put his EGO needs out of the way and put principles, plans and policies into such effective action that the rest will want to follow, help, support and back up the ideas and actions. In this concept Bill Wilson provided an article he wrote in 1959 entitled LEADERSHIP IN AA: EVER A VITAL NEED, which categorizes a leader similar to what an Eagle Scout must learn to be. "Good leadership originates plans, policies, and ideas for the improvement of our Fellowship and its services."..."Good leadership never passes the buck"... A leader is a "Statesman who can carefully discriminate...and take a stand against the storm, using every ability of authority and persuasion to effect a change" for the well being of the whole... "Another qualification for leadership is ...the ability to compromise cheerfully whenever a proper compromise can cause a situation to progress in what appears to be the right direction"..."Leadership is often called upon to face heavy and sometime long-continued criticism"...Leaders have "vision, the ability to make good estimates, both for the immediate and for the more distant future"... "Leaders exhibit prudence"...Leaders "demonstrate an aptness for foresight in their own business or professional careers"...All levels of leaders "have the same attributes -- tolerance, responsibility, flexibility and vision"...What the leader "does and says, how well he handles criticisms and how well he leads... by spiritual examples-- these qualities of leadership can make all the difference" in an effective or corrupt society. (AA) The article also points out that leader can be a friend, teacher, delegate, manager, employee, director, trustee and leadership is the essence of the 12th Step of living by spiritual principles and carrying the message by example to others. There are other types of leaders, too, with much less integrity that can easily persuade and influence large numbers of EGO oriented people. They know how to wake up EGO in a heartbeat. They are often popular because of their misdeeds rather than their moral conviction. They are skilled at flattery and cunningly know how to stroke the powerful ones when they address the membership. They are often skilled at misinforming every one of the virtues of EGO. They often demonstrate the immediate gratifying rewards of EGO and can convince large numbers not to try too hard or what's the use anyway. We're never going to make it. And they can keep many distracted from HOLY SPIRIT for a long time with a seemingly easier and softer way. Since future efficacy depends upon ever new generations of good, moral service leaders, ACIM should have established ways and means to find and pick the right people for the many service tasks. Hence, great care needs to be taken by the members as they choose their representatives. Personal ambitions, feuds and controversy must be caste aside for the good of the whole. It is a matter of increased care, responsibility and education with an attempt to continually strengthen the composition of leadership with dedicated and competent people. "No matter how carefully we design our service structures of principles and relationships, no matter how well we apportion authority and responsibility, the operating results of our structure can be no better than the personal performance of those who must man it and make it work. Good leadership cannot function well in a poorly designed structure…Weak leadership can hardly function at all, even in the best of structures." "Good leadership will also remember that a fine plan or idea can come from anybody, anywhere. Consequently, good leadership will often discard its own cherished plans for others that are better, and it will give credit to the source."… "We cannot, however, compromise always. Now and then, it is truly necessary to stick flat-footed to one's convictions about an issue until it is settled". ACIM "leaders serve, they never govern".

CONCEPT X:

Every Service Responsibility Or Position Should Be Matched By An Equal Service Authority -- The Scope Of Which Is Always Well Defined By Specific Job Description, Charter, Bylaw, Resolution Or Tradition. (Aa)

An ACIM service structure will not be able "to function effectively and harmoniously unless, at every level of service, each operational responsibility is matched by corresponding authority to discharge it." This requires that responsibility and the delegated authority are well defined and clearly understood. An outstanding characteristic of good operational structure is relating authority with responsibility so none can doubt the leader's role and position. "Unless attributes are well defined; unless those holding the final authority are able and willing to properly delegate and maintain a suitable operation authority, unless those holding such delegated authority feel able and willing to use their delegated authority freely as trusted servants; and unless there exists some definite means of interpreting and deciding doubtful situations--then personal clashes, confusion and ineffectiveness will be inevitable... When delegated authority is operating well, it should not be constantly interfered with; otherwise those charged with the operating responsibility will be demoralized...There should be an abundance of ultimate authority to correct or reorganize; but there should be equally enough authority so that service workers are clear and able to do their daily work and discharge their responsibilities with esteem. (AA) However, neither ultimate authority nor delegated authority should be used indiscriminately. Boards cannot be made into timid rubber stamps by the delegates and managers should not micro manage their employees. Extraordinary precautions should be applied to maintain the operating authority and integrity of active services. Requisite cooperation between committees, office, boards, assemblies conferences and subsidiary operations having primary and secondary jurisdiction in certain service functions should always occur. Therefore in all matters of joint or conflicting authority, a senior jurisdiction should be established and defined. However all parties should be heard regardless of the question involved. Authority can never be adequately divided into halves; therefore it must always be clear at the end of the discussion where the final authority lies. (AA)

Again, all official meetings, discussions, assemblies, conferences, boards and committee meetings should always open and close in prayer and a five minute meditation to consult with HOLY SPIRIT should be taken prior to making any decision, recommendation, resolution, election, etc. The 12 steps, 12 traditions, 12 concepts and 12 warranties are based upon human dignity, respect, esteem, and individuality; Let's always keep these spiritual principles foremost in our minds prior to deciding on taking action.

CONCEPT XI:

ACIM service administration should always have the best possible and available staff, executives, consultants, delegates, etc. Matters for serious care and concern at all levels are as follows (in no order of priority):
- A. Personnel composition of staff, boards, committees, etc.
- B. Personal qualifications
- C. Induction and selection procedures
- D. Terms, tenure and rotation
- E. Service job descriptions, responsibilities, authority, rights & duties
- F. Democratic, hierarchical and lateral interaction
- G. Proper compensation, re-imbursement, respect, dignity and esteem (AA)

Although the membership in AA is set up as a representative democracy and the actual service operations are set up as a corporate hierarchy, quality, spiritual principles, respect for human rights, dignity and esteem were preeminent in their development. It is evident that ACIM could benefit greatly by following such sensible, reliable and virtuous principles of operation. The information in the AA Service manual is rather extensive and the editor will highlight most of the major topics presented in the explanation of Concept XI.

As AA is set up, it has subsidiary organizations and committees that require competent leadership and staff and harmonious association amongst them selves and other entities. The AA service organizational chart is set up with two subsidiary operations owned by the board and several committees assigned to the General Service Board chairman which are: Nominating, Finance & Budgetary, Public Information, Literature and General Policy. ACIM may naturally evolve differently and have different needs or committees. Each committee includes a suitable proportion of the Board Trustees, non trustee experts or consultants, an executive and staff. Bill Wilson provides some absolute sage advise for each committee function that is apropos to any committee conscience and satisfactory operation. For instance the following is what he wrote for the nominating committee: "This committee aids the Trustees in discharging their prime obligation to see that all vacancies -- whether within their own ranks or among key service directors, executives and staff members-are properly filled with members and workers of the greatest possible competence, stability, and industry. The recommendations of this committee to a large extent will determine the continuous success of our service. Its members will have the primary voice in choosing our future Trustee and nontrustee workers. Careful deliberation, painstaking investigation and interviewing, refusal to accept casual recommendations, preparation well in advance of lists of suitable candidates-- these will need to be the principal attitudes and activities of this committee. All temptation to haste or snap judgment will need to be faithfully and constantly revisited. Another problem that future committees may have to face is the subtle tendency toward deterioration in the caliber of personnel due to the very natural and usually unconscious tendency of those who suggest nominees to select individuals of somewhat less ability than themselves. Instinctively we look for associates rather like ourselves, only a little less experienced and able. For example, what executive is likely to recommend an assistant who is a great deal more competent than he is? What group or staff members will suggest a new associate whose capabilities are a great deal above their own average? The reverse is the more likely. Government bureaus, institutions, and many commercial enterprises suffer this insidious deterioration. We have not yet experienced it to any extent, but let us be sure that we never do. All of us need to be on guard against this ruinous trend, especially the Nominating committee, whose first and last duty is to choose only the best obtainable for each vacant post." This example depicts Bill's background, savvy and experience in knowing the do's and don'ts for organizational success. Bill provides such a narrative for each committee with pertinent explanations why certain ideas didn't work for the benefit of the wise; ideas such as "Money and spirituality do have to mix", and "The safe course will usually lie between reckless budget slashing and imprudent spending." (AA)

Bill then identifies several more principles and problems which are common to the subsidiary company operations:

A. <u>Status of Executives</u>: A board of a committee can never actively and continuously manage anything; the function has to be delegated to a sustained and competent executive. The executive should have ample freedom and authority to do his job, and he should not be interfered with as long as he does his job well. Lack of funds should not take precedence over choice of quality executives.(AA)

B. <u>Compensation and re-imbursement of executives, staff, experts and consultants</u>: Paid employees should be recompensed in relative value of their service in commercial enterprises. Cheap help is very costly in the long run and neither good spiritually nor good businesswise. (AA)

C. <u>Sustained executives, rotated staff</u>: Each staff member is expected to possess the general ability to do or to learn how to do, any job in the place--excepting for office management. Therefore it is desirable to sustain the executives in their positions and rotate the staff in the various essential underlying positions. Also the basis of compensating these essential underlying staff is identical (the same pay scale for all employees working for the directors or managers) and pay increases are from longevity only. Although this concept departs from the corporate business structure, it has proved beneficial in times of indisposition, absence or attrition. It also has a way of developing the right ingredients of personality, ability, stability, and business experience. The periods and tenures in the relative positions are designated by charters, bylaws, resolution, or ground rules and should be easily amenable to meet current needs and changing conditions. (AA)

D. <u>Full participation with the ACIM fellowship is available to all paid workers above "group" level (however it is recommended to include paid "group" offi ce staff and managers in pertinent collective conscience decisions):</u> Naturally all a person has to do to become a member is say that they have a desire to learn and live ACIM, but it is not a mandatory condition of employment. However all ACIM paid employees or consultants do have the "Right to Participate" in all service functions above the level of group that pertain to the performance of their duties. Meetings, business discussions and group activities are by membership only; paid services including office staff and management for meetings and groups are not included in this concept; (but it is highly recommended to allow it by a collective conscience decision). Club houses, meeting halls, their subsequent memberships and boards should have no affiliation with ACIM, lest problems of property, money and prestige interfere with the primary purpose and message of ACIM. (AA)

STEVEH.

Not only should we give the paid workers a place at the convention table, we ought to treat them with respect as our friends and co workers. They are members of the team and no shunning, prejudice, segregation or discrimination of anyone or any group of people in ACIM service or membership under any circumstances is valid.

Concept XII: AA provides six warranties to the membership and paid staff: The editor has suggested six more warranties to make a total of

12 WARRANTIES RECOMMENDED TO ACIM:

1	ACIM at any level should never become the seat of perilous wealth or power. (AA)

2	Sufficient operating funds, ample reserve, and financial prudence and husbandry are recommended principles for ACIM fellowship longevity. (AA)

3	No ACIM member or paid employee should ever be placed in a position of absolute tyrannical control over another. (AA)

4	All important ACIM decisions ought to be made with a collective conscience of those present for participation in the discussion (except for scheduled elections, where the necessary information has been previously provided to all eligible to voters). Prior to the collective conscience vote a five minute meditation should occur for each to consult with HOLY SPIRIT. Prayer should always begin and end all sessions concerning important decisions; the hat or basket should always be passed in order to be self supporting through voluntary contributions. All decisions should have a substantial unanimity of greater than 80% (at meeting & group levels -- always including the abstained voters in the count), substantial majority of greater than 67% (at assembly and conference levels -- not counting abstained votes) or no decision is rendered and further discussion is required. All decisions should attempt to either provide an effective compromise between majority and minority opinion or choose the best idea. If necessary "No Decision" can be resolved by putting all solutions or candidates into a "Hat" and the chairman randomly pull out a solution or candidate which will be the accepted remedy. (AA)

5	ACIM should not approve punitive action of members or incitement of public controversy. Forgiveness is our only function. ACIM encourages praise, recognition, helpfulness and support to all. (AA)

6.	ACIM should always remain democratic in thought and action; ACIM governs no one. (AA)

The AA literature discusses these warranties further. The above has been altered somewhat from the wording used by AA. It was done to reflect some collateral ideas for ACIM. If you look for the similarities you will find them. Everything that Bill Wilson incorporated into the traditions, concepts and warranties about respect, dignity, and a genuine concern for the well being of your fellows whether cooperating with them as peers, attending them as trusted servants or aiding them as teachers is actually about Holy Relationships and is the basis for the convention of members and the service structural system previously described. As the editor, I would like to suggest six additional warranties:

7.	No one ACIM member, convention of members, paid employee or service function should be the arbiter or judge of another's personal life, sexual conduct or preference or of the manner they choose to earn a living.

8.	As ACIM members and employees, we should refrain from gossip, hearsay, accusation or condemnation of others taking special care not to damage the life, reputation or livelihood of another or others by our words or actions.

9.	As ACIM members and employees, we should always strive to maintain the highest level of honesty in our words and actions. We should be candidly honest when to do so would help another; cash register honest in the performance of our duties, self honest in following our conscience, but never brutally honest when to do so would hurt another or others. As ACIM members and employees, we should always strive to remain non- judgmental in our words and actions reminding ourselves that criticism, condemnation, cynicism and sarcasm are always on the debit side of the ledger and are tools of EGO.

10. As ACIM members and employees, we should always strive to maintain the spiritual principle of equality, remembering that we can only be equal in HOLY SPIRIT and unequal with EGO.

11. As ACIM members and employees, we should always strive to practice unconditional love and forgiveness for everyone we encounter.

12. If in the event that you have tried ACIM and the steps, and have failed to achieve the spiritual enlightenment and miracles guaranteed by the process, ACIM will gladly refund you your misery and suffering at the door. Remember the door to the meetings always swings both ways. Keep coming back.

Again the words are not permanent (neither is the body) and are only used to convey a thought. The proposal is nothing more than that--a proposed guideline using AA information for the future of ACIM. The AA Service Manual goes into great detail about service descriptions and functions that will not be part of this writing, but it should not be neglected and therefore its table of contents will be provided in Appendix A. At this time the editor will close this work and attempt to get it out to key self proclaimed students of ACIM for review and maybe sometime in the future have this work published for the benefit of any interested AA members, ACIM teachers and students or the general public.

EPILOG:

As a postscript and for the sake of being honest with the reader, I would like to say that the first four chapters were rather easy and enjoyable to do. Mostly because of the experience and familiarity I had acquired with the material. The chapter on the concepts and warranties was a bit more difficult. At first I thought it was because I wasn't aligned with HOLY SPIRIT (which still may be true because there is only a small percentage of time each day that I am spiritually awake, and as the work pressed on I became more compulsive about finishing, and didn't practice most of the principles in which I was writing about). However, it may have also been because of my unfamiliarity with the AA Concepts for World Service. I have danced around them and I have slung them at others in defensive actions (not recommended ACIM behavior), but this time I really had to dig into them. And I am further amazed at the genius of Bill Wilson. Sure I took a couple of jabs at him and I referenced the AA dirt book by Nan Robertson (I'm sure that Bill would of had it this way because I envision him as having a genuine open-mindedness and sense of fair play). But what Bill had the great opportunity to develop with his new society was not only a system to ensure longevity and survival for his healing, recovery and altruistic organization, but a blueprint for a society to function in accordance with spiritual principles. I am sure we could spend a great deal of time discussing the great theologians of the past that developed various concepts for a utopian society, but Bill pulled it off; with seventy years of experience; and with society's rejects, to boot!

The other side of the coin is that alcoholics and drug addicts are highly motivated because of their reckless and painful past experiences and of the grave emotional, financial, physical and spiritual low point they reached in their lives, and after experiencing some of the fruits of recovery they become extremely willing to maintain their spiritual condition because of a memory of despair they are not likely to forget. For others, the act of vigilance may be more difficult especially if your life is comfortable. During my experience of writing this document, at first I started off slowly and maintained balance in my life, but slowly at first, then faster and faster, I became so compulsive that I would spend the entire weekend working on this proposal and neglecting my spiritual maintenance activities such as daily AA meetings, attendance to other spiritual congregations, participating in a Prayer Therapy class, etc. My attitude progressively deteriorated and I began to open my bag of life's resentments and self pity all the while rationalizing that my work on this document would maintain me until I finished. I grossly miscalculated and began to experience anxiety attacks and subtle forms of insanity. This result is not new to me, I have conducted numerous experiments with slacking off on my spiritual maintenance with similar results and it is not easy to get back into spiritual health right away. However from this experience I did come away with one valuable insight. During this period, when I was in idle thought or when I awoke from sleep, I was extremely upset with people who are in responsible positions or are of a known religious persuasion and often do very cruel things to others in their employment, especially to those who appear weak. (I have observed that people who practice spiritual principles in their life are perceived as weak by those who do not.) They sometimes behave as wild animals picking on the one they decided doesn't belong in their herd and they unite in the cause, taking turns being brutal to the one outcast. To me it is like a group EGO. Some of these people acting out are highly educated

STEVEH.

professionals and others are spiritual leaders in church, etc., yet they get caught up in the mob psychology, believe the hearsay and do bad things to others. ACIM explains what it is over and over; they project their guilt onto that individual. They must be carrying around a tremendous amount of guilt and pain for the extent of their actions and rationalization, but they are able to tolerate and deny it. For me, when I return to those levels (for I am not above the same thing), I find that the pain I was once able to tolerate and deny is overwhelming and makes me physically sick. I have no choice but to return to the level of spiritual maintenance I achieved (with no vacations). It's kind of like a person who has become a vegetarian trying to go back to meat. I guess the point I am trying to make is that we can't evangelize, convert or rescue others. We all have our own chosen paths to follow and as equals, we really aren't the judge to know what is always best, or who is winning. Some must continue down before they can come up. Some of us are looking down and thinking we are looking up. All we can do is forgive, pray and meditate to the best of our ability (which isn't saying that much for me sometimes).

ACIM and the steps may not be for you. You may have tapped into something and are at a level that we may only hope to achieve in this lifetime. Nevertheless, if this be the case, I would suspect that you are in a very high percentile of our population because most of us are still greatly influenced by EGO. Whether we admit it or not, we are still trying to serve two masters. And who out there knows the meaning of unconditional love. A friend told me that he loves his son unconditionally and I replied from what I have learned about what is unconditional love; it would mean that he would love his neighbor's son equally as he does his own. To take from one of the copious altruistic writings on ACIM by the very comprehensible author, Robert Perry as an experiment to demonstrate to the reader how far along the path of spiritual progress we may be, please evaluate and recognize

WHAT LOVE IS NOT:

1. Love is not having external things – money, status, things, human love—that tell me I'm lovable. (Perry)

You know not what love means because you have sought to purchase it with little gifts, thus valuing it too little to understand its magnitude. Love is not little and love dwells in you, for you are host to Him. Before the greatness that lives in you, your poor appreciation of yourself and all the little offerings you give slip into nothingness. (ACIM)

2. Love is not filling the hole inside me, gaining something that isn't yet mine. ACIM points out that if you believe there is lack in you and if you believe that you can gain and you can lose, then you cannot know that perfect love is in you. (Perry)

Yet part of the meaning of love is that perfect love is in you. Thus, the mere fact that you believe there is a hole in you that can be filled or widened shows you do not know the meaning of love. (ACIM)

3. Love is not sacrificing for another so that he will be obligated to sacrifice for me. In our eyes, love is synonymous with making sacrifices on behalf of the beloved. And that is exactly what we expect from our loved ones. We expect them to show their love by sacrificing for us, by expending time and energy and passion and money on us. Yet, sacrifice is loss, and so to demand that our loved ones sacrifice for us is to demand that they lose for our sake. If that is what love is, then we must be inseparable from attack and fear; to be intensely loved is to be sucked dry. (Perry)

You who believe that sacrifice is love must learn that sacrifice is separation from love. (ACIM)

4. Love is not empathizing with my brother's weakness and suffering. When someone is hurting, it feels loving to empathize with his or her vulnerability and pain; "I feel your pain," we say. Yet, according to ACIM, this amounts to trying to find love in weakness, and thus equates love with weakness. (Perry)

The power of love, which is its meaning, lies in the strength of God that hovers over it and blesses it silently by enveloping it in healing wings. Let this be, and do not try to substitute your "miracle" for this. (ACIM)

5. Love is not having a special bond from which others are excluded. In our eyes, the ideal loving relationship is a private connection from which others are excluded. This, of course, is the very meaning of "Special Relationship" as opposed to "Holy Relationships". Strangely, this means that love is exclusion. (Perry)

In Heaven, where the meaning of love is known, love is the same as union. Here, where the illusion of love is accepted in love's place, love is perceived as separation and exclusion. (ACIM)

6. Love is not sharing our bodies. ACIM points out that bodies cannot really love; they are just things. Love is sharing, but can bodies really share. (Perry)

STEVEH.

The love of them has made love meaningless. They can be loved, but they cannot love. (ACIM)

7. Love is not being special. Who of us could see ourselves as lovable if we were nobody special? Being special and being lovable seem to be synonymous. Yet, special means being better than and above others. (Perry)

Can love have meaning where the goal is triumph. (ACIM)

8. Love is not having love for some people and not others. Love is not selective. We think we can love in compartments, that our love for one can be genuine even while we hate others. (Perry)

You cannot love parts of reality and understand what love means. If you would love unlike God, Who knows no special love, how can you understand it? To believe that special relationships, with special love, can offer you salvation is the belief that separation is salvation. (ACIM)

If you have mastered and can express the meaning of love, you may just be beyond any information provided in this document. Most of this document consists of rudimentary spiritual principles extracted, often word for word from other spiritual books; and there are a great many more such magnificent books. However, I believe that the information presented in this document can not only help the individual achieve spiritual enlightenment but can effectively establish a lasting design and continuing system of organization for a spiritual society to support one another in their pursuit of miracles, atonement and holy relationships.

Although I am an AA member and an ACIM student, I am more biased toward AA, therefore in my encounters with fellow ACIM students I always thought (by my biased judgment) that they could greatly benefit from the AA steps. Now hopefully and at least the steps are available in a form that an ACIM student could comprehend and relate. The information about traditions and meetings is for the select few that may be interested in forming ACIM meetings; and the concepts are perhaps just for those in an elevated teacher status that with the help of HOLY SPIRIT may use the design and experience of the AA fellowship to create a unified approach to the dissemination of ACIM to the world. And although my present spiritual growth from EGO to HOLY SPIRIT may still have quite a few limitations and drawbacks, I have a very deep respect and knowing that both the AA and ACIM literature represent the Truth. I know that either one is sufficient to keep one very busy with spiritual growth for their days of this life, but I (and hope others will too) do see how each could benefit the other synergistically. It has been a great honor to endeavor this proposal and my hope is that will serve to help others.

For those who may not be familiar with the ACIM text and workbook, I would like to close this proposal with LESSON 138 – **Heaven is the decision I must make.**

"In this world Heaven is a choice, because here we believe there are alternatives to choose between. We think that all things have an opposite, and what we want we choose. If Heaven exists there must be hell as well, for contradiction is the way we make what we perceive, and what we think is real. Creation knows no opposite. But here is opposition part of being "real". It is this strange perception of the truth that makes the choice of Heaven seem to be the same as the relinquishment of hell. It is not really thus. Yet what is true in God's creation cannot enter here until it is reflected in some form the world can understand. Truth cannot come where it could only be perceived with fear. For this would be the error that truth can be brought to illusions. Opposition makes the truth unwelcome, and it cannot come. (ACIM)

Choice is the obvious escape from what appears as opposites. Decision lets one of conflicting goals become the aim of effort and expenditure of time. Without decision, time is but a waste and effort dissipated. It is spent for nothing in return, and time goes by without results. There is no sense of gain, for nothing is accomplished; nothing learned. (ACIM)

You need to be reminded that you think a thousand choices are confronting you, when there is really only one to make. And even this but seems to be a choice. Do not confuse yourself with all the doubts that myriad decisions would induce. You make but one. And when that one is made, you will perceive it was no choice at all. For truth is true. There is no opposite to choose instead. There is no contradiction to be truth. (ACIM)

Choosing depends on learning. And the truth cannot be learned, but only recognized. In recognition its acceptance lies, and as it is accepted it is known. But knowledge is beyond the goals we seek to teach within the framework of this course. Ours are teaching goals, to be attained through learning how to reach them, what they are, and what they offer you. Decisions are the outcome of your learning, for they rest on what you have accepted as the truth of what you are, and what your needs must be. (ACIM)

In this insanely complicated world, Heaven appears to take the form of choice, rather than merely being what is. Of all the choices you have tried to make this is the simplest, most definitive and prototype of all the rest, the one which settles all decisions. If you could decide the rest, this one remains unsolved. But when you solve this one, the others are resolved with it, for all decisions but conceal this one by taking different forms. Here is the final and the only choice in which is truth accepted or denied. (ACIM)

So we begin today by considering the choice that time was made to help us make. Such is its holy purpose, now transformed from the intent you gave it; that it be a means for demonstrating hell is real, hope changes despair, and life itself must in the end be overcome by death. In death alone are opposites resolved, for ending opposition is to die. And thus salvation must be seen as death, for life is seen as conflict. To resolve the conflict is to end your life as well. (ACIM) These mad beliefs can gain unconscious hold of great intensity and grip the mind with terror and anxiety so strong that it will not relinquish its ideas about its own protection. It must be saved from salvation, threatened to be safe, and magically armored against truth. And these decisions are made unaware, to keep them safely undisturbed; apart from question and from reason and from doubt.(ACIM)

Heaven is chosen consciously. The choice cannot be made until alternatives are accurately seen and understood. All that is veiled in shadows must be raised to understanding, to be judged again, this time with Heaven's help. And all mistakes in judgment that the mind had made before are open to correction, as the truth dismisses them as causeless. Now are they without effects. They cannot be concealed, because their nothingness is recognized. (ACIM)

The conscious choice of Heaven is as sure as is the ending of the fear of hell, when it is raised for its protective shield of unawareness, and is brought to light. Who can decide between clearly seen and the unrecognized? Yet who can fail to make a choice between alternatives when only one is seen as valuable; the other as a wholly worthless thing, but an imagined source of guilt and pain? Who hesitates to make a choice like this? And shall we hesitate to choose today? (ACIM)

We make the choice for Heaven as we wake, and spend five minutes making sure that we have made the one decision that is sane. We recognize we make a conscious choice between what has existence and what has nothing but appearance of the truth. Its pseudo-being, brought to what is real, is flimsy and transparent in the light. It holds no terror now, for what was made enormous, vengeful, and pitiless with hate, demands obscurity for fear to be invested there. Now it is recognized as but a foolish, trivial mistake. (ACIM)

Before we close our eyes in sleep tonight, we reaffirm the choice that we have made each hour in between. And now we give the last five minutes of our waking day to the decision with which we awoke. As every hour passed, we have declared our choice again, in a brief quiet time devoted to maintaining sanity. And finally, we close the day with this acknowledging we chose but what we want: (ACIM)

Heaven is the decision I must make. I make it now and will not change my mind, because it is the only thing I want. (ACIM)

The editor's conclusion is that judgment day has already come and gone and God has ruled His verdict "Not Guilty" and has passed His loving sentence "Eternity in Heaven for all Mankind." This is the only possibility that there could be

APPENDIX A - THE A.A. SERVICE MANUAL COMBINED WITH TWELVE
CONCEPTS FOR WORLD SERVICE BY BILL W.

Contact AAWS

ALCOHOLICS ANONYMOUS® is a fellowship of men and women who share their experience, strength and hope with each other that they may solve their common problem and help others to recover from alcoholism.
The only requirement for membership is a desire to stop drinking. There are no dues or fees for A.A. membership; we are self-supporting through our own contributions.
A.A. is not allied with any sect, denomination, politics, organization, or institution; does not wish to engage in any controversy; neither endorses nor opposes any causes.
Our primary purpose is to stay sober and help other alcoholics to achieve sobriety.
Copyright© by the A.A. Grapevine Inc.; reprinted with permission

A Declaration of Unity

This we owe to A.A.'s future; to place our common welfare first; to keep our Fellowship united. For on A.A. unity depend our lives, and the lives of those to come.

I Am Responsible…

When anyone, anywhere, reaches out for help, I want the hand of A.A. always to be there. And for that: I am responsible.

Copyright© 1962, 1969, 1986, 1987, 1988, 1989, 1990, 1991,1992, 1993, 1994, 1995, 1996, 1997, 1998, 1999,

2000, 2001, 2002, 2003, 2004, 2005 First printing of Revised Edition, 1999

Alcoholics Anonymous World Services, Inc. 475 Riverside Drive, New York, N.Y. 10115 Mail address: Box 459, Grand Central Station New York, N.Y. 10163 www.aa.org

A.A. and Alcoholics Anonymous are registered trademarks® of Alcoholics Anonymous World Services, Inc. 40M-8/05 (INTRA) Printed in U.S.A.

APPENDIX B

ORIGINAL CONFERENCE CHARTER — 1955 (NORTH AMERICAN SECTION)

1   Purpose: The General Service Conference of Alcoholics Anonymous is the guardian of the World Services and of 1 the Twelve Traditions of Alcoholics Anonymous. The Conference shall be a service body only; never a government for Alcoholics Anonymous.

2   Composition: The Conference (North American Section) shall be composed of State and Provincial Delegates, the Trustees of the General Service Board, Directors and staff members of the New York Headquarters and such ex-Trustees or foreign Delegates as the Conference may wish to invite. Other Sections of the Conference may sometimes be created in foreign lands as the need arises out of language or geographical considerations. The North American Section of the General Service Conference will then become the Senior Section, related to the other Sections by ties of mutual consultation and a cross linking of Delegates. But no Conference Section shall ever be placed in authority over another. All joint action shall be taken only upon two-thirds vote of the combined Sections. Within its boundaries each Conference ought to be autonomous. Only matters seriously affecting A.A.'s worldwide needs shall be the subject of joint consideration.

3   Conference Relation to A.A.: The Conference will act for A.A. in the perpetuation and guidance of its World Services, and it will also be the vehicle by which the A.A. movement can express its views upon all matters of vital A.A. policy and all hazardous deviations from A.A. Tradition. Delegates should be free to vote as their conscience dictates; they should also be free to decide what questions should be taken to the group level, whether for information, discussion or their own direct instruction. But no change in the A.A. Tradition itself may be made with less than the written consent of two-thirds of all the A.A. groups.

4   Conference Relation to A.A. Headquarters: The Conference will replace the founders of Alcoholics Anonymous who formerly functioned as guides and advisors to The General Service Board and its related Headquarters services. The Conference will be expected to afford a reliable cross-section of A.A. opinion for this purpose. To effectively further this same purpose it will be understood, as a matter of tradition, that a two-thirds vote of a Conference quorum shall be considered binding upon the General Service Board and its related corporate services. A quorum shall consist of two-thirds of all the Conference members registered. But no such vote ought to impair the legal rights of the General Service Board and the service corporations to conduct routine business and make ordinary contracts relating thereto. It will be further understood that, as a matter of tradition, a three-quarters vote of all Conference members may bring about a reorganization of the General Service Board and the Headquarters, if or when such reorganization is deemed essential. Under such a proceeding, the Conference may request resignations, may nominate new Trustees and may make all other necessary arrangements regardless of the legal prerogatives of the General Service Board.

5   State and Provincial Assemblies: Composition of: State and Provincial Assemblies are composed of the elected Representatives of all A.A. groups desiring to participate, in each of the United States and each of the Provinces of Canada. Each State and Province will always be entitled to one Assembly. But States and Provinces of large A.A. populations will be entitled to additional Assemblies, as provided by this Manual of World Service, or by any future

amendment thereto.

6   State and Provincial Assemblies: Purpose of: State and Provincial Assemblies convene every two years for the election of State and Provincial Committeemen, from which are selected Delegates to the General Service Conference of Alcoholics Anonymous held at New York. Such State or Provincial Assemblies are concerned only with the World Service affairs of Alcoholics Anonymous.

7   State and Provincial Assemblies: Method of Electing Committeemen and Delegates: Whenever practicable, Committeemen are elected by written ballot without personal nomination. And Delegates are selected from among such Committeemen by a two-thirds written ballot or by lot, as provided in the Manual of World Service .

8   State and Provincial Assemblies: Terms of Office for Group Representatives, Committeemen and Delegates: Unless otherwise directed by the Conference, these terms of office shall all be concurrent and of two years duration each. In half the States and Provinces, Assembly elections will be held in the even years; the remaining half of the Assemblies will elect in the odd years, thus creating rotating Panels One and Two of the Conference as further described in the Manual of World Service.

9   The General Service Conference Meetings: The Conference will meet yearly in the City of New York, unless otherwise agreed upon. Special meetings may be called should there be a grave emergency. The Conference may also render advisory opinions at any time by a mail or telephone poll in aid of the General Service Board or its related services.

10   The General Service Board: Composition, Jurisdiction, Responsibilities: The General Service Board of Alcoholics Anonymous shall be an incorporated Trusteeship composed of alcoholics and non-alcoholics who choose their own successors, these choices being subject, however, to the approval of the Conference or a committee thereof. Alcoholic out-of-town Trustees are, however, first nominated by their areas or by their State or Provincial Committees after being cleared by the Conference Nominating Committee. They are then elected to the General Service Board, the Trustees being obligated by tradition so to do.

11   The General Service Conference: Its General Procedures: The Conference will hear the financial and policy reports of the General Service Board and its related Headquarters Services. The Conference will advise with the Trustees, Directors and Staff members of the Headquarters upon all matters presented as affecting A.A. as a whole, engage in debate, appoint necessary committees and pass suitable resolutions for the advice or direction of the General Service Board and the Headquarters. The Conference may also discuss and recommend appropriate action respecting serious deviations from A.A. Tradition or harmful misuse of the name, "Alcoholics Anonymous." The Conference may draft any needed bylaws and will name its own officers and committees by any method of its own choosing. The Conference, at the close of each yearly session, will draft a full report of its proceedings to be supplied to all Delegates and Committeemen; also a condensation thereof which will be sent to A.A. Groups throughout the world.

12   General Warranties of the Conference: In all its proceedings, the General Service Conference shall observe the spirit of the A.A. Tradition, taking great care that the two service corporations, A.A.W.S., Inc. and the

A.A. Grapevine, Inc., although affiliates and not "subsidiaries," of the General Service Board of Alcoholics Anonymous, Inc., are organized as separate, not-for-profit corporations, and, as such, the routine conduct of policy and business affairs and the creation of "suitable committees," respecting each, resides in the respective boards of the two corporations. However, the trustees of the General Service Board, when acting in their capacity as members of the A.A. World Services, Inc., and/or the A.A. Grapevine, Inc., do elect the directors of the two service corporations.

The General Service Board is the chief Service Arm of the Conference, and is essentially custodial in its character. Excepting for decisions upon matters of policy, finance, or A.A. Tradition, liable to seriously affect

22   A.A. as a whole, the General Service Board has entire freedom of action in the routine conduct of the policy and business affairs of the A.A. General Headquarters at New York and may name suitable committees and elect directors to its subsidiary corporate service entities in pursuance of this purpose. The General Service Board is primarily responsible for the financial and policy integrity of its subsidiary services: A.A. Publishing, Inc. and A.A. Grapevine, Inc. and for such other service corporations as the Conference may desire to form, but nothing herein shall compromise the Grapevine editor's right to accept or reject material for publication. The Charter and Bylaws of the General Service Board, or any amendments thereto, should always be subject to the approval of the General Service Conference by a two-thirds vote of all its members.11 Except in a great emergency, neither the General Service Board nor any of its related services ought ever take any action liable to greatly affect A.A. as a whole, without first consulting the Conference. It is nevertheless understood that the Board shall at all times reserve the right to decide which of its actions or decisions may require the approval of the Conference.

Conference never becomes the seat of perilous wealth or power; that sufficient operating funds, plus an ample reserve, be its prudent financial principle; that none of the Conference members shall ever be placed in a position of unqualified authority over any of the others; that all important decisions be reached by discussion, vote and, whenever possible, by substantial unanimity; that no Conference action ever be personally punitive or an incitement to serious public controversy; that though the Conference may act for the service of Alcoholics Anonymous, it shall never perform any acts of government; and that, like the Society of Alcoholics Anonymous which it serves, the Conference itself will always remain democratic in thought and action. The principles on which this Charter operates are outlined in "Twelve Concepts" and they should be read.

1 Updated by the 1969 Conference to include the words: "the Twelve Steps."

2 Revised by the 1979 Conference to read: "Composition: The Conference (U.S. and Canada) shall be composed of area delegates, the trustees of the General Service Board, directors of A.A. World Services and A.A Grapevine, and staff members of the Grapevine and General Service Office."

3 Updated by the 1987 Conference to read: "Foreign lands in many cases have created autonomous General Service Conferences of their own, which rely on the Steps and Traditions protected by the Conference (U.S. and Canada) and in other ways often turn to the actions of the Conference for guidance. "Consultation between Conferences is encouraged. And a formal meeting — the World Service Meeting of delegates from the various Conferences is held once every two years. The US./Canada delegates are chosen from the General Service Board. "In countries where General Service structure exists, the U.S./Canada Conference will delegate sole right to publish our Conference-approved literature to the General Service Board of the structure. "Only matters seriously affecting A.A.'s worldwide needs shall be the subject of joint consideration." Further clarified by the 1988 Conference to read: "Other countries have created autonomous General Service Conferences of their own, which rely on the Steps and Traditions that are protected by the United States/Canada Conference. In addition, these other Conferences often

turn to the actions of the United States/Canada Conference for guidance. "Consultation between Conferences is encouraged, and a World Service Meeting of delegates from the various Conferences is held once every two years. The United States/Canada delegates to the World Service Meeting are chosen from the General Service Board. "In countries where a General Service Structure exists, the United States/Canada Conference will delegate sole right to publish our Conference-approved literature to the General Service Board of that structure."

4 Revised by the 1957 Conference as follows: "Bill has suggested that the third article of the Conference Charter, i.e., Conference Relation to A.A. (Second paragraph page 58 of the Third Legacy Manual), be amended to read: "But no change in Article 12 of the Charter or in A.A. Tradition or in the Twelve Steps of A.A. may be made with less than a written consent of three-quarters of the A.A. groups, as described in the resolution adopted by the 1955 Conference and Convention." If this amendment is made the seventh paragraph on page 57 of the Third Legacy Manual must also be amended to read: "excepting, however that any amendment of Article 12 of the Charter or of A.A.'s Twelve Steps and Twelve Traditions must have the consent of A.A. groups as provided in Article 3 of the Charter." It was recommended that these amendments be made." Subsequently revised by the 1969 Conference to replace the words "A.A. Tradition" with "The Twelve Traditions of A.A."

5 Revised by the 1986 Conference as follows: A quorum shall consist of two-thirds of all the Conference members registered. It will be understood, as a matter of tradition, that a two-thirds vote of Conference members voting shall be considered binding upon the General Service Board and its related corporate services, provided the total vote constitutes at least a Conference quorum.

6 Article 5, paragraph 2 reworded by the 1971 Conference to read: "Generally speaking, each state and province will be entitled to one assembly. However, more than one state or province may be joined to another state or province to form one assembly area. But states and provinces of large A.A. populations and/or whose geography presents communication problems may be entitled to additional assemblies, as provided by the A.A. Service Manual, or by any further amendment thereto." Subsequently, the 1978 Conference made a further amendment to Article 5 as follows: "Area Assemblies: Composition of: Assemblies, designated as area assemblies, are composed of the elected general service representatives of all A.A. groups desiring to participate, district committee members, and area committee officers in each of the delegate areas of the United States and Canada."

7 The 1970 Conference revised the title indicated here as Alcoholic out-of-town Trustee (later appearing as General Service Trustee-at-Large) to be "Regional General Service Trustee." By 1978, this Board title appeared as Trustee-at-Large.

8 By 1969, the following sentence had been added: "The same procedure is followed for general service trustees in the United States and Canada, except that the Board will specify certain business or professional qualifications." The 1979 Conference substituted the word "will" with "may."

10 See preceding footnote.

11 The approval of the Bylaws by the Conference is a matter of tradition, rather than a legal requirement.

12 The 1981 Conference recommended that this note appear immediately following the Conference Charter.

APPENDIX C -

THE HOLY SPIRIT (EXCERPT FROM ACIM MANUAL FOR TEACHERS – CLARIFICATION OF TERMS)

1   The HOLY SPIRIT is described as the remaining communication link between God and His separated Sons. In order to fulfill this special function the HOLY SPIRIT has assumed a dual function. He knows because He is part of God; He perceives because He was sent to save humanity. He is the great correction principle: the bringer of true perception, the inherent power of the vision of Christ. He is the light in which the forgiven world is perceived; in which the face of Christ alone is seen. He never forgets the Creator or His Creation. He never forgets the Son of God. He never forgets you. And He brings the Love of your Father to you in eternal shining that will never be obliterated because God has put it there.

2   The HOLY SPIRIT abides in the part of your mind that is part of the Christ Mind. He represents your Self and your Creator, Who are one. He speaks for God and also for you, being joined with both. And therefore it is He Who proves them one. He seems to be a Voice, for in that form He speaks God's Word to you. He seems to be a Guide through a far country, for you need that form of help. He seems to be whatever meets the needs you think you have. But He is not deceived when you perceive your self entrapped in needs you do not have. It is from these He would deliver you. It is from these that He would make you safe.

2. The HOLY SPIRIT is described throughout the course as giving us the answer to the separation and bringing the plan of the Atonement to us, establishing our particular part in it and showing us exactly what it is. He has established Jesus as the leader in carrying out His plan since he was the first to complete his own part perfectly. All power in Heaven and earth is therefore given Him and He will share it with you when you have completed yours. The Atonement principle was given to the HOLY SPIRIT long before Jesus set it in motion.

Editorial note: For myself, reading A Course In Miracles alone is like trying to read and comprehend Emmerson, William James or an Old English Bible. It is too difficult to comprehend and I easily give up. However, when I read the same words with a group joined with HOLY SPIRIT, a light comes on and I am lifted. The meanings are clear and I am overwhelmed by a sense of joy and knowing. The

feeling I get makes a great substitute for what at one time in my life I used alcohol to create.

APPENDIX D

ACIM DEFINITION OF JESUS CHRIST (EXCERPTS FROM ACIM WORKBOOK - WHAT IS CHRIST?; MANUAL FOR TEACHERS – DOES JESUS HAVE A SPECIAL PLACE IN HEALING?; & CLARIFICATION OF TERMS – JESUS CHRIST.)

"The name of Jesus is the name of one who was a man but saw the face of Christ in all his brothers and remembered God. So he became identified with Christ, a man no longer, but at one with God. The man was an illusion, for he seemed to be a separate being, walking by himself, within a body that appeared to hold his self from Self, as all illusions do. Yet who can save unless he see illusions and then identifies them as what they are? Jesus remains a Savior because he saw the false without accepting it as true. And Christ needed his form that He might appear to men and save them from their own illusions."

"Jesus has led the way. Why would you not be grateful to him? He has asked for love, but only that he might give it to you. You do not love yourself. But in his eyes your loveliness is so complete and flawless that he sees in it an image of his Father. You become the symbol of his Father here on earth. To you he looks for hope, because in you he sees no limit and no stain to mar your beautiful perfection. In his eyes Christ's vision shines in perfect constancy. He has remained with you. Would you not learn the lesson of salvation through his learning? Why would you choose to start again, when he has made the journey for you?"

"No one on earth can grasp what Heaven is, or what its one Creator really means. Yet we have witnesses. It is to them that far exceeds what we can learn. Nor would we teach the limitations we have laid on us. No one who has become a true and dedicated teacher of God forgets his brothers. Yet what he can offer them is limited by what he learns himself. Then turn to the one who laid all limits by, and went beyond the farthest reach of learning. He will take you with him, for he did not go alone. And you were with him then, as you are now."

"This course has come from him because his words have reached you in language you can love and understand. Are other teachers possible, to lead the way to those who speak in different tongues and appeal to different symbols? Certainly there are. Would God leave anyone without help in time of trouble a very present savior who can symbolize Himself? Yet we need a many faceted curriculum, not because of content differences, but because symbols must shift and change to suit the need. Jesus has come to answer yours. In him you find God's Answer. Do you then, teach with him, for he is with you; he is always there."

Editorial note: A word to those who may not be <u>A Course In Miracles</u> students; if for any reason, you may harbor any resentment against words such as Jesus, Christ, God, Holy Spirit, etc., the editor has had some luck with hypnotherapy; going back to where the resentment was created and identifying the resentment as a defense mechanism. Under hypnosis, I could re-evaluate the defense mechanism and decide with an adult mind whether or not this defense mechanism was serving me in a positive manner. As for myself, these words were an obstacle that kept me in ignorance and pain, and the resentment stunted my spiritual growth.

APPENDIX E

What is the HOLY SPIRIT? (excerpt from ACIM Workbook)

1   The HOLY SPIRIT mediates between illusions and the truth. Since He must bridge the gap between reality and dreams, perception leads to knowledge through the grace that God has given Him, to be His gift to everyone who turns to Him for truth. Across the bridge that He provides are dreams all carried to the truth, to be dispelled before the light of knowledge. There, are sights and sounds forever laid aside. And where they were perceived before, forgiveness has made possible perception's tranquil end.

2   The goal the HOLY SPIRIT's teaching sets is just this end of dreams. For sights and sounds must be translated from the witnesses of fear to those of love. And when this is entirely accomplished, learning has achieved the only goal it has in truth. For learning, as the HOLY SPIRIT guides it to the outcome He perceives for it, becomes the means to go beyond itself, to be replaced by the Eternal Truth.

3   If you but knew how much your Father yearns to have you recognize your sinlessness, you would not let His Voice appeal in vain, nor turn away from His replacement for the fearful images and dreams you made. The HOLY SPIRIT understands the means you made, by which you would attain what is forever unattainable. And if you offer them to Him, He will employ the means you made for exile to restore your mind to where it truly is at home.

4   From knowledge, where He has been placed by God, the HOLY SPIRIT calls to you, to let forgiveness rest upon your dreams, and be restored to sanity and peace of mind. Without forgiveness will your dreams remain to terrify you; And the memory of all your Father's Love will not return to signify the end of dreams has come.

5   Accept your Father's gift. It is a call from Love to Love, that It be but Itself. The HOLY SPIRIT is His gift, by which the quietness of Heaven is restored to God's beloved Son. Would you refuse to take the function of completing God, when all He wills is that you be complete?

APPENDIX F

What is a Miracle? (excerpt from ACIM Workbook).

1. Miracles fall like drops of healing rain from Heaven on a dry and dusty world, where starved and thirsty creatures come to die. Now they have water. Now the world is green. And everywhere the signs of life spring up, to show that what is born can never die, for what has life has immortality.

2   A miracle is a correction. It does not create, nor really change at all. It merely looks on the devastation, and reminds the mind that what it sees is false. It undoes error, but does not attempt to go beyond perception, nor exceed the function of forgiveness. Thus it stays within time's limits. Yet it paves the way for the return of timelessness and love's awakening, for fear must slip away under the gentle remedy it brings.

3   A miracle contains the gift of grace, for it is given and received as one. And thus it illustrates the law of truth the world does not obey, because it fails entirely to understand its ways. A miracle inverts perception which was upside down before, and thus it ends the strange distortions that were manifest. Now is perception open to the truth. Now is forgiveness seen as justified.

4. The miracle is taken first on faith, because to ask for it implies the mind has been made ready to conceive of what it cannot see and does not understand. Yet faith will bring its witnesses to show that what it rested on is really there. And thus the miracle will justify your faith in it. And show it rested on a world more real than what you saw before; a world redeemed from what you thought was there.

   3. Forgiveness is the home of miracles. The eyes of Christ delivers them to all they look upon in mercy and in love. Perception stands corrected in His sight, and what was meant to curse has come to bless. Each lily of forgiveness offers all the world the silent miracle of love. And each is laid before the Word of God, upon the universal alter to Creator and creation in the light of perfect purity and endless joy.

APPENDIX G

EGO Reduction - Dr. Harry Tiebout, AA World Conference, St. Louis, 1955
(excerpt from "Alcoholics Comes of Age")

..."...my first two or three years of contact with AA were the most exciting in my whole professional life. AA was then in its miracle* phase. Everything that happened seemed strange and wonderful. Hopeless drunks were being lifted out of the gutter. Individuals who had sought every known means of help without success were responding to this new approach. To be close to any such group, even by proxy, was electrifying.

In addition, from a professional point of view, a whole new avenue of treatment for the problems of alcohol had opened up. Somewhere in the AA experience was the key to sobriety. Here was the first authentic clue after many years of fruitless effort. The possibilities ahead were most intriguing. Perhaps I could learn how AA worked and thus learn something about how people stopped drinking. Yes, I shared in the general excitement of those days. I could see some day light ahead.

The future in this regard was now clear. I would try to discover what made AA tick. In this quest for understanding I would never have gotten beyond first base if it had not been for Bill and many of the early members. A study of the Twelve Steps helped a little, but of far greater importance were the many insights already possessed by Bill and the others into the process through which AA brought about its results.

I heard of the need to hit bottom, of the necessity for accepting a higher Power, of the indispensability of humility. These were ideas which had never crossed my professional thinking or attitudes. Revolutionary as they were, they nevertheless made sense, and I found myself embarked on a tour of discovery.

I began to recognize more clearly what hitting bottom really implied, and I began to do what I could to induce the experience in others, always wondering what was happening inside the individual as he went through the crisis of hitting bottom.

Finally, fortune smiled on me again, this time from another patient. For some time she had been under my new brand of psychotherapy, designed to promote hitting bottom. For reasons completely unknown, she experienced a mild but typical conversion which brought her into a positive state of mind. Led by the newly found spiritual elements, she started attending various churches in town. One Monday morning she entered my office, her eyes ablaze, and at once commenced talking, "I know what happened to me! I heard it in church yesterday. I surrendered." With that word "surrender" she had handed me my first real awareness of what happens during the period of hitting bottom.

The individual alcoholic was always fighting an admission of being licked, of admitting that he was powerless. If and when he surrendered, he quit fighting, admitted he was licked, and accepted the fact that he was powerless and needed help. If he did not surrender, a thousand crises could hit him and nothing constructive would happen. The need to induce surrender became a new therapeutic goal. The miracle of AA was now a little clearer, though the reason was still obscure why the program and the fellowship of AA could induce a surrender which could in turn lead to a period of no drinking.

As might be expected, I enjoyed a thrill of my own. I was getting in on what was happening, all of it an enjoyable experience. Still questing eagerly, I shifted my therapeutic attack. The job now was to induce surrender. But I ran into a whole nest of resistances to that idea. Totally new territory had to be explored. As I continued my tour it became ever more apparent that in everyone's psyche there existed an unconquerable EGO which bitterly opposed any thought of defeat. Until that EGO was somehow reduced or rendered ineffective no likelihood of surrender could be anticipated. The shift in emphasis in hitting bottom to surrender, to EGO reduction, occurred during the first five or six years of my initial contact with AA.

I well remember the first AA meeting to which I spoke on the subject of EGO reduction. AA, still very much in its infancy, was celebrating a third or fourth anniversary of one of the groups. The speaker immediately preceding me told in detail of the efforts of his local group, which consisted of two men, to get him to dry up and become its third member. After several months of vain efforts on their part, and repeated nose dives on his, the speaker went on to say, "Finally I got cut down to size, and I've been sober ever since." When my turn came to speak I used his phrase, "cut down to size," as a text around which to weave my remarks. Before long, out of the corner of my eye, I was conscious of a disconcerting stare. It was coming from the previous speaker. Looking a little more directly, I could see his eyes fixed on me in wonder. It was perfectly clear that he was utterly amazed that he had said anything that would make sense to a psychiatrist. The look of incredulity never left his face during my entire talk. The incident had one value in my eyes. It showed that two people, one approaching the matter clinically, and the other relying on his own intuitively experienced report of what had happened to him, both came up with exactly the same observation: the need for EGO reduction.

During the past decade my own endeavors have centered primarily upon the problem of EGO reduction. How far I have been able to explore the territory is not at all certain. I have made, however, a little progress, and in the minutes remaining I shall try, first, to acquaint you with some of my findings, and second, to relate them to the AA scene as I see it.

As I have already stated, the fact of hitting bottom to produce surrender which cut the EGO to size was evident fairly soon. In time two additional facts manifested themselves. The first was that a reduced EGO has marvelous recuperative powers. The second was that surrender is an essential disciplinary function and experience.

The first is merely repeating a fact known to you all. It is common knowledge that a return of the full-fledged EGO can happen at any time. Years of sobriety are no insurance against its resurgence. No AA member, regardless of his veteran status, can ever relax his guard against the encroachments of a reviving EGO. Recently one AA member, writing to another, reported that he was suffering, he feared, from "halo-tosis," a reference to the smugness and self-complacency which so easily can creep into the individual with years of sobriety behind him.

The assumption that one has all the answers, and the contrary, that one needs to know no answers, but just to follow AA, are two indicators of trouble. In both cases open-mindedness is notably absent. Perhaps the commonest manifestation of the return to EGO is witnessed in the individual who falls from his pink cloud, a state of mind familiar to you all. The blissful pink cloud state is a logical aftermath of surrender. The EGO, which is full of striving, just quits, and the individual senses peace and quiet within. The result is an enormous feeling of release, and the person flies right up to his pink cloud and thinks he has found heaven on earth. Everyone knows he is doomed for a fall. But it is perhaps not equally clear that it is the EGO slowly making his comeback which forces the descent from the pink cloud into the arena of life, where with the help of AA, he can learn how to become a sober person and not an angel. I could go on with many more examples familiar to you all, to show you the danger of ever assuming that the EGO is dead and buried. Its capacity for rebirth is utterly astounding and must never be forgotten.

My second finding, that surrender is a disciplinary experience, requires explanation. In recent articles I have shown that the EGO, basically, must be forging continuously ahead, and that it operates on the unconscious assumption that it, the EGO, should never be stopped. It takes for granted that it is right to go ahead. It has no expectation of ever being stopped and hence no capacity to adjust to the eventuality. Stopping says in effect, "No, you cannot continue," which is the essence of disciplinary control. The individual who cannot take a stopping is fundamentally an undisciplined person. The function of surrender in AA is now clear. It produces that stopping by causing individuals to say, "I quit. I give up my headstrong ways. I've learned my lesson." Very often for the first time in that individual's adult career he has encountered the necessary discipline which halts him in his headlong pace. And this happens because we can surrender and truly feel, "Thy will, not mine be done." When that is true we have become in fact obedient servants of God. The spiritual point, at that moment, is a reality. We have become members of the human race.

I have presented the two points I wished to make, namely, first the EGO is revivable, and second, surrender is a disciplinary experience. I next wish to discuss their significance to AA as I see it…

…The single act of surrender can produce sobriety by its stopping effect upon EGO. Unfortunately, that EGO will return unless the individual learns to accept a disciplined way of life, which means that a tendency for EGO to comeback is permanently checked. This is not new to AA members; they have learned that a single surrender is not enough. Under the wise leadership of the founding fathers, the need for continued endeavor to maintain that miracle has been steadily stressed. The Twelve Steps, repeated inventories, not just one, and the Twelfth Step itself, a routine reminder that one must work at deserving sobriety, are all essential…

* The term "miracle" used in this document may be significantly different than what is described as a "miracle" in the ACIM literature or in this Proposal.

"I have decided to stick with love; hate is too great a burden to bear…" **Dr. Martin Luther King Jr.**

Excerpt from Nobel Peace Prize acceptance speech, Oslo, Norway 1964

Appendix H - The Need for a World Wide Spiritual Awakening - Dr. Samuel Shoemaker, AA World Conference, St. Louis 1955 (excerpt from "Alcoholics Comes of Age")

"...Last autumn at his twentieth anniversary dinner, I first heard Bill give the story of various strands which, woven together, have made the strong cable of AA. We all know by now that the first thing that got into his mind as offering any real hope was talking with some men in whom there was the beginning of a real religious experience. One of them is here now. They had begun to find this through the old Oxford Groups in its earlier and, I think, better days. Much of its work centered at that time in my old parish, Calvary, on Gramercy Park in New York.

I take it that it began to be clear quite early in the life of AA that Dr. Jung's simple declaration that science had no answer, and Dr. Silkworth's incalculable help from the medical angle, and William James' great wisdom in his Varieties of Religious Experience, still left the need for a spiritual factor that would create a kind of synthesis and offer a kind of positive dynamic. The problem was: how to translate the spiritual experience into universal terms without letting it evaporate into mere ideals and generalities. And so, immediately after Step One, which concerned the unmanageableness of life, came Step Two: We came to believe in a power greater than ourselves that could restore us to sanity. The basis of that belief was not theoretical; it was evidential. Right before us were people in whose lives were the beginnings of a spiritual transformation. You could question the interpretation of the experience, but you couldn't question the experience itself.

In the third and fourth chapters of Acts is the story of the healing of a lame man by Peter and John. A lot of the ecclesiastics wanted to know how this came about. The Apostles told them that it was through the name of Christ that this man was healed. The story says, "And beholding the man which was healed standing with them, they could say nothing against it." Now you can fight a theory about an experience, but you've got to acknowledge the experience itself.

AA has been supremely wise, I think, in emphasizing the reality of the experience, and acknowledging that it came from a higher Power than human, and leaving the interpretation part pretty much at that. It would have been easy and must have been something of a temptation to not go into the theological side. Here was evidence of spiritual power. All right then, lets define the power. But that would have run against several possible difficulties. If AA's had said more, some people would have wanted them to say a great deal more and define God in a way acceptable and congenial to themselves. It would have taken only two or three groups like this, dissenting from one another, to wreck the whole business. Moreover, there were people with an unhappy association with religion, a dead church or a dull parson, or some churchgoing people whose workaday-weekday lives did not support their Sunday professions. That would have added another factor to be overcome, as if we didn't have enough already. Also, there are the agnostics and the atheists, who either say that they don't know anything at all about these ultimate realities or that they disbelieve in God altogether.

I would like to quote for those who believe themselves still to be without faith in God a wonderful work from the Roman Catholic Spanish philosopher Unamuno y Jugo, who said, "Those who deny God deny Him because of their despair at not finding Him." For an outfit

like AA to become dogmatic would have been fatal, I think. So they stuck to the inescapable experiences and told people to turn their will and lives over to the care of God as they understood Him. That left the theory and the theology ... to the churches to which people belong. If they belonged to no church and could hold no consistent theory, then they had to give themselves to the God that they saw in other people. That's not a bad way to set in motion the beginnings of a spiritual experience. Maybe that's what we all do at the point where religion changes over for us from a mere tradition to a living power.
I believe in the psychological soundness of all this. Don't think it applies to alcoholics alone. I think it applies to everybody who is seeking genuine spiritual faith and experience. When one has done the best he can with intellectual reasoning, there yet comes a time for decision and for action. It may be a relatively simple decision, such as to enter fully into the experiment. I think the approach is much more like science than it is like philosophy. We don't so much try to reason it out in abstract logic. We choose a hypothesis. We act as if it were true and see whether it works. If it doesn't we discard it, and if it does we are free to call the experiment a success.

You can consider an idea in a vacuum, whether it be in the privacy of your own room or in an academic classroom or indeed in a pulpit, and you can discuss the truth of a theory forever, and it may do you no good; But when you let truth go into action, when you hurl your life after your held conception of truth, then things start to happen. If it is genuine truth it will accomplish things on the plane of actual living. If God is what Christ said He is, He is more eager to help us than we are to be helped. He does not trespass on man's freedom, and we can reject Him and deny Him and ignore Him as long as we like. But when we open the door on a spiritual search with our whole life thrown into it, we shall find Him always there ready to receive our feeblest approaches and our most selfish and childish prayers and our always entirely unworthy selves. He is always ready to get down to business with us. The experimental approach seems to me to be the essence of our finding the help of a higher Power. We first lean on another human being who seems to be finding the answer, and then we lean on the higher Power that stands behind him.

William James, in the famous passage in Varieties of Religious Experience, says this: "The crisis of self surrender is the throwing of our conscious selves on the mercy of powers which, whatever they may be, are more ideal than we are actually, and make for our redemption. Self surrender has been and always must be regarded as the vital turning point in religious life." That was almost the turning point in my own thinking, that sentence. He goes on to say, "One may say that the whole development of Christianity in inwardness has consisted in little more than the greater and greater emphasis attached to this crisis of self surrender." That, of course becomes the heart of real religion. Most of us come to God in the first instance from a need. But I would like to point out that before we can possibly be of any use to anybody else we must find the beginnings of an answer for ourselves, so that kind of selfishness may represent a necessary step in the progress.

There is a great hue and cry today on the part of some people about those who seek benefits from God. I would like to know where in Heaven's name a bewildered and defeated person is going to go for the help he desperately needs if he doesn't go to God for it. Of course he is concerned about himself. He can't help it. He ought to be. He must be, if he is ever going to be made useful to other people. But later on he must also grow up and stop just using God and begin to ask God to use him. Stop asking God to do what he wants, and begin to try to find out what it is that God wants. Many people tell you they've given up faith. They prayed for something they wanted and it didn't come, and either there is no God or else He has no interest in them. What childish nonsense! How can anybody expect God to acquiesce in the half-baked prayers that a lot of us send up to Him. He would have the world in a worse chaos than it is now in five minutes.

Real prayer is not telling God what we want. It is putting ourselves at His disposal so that He can tell us what He wants. Prayer is not trying to get God to change His will. It is trying to find out what His will is, to align ourselves or realign ourselves with His purpose for the world and for us. That's why it is so important for us to listen as well as talk when we pray. That is why it is good to begin these meetings with silence. Oftentimes we come feverishly and willfully, and we have just got to quiet down before God can do anything for us. While our own voices are clamorous and demanding, there is no place for the voice of God. That is the thing most of us non-alcoholics get drunk on, just willfulness, just wanting life on our own terms, and it is as neurotic as any neurosis ever was. Everybody that is away from God and tries to do his own will in defiance of God is half-crazy. Till our own clamorous, demanding voices quiet down we cannot hear the voice of God. When we let willfulness cool out of us, God can get His will across to us as far as we need to see ahead of us. Dante said, "In His will is our peace."

There are a lot of people who don't like the weakness that is implied in that word "surrender." I was deeply thankful to hear Dr. Tiebout use that word. People like to think they are strong characters who can take care of their own destinies. That is always fictitious thinking. Everybody in this world is some kind of weakling, and if he thinks he is not, then pride is his weakness, and that is the greatest weakness of all.

People may think that they have overcome, or else they have never been overcome by the overtly disputable sins, but who of us avoids selfishness and self-centeredness and the love of adulation and the lover of power and pride? I think that a man is fortunate whose problems are of such a kind that they really get him into trouble, so he has got to do something about it. Temper and prided and laziness and scornfulness and irritability and indifference to human trouble and God-awful littleness – which is the worst thing about most of us in a day when everybody is meant to be bigger—these things get us non-alcoholics into difficulties, and they are just as bad as anything that ever got you alcoholics into difficulties. Nobody is strong and the people who think they are strong are self-deceived.

We act as if character and reasonably good behavior were the end of all existence. The real questions in life which underlie these matters of behavior are definitely of religious nature. And they have only a religious answer, an answer that comes from God. Where did I come from, and what am I supposed to be doing here, and where do I go when I die? Those questions which, unanswered, leave us without direction, without moorings, and without values. Science hasn't got any answer to those things, and philosophy only has the answers of good human guesses. Religious faith is the one candle in man's darkness in the mystery of life. If Christ came down from Heaven to represent God and speak for Him, we have got an answer. The lesser revelations to prophets and seers are of the same nature, but not of the same authority…but all truly wise men begin with the acknowledgement of their finiteness, their darkness, and their needs. When we get through to God, by whatever name we call Him, or rather when we let Him get through to us, then we begin finding light and the answer.

STEVEH.

I think the great need of our time is for vast, worldwide spiritual awakening. There are many signs that it is upon us. Western man is gradually getting it through his head that he owes the greatest of all human blessings, the blessing of liberty; then we begin finding light and the answer…

<u>Bernard B. Smith, AA Trustee from 1944 to 1956</u>

APPENDIX I -
Fellowship, Surrender and Humility as a Way of Life - Bernard Smith
(excerpt from "Alcoholics Comes of Age")

As the time approached when I would cease to serve as Chairman, I found myself thinking of many things—of those exciting, early struggling days when AA was taking form; of the many friendships that AA has made possible for me, a non-alcoholic; of the countless heart warming experiences that have been mine with the fellowship of AA; of the wonder that, in so short a time, AA could have produced a General Service Conference with so large a part of our Society represented by its chosen delegates.

More than anything else, perhaps, I thought of the miracle of timing in AA, how things seem to get started in AA only when the time is ripe; how we may be vexed at things delayed only to realize and appreciate later that they were delayed solely because the time for doing them had not yet arrived.

And I thought of the finger of God determining our course—as individuals, as a fellowship, and in our relations to the world about us. Clearly, I thought, the Twelve Steps of AA, must have been spiritually conceived to meet a serious and growing challenge to all of us, nonalcoholic as alcoholic. What is that challenge? It is the challenge to a generation that would deny the spiritual basis for human existence and accept in its place a currently socially accepted basis that is mechanistic and materialistic. It is a challenge to which AA will never yield, for the tenet of its faith and indeed its existence is founded on the certainty of a spiritual basis for life on earth.

I confess that when I was first exposed to AA, I did not think in terms of broad social concepts or the application of great spiritual truths to the problems all men share in their pursuit of what each may dimly regard as happiness.

The circumstances of this first exposure were rather prosaic. The early members of AA and certain of the non-alcoholic friends, conscious of the need to create a simple but effective service structure for the fledging movement, needed a lawyer to help frame the document leading to incorporation of the Alcoholic Foundation, now known as the General Service Board of AA.

A friend of mine who was—and is—a member of AA suggested that I meet Bill. I shall never forget that first meeting in my office, late one afternoon fifteen years ago, and the evening we then spent together. And I shall always be grateful to my friend who brought Bill and me together on that memorable afternoon and evening, for in some mysterious way I was ready for Bill's message. I learned something then from Bill for which all my life up to then seems to have been a preparation. What Bill was getting through to me was the then-startling fact that in AA, when men cease to drink by applying the Twelve Steps to their lives, they are in effect beginning to live on a spiritual basis.

And it struck me, as a non-alcoholic, the AA was a way of life for me, too, and for countless others like me who had never sought escape in a bottle or in those other refuges to which men turn from the pressures of a materialistic world. The still-drinking alcoholic, as should be clear

STEVE H.

to all who observe mankind today, has no monopoly on unhappiness or on the feeling that life lacks purpose and fulfillment.

In all the years since that first meeting with Bill, wonderful years, when it has been my privilege to serve as a member and as a Chairman of the General Service Board, I have never lost my initial awareness that AA is more than a fellowship for recovered alcoholics, that it is indeed a way of life for all who have lost their way in a troubled world.

I have frequently attempted to define the fellowship of AA with little success, until one day while in England I listened to a broadcast delivered by Canon C.E. Raven, a noted British religious leader. In the course of this broadcast, Canon Raven set forth the condition of a true fellowship in these words:

Three conditions are necessary for true fellowship: (1) The possession of a common ideal involving a complete release from selfishness and division. (2) The discharge of common task big enough to capture the imagination and give expression to loyalty. And (3) the comradeship, the "togetherness" thus involved as we find out the joy and power of belonging to an organic society and engaging in a whole-time service. We can find it at its fullest extent where the ideal is highest and most exacting, where the task extends and integrates every ounce of our strength and every element of our being, where the comradeship is so solid and deep that we respond one to another without conscious effort, realize the unspoken need, and react to it spontaneously and at once.

Under such conditions, all the vitality that we usually waste upon our jealousies and vanities —upon keeping up appearances and putting other people in their proper place—becomes available for creative use.

These words have meaning for AA, I believe, not only as a definition of a true fellowship and of our goals and attitudes but as reminders that AA is not a static, passive social organism but, in its largest sense, a dynamic, creative force that releases our latent power to live and act constructively…

…When alcoholics live materialistically, and drink excessively, they refuse to accept the label of "alcoholic." Yet when they cease to drink and when they say to them selves and to the world, "We are alcoholic," the world refuses to see them as such.

What an unthinking world may look upon as defeat, alcoholics in AA know as a triumph of the spirit, a triumph of humility over false pride and self-centeredness. How few human beings ever have the courage to stand up before their neighbors and, in humility, describing them selves truthfully, to say: This is what I truly am."

There are two moments in which utterance of the words "I am an alcoholic" have great significance. There is the first time a member speaks those words at an AA meeting. There is, however, another and earlier time which is perhaps of greater significance. That is the moment when a man says to his sponsor, in the darkness and desperation of his soul, "I am an alcoholic." And this moment points to another paradox in AA.

The paradox is that the member of AA approaches his suffering alcoholic brother not from the superiority and strength of his position of recovery but from the realization of his own weakness. The member talks to the newcomer not in a spirit of power but in a spirit of humility and weakness. He does not speak of how misguided the still suffering alcoholic is; he speaks of how misguided he once was. He does not sit in judgment of another but in judgment of himself as he had been.

Society, in referring to the alcoholic, employs the expression "the enslavement of alcohol." For the AA member, this statement is in a very special sense paradoxical too, if indeed it is true at all. In sober fact, the member was never enslaved by alcohol. Alcohol simply served as an escape from personal enslavement to the false ideals of a materialistic society. Yet if we accept society's definition of the alcoholic's earlier state of enslavement by alcohol, the AA member can no longer resent it, for it has served to set him free from all the materialistic traps with which the paths through the jungle of our society are set; For the alcoholic first had to face materialism as a disease of society before he could free himself of the illness of alcoholism and be free of the social ills that made him an alcoholic.

Men and women who use alcohol as an escape are not the only ones who are afraid of life, hostile to the world, fleeing from it into loneliness. Millions who are not alcoholics are living today in illusionary worlds, nurturing the basic anxieties and insecurities of human existence rather than face themselves with courage and humility. To these people, AA offers as a cure what no magic potion, no chemical formula, no powerful drug can. But it can demonstrate to them how to use the tools of humility, honesty, devotion, and love, which indeed are the heart of the Twelve Steps of recovery.

There is still another paradoxical statement by human society which has special application to AA. That statement is the saying that "A chain is as strong as its weakest link." The accepted connotation is that a chain is strong only if it has no weak links.

The paradox of this statement as applied to AA is that, in AA, the chain is as strong as its weakest links. For the endless chain of AA grows in strength to the extent that it is able to reach the weak links, the still-suffering alcoholic men and women about us. It is upon this paradoxical truth that the assurance of the survival of the fellowship rests. The perpetuation of AA is grounded in the so-called weakness of those human beings who escape the materialistic bases of society through the medium of alcohol.

It is because we know of the tremendous impact that AA can have on generations that will follow us that we have been so painstaking in building a structure of service of AA in the General Service Board, the General Service Conference, and the many service agencies that perform the essential daily tasks of carrying the AA message through out the world. It is with good reason that Bill has described this structure of service as a legacy, deserving of the same attention and understanding accorded the First Legacy of the Twelve Steps and the Second Legacy of the Twelve Traditions.

But this Third Legacy of Service has a string to it. And the string is that we are granted the use of this legacy for our lifetime upon the condition that we will not only look after it but increase its spiritual content for the generations that will follow us. Each succeeding generation, as it receives this legacy, must similarly protect it if they wish to employ it and gain life by it and pass it on to the next generation with an enriched spiritual content.

STEVEH.

The General Service Conference of AA is, of course, the practical instrument for preserving, enhancing, and administering this great Third Legacy of Service. The concept of the Conference from the beginning has been simple and compelling. It is grounded in the belief that all of us who have been associated with AA during its early growth and development owe an obligation to society. That obligation is to insure that this fellowship survives, that this flame of faith, this beacon light of hope for the world, must never be extinguished.

We may not need a General Service Conference to insure our own recovery. But we do need it to insure the recover of the alcoholic who still stumbles in the darkness, seeking the light. We need it to insure the recovery of some newborn child, inexplicably destined to alcoholism. We need it to provide, in keeping with the Twelfth Step, a permanent haven for all alcoholics who in the ages ahead can find in AA that rebirth which brought its first members back to life.

We need it because we are conscious of the devastating effect of the human urge for power and prestige which must never be permitted to invade AA. We need a Conference to insure AA against government while insulating it against anarchy; we need it to protect the fellowship against disintegration while preventing over-integration. We need it so that Alcoholics Anonymous and Alcoholics Anonymous alone may be the ultimate repository of its own Twelve Steps, its Twelve Traditions, and all its Services.

We need a Conference to insure that changes within AA come only as a response to the needs and wants of all AA, and not of any few. We need it to insure that the doors of the halls of AA shall never have locks on them, so that all people with an alcoholic problem for all time to come may enter these halls unmasked and feel welcome. We need it to help insure that Alcoholics Anonymous never asks of anyone who needs help what his or her race is, what his or her creed is, or what his or her social position is.

I have considered it a priceless privilege and a great inspirational experience to have been able to serve AA as Chairman of the General Service Board for so many years, a position which also enabled me to serve as Chairman of the first six General Service Conferences. When I retired as Chairman, following the Sixth Conference in April 1956, I did not feel that I was stepping out of AA. No one who is a part of AA, as I feel I have been, steps out. He just steps aside. He continues to serve in the ranks, giving of himself as humbly and as ably as he can.

I did not tender my resignation as Chairman because I no longer wanted to be Chairman. I have enjoyed the responsibility. I have found, as a non-alcoholic, great self-fulfillment in the trust that so many have granted me. To state one more paradox, I am resigning as Chairman out of my love for, and devotion to AA. For I declared many years ago, and have continued to believe, that AA must insulate itself against the "propriety right to serve." No man must have the right to remain in office in AA indefinitely.

The very fact that no one has sought my resignation, and indeed that the contrary is happily true, is all the more reason to reaffirm the tradition of rotation in all AA service positions. Some day this tradition that no one should serve as chairman for an indefinite period may prove more valuable than we appreciate today. Certainly it is in keeping with the expanding unwritten body of tested tradition that is being accepted throughout AA: that while AA is important to existence of the individual, no individual must be vital to the existence of AA. It is AA that is important, important to those whom society has rejected and to those who have rejected society, important indeed to all of human society as a symbol of the power of the great spiritual reservoir upon which all may draw who aspire to a true way of life.

This precious message which we have received, and by which we try to live, has resulted in our achieving a far greater measure of human happiness than is the lot of the average human being who walks the earth today and who has not been subjected to the acute suffering of alcoholism. We must, however, as individuals and as a fellowship, always be concerned with the structure of server of Alcoholics Anonymous which protects and expands our way of life. For we will continue to owe to the generations yet unborn a solemn obligation to insure that this way of life is available to them, as it has been to us.

And as a non-alcoholic and as a student of those great social movements from which we derive the best of our heritage today, I regard the fellowship of Alcoholics Anonymous as the outstanding spiritual phenomenon of our century. I see in the concept of living which is embodied in Alcoholics Anonymous a glorious hope for all of mankind. For the members of this fellowship are truly witnesses of the living truth that man can live the life of the spirit and still function effectively in a materialistic world.

And so this first generation in the life of AA draws to a close. It is rich in its faith, large in its numbers, and dedicated to its purpose. I am grateful that I have been privileged to observe its emergence in our society.

In now stepping aside as Chairman of AA's movement-wide service agency, I confess to having only one regret. And that is that I did not have the skill or the gifts that would have enabled me to do more than the little I have tried to do to further the purposes of this great and enduring fellowship.

APPENDIX J

THE PAIN-BODY BY ECKHART TOLLE (EXCERPT FROM <u>A NEW EARTH – AWAKENING TO YOUR LIFE'S PURPOSE</u>, CHAPTER FIVE)

EMOTIONS AND THE EGO – The ego is not only the unobserved mind, the voice in the head which pretends to be you, but also the unobserved emotions that are the body's reaction to what the voice in the head is saying.

We have already seen what kind of thinking the egoic voice engages in most of the time and the dysfunction inherent in the structure of its thought processes, regardless of content. This dysfunction thinking is what the body reacts to with negative emotion.

The voice in the head tells a story that the body believes in and reacts to. Those reactions are the emotions. The emotions, in turn, feed energy back to the thoughts that created the emotion in the first place. This is the vicious circle between unexamined thoughts and emotions, giving rise to emotional thinking and emotional story-making.

The emotional component of ego differs from person to person. In some egos, it is greater than in others. Thoughts that trigger emotional responses in the body may sometimes come so fast that before the mind has had time to voice them, the body has already responded with an emotion, and the emotion has turned into a reaction. Those thoughts exist at a preverbal stage and could be called unspoken, unconscious assumptions. They have their origin in a person's past conditioning, usually from early child-hood. "People cannot be trusted" would be an example of such an unconscious assumption in a person whose primordial relationships, that is to say, with parents or siblings, were not supportive and did not inspire trust. "Nobody respects me and appreciates me. I need to fight to survive. There is never enough money. Life always lets you down. I don't deserve abundance. I don't deserve Love." Unconscious assumptions create emotions in the body which in turn generate mind activity and/or instant reaction. In this way, they create your personal reality.

The voice of the ego continuously disrupts the body's natural state of well-being. Almost every human body is under a great deal of strain and stress, not because it is threatened by some external factor but from within the mind. The body has an ego attached to it, and it cannot but respond to all the dysfunctional thought patterns that make up the ego. Thus, a stream of negative emotion accompanies the stream of incessant and compulsive thinking.

What is negative emotion? : An emotion that is toxic to the body and interferes with its balance and harmonious functioning. Fear, anxiety, anger, bearing a grudge, sadness, hatred or intense dislike, jealousy, envy—all disrupt the energy flow through the body, affect the heart, the immune system, digestion, production of hormones, and so on. Even mainstream medicine, although it knows very little about how the ego operates yet, is beginning to recognize the connection between negative emotional states and physical disease. An emotion that does harm to the body also infects the people you come into contact with and indirectly, through a process of chain reaction, countless others you never meet. There is a generic term for all negative emotions: unhappiness.

Do positive emotions then have the opposite effect on the physical body? Do they strengthen the immune system, invigorate and heal the body? They do, indeed, but we need to differentiate between positive emotions that are ego-generated and deeper emotions that emanate from your natural state of connectedness with Being.

Positive emotions generated by the ego already contain within themselves their opposite into which they can quickly turn. Here are some examples: What the ego calls love is possessiveness and addictive clinging that can turn into hate within a second. Anticipation about an upcoming event, which is the ego's overvaluation of future, easily turns into its opposite—letdown or disappointment— when the event is over or doesn't fulfill the ego's expectations. Praise and recognition make you feel alive and happy one day; being criticized or ignored make you dejected an unhappy the next. The pleasure of a wild party turns into bleakness and a hangover the next morning. There is no good without bad, no high without low.

Ego-generated emotions are derived from the mind's identification with external factors which are, of course, all unstable and liable to change at any moment. The deeper emotions are not really emotions at all but states of Being. Emotions exist within the realm of opposites. States of Being can be obscured, but they have no opposite. They emanate from within you as the love, joy, and peace that are aspects of your true nature.

THE DUCK WITH A HUMAN MIND - ...after two ducks get into a fight, which never lasts long, they will separate and float off in opposite direction. Then each duck will flap its wings vigorously a few times, thus releasing the surplus energy that built up during the fi ght. After they flap their wings, they float off peacefully, as if nothing had ever happened.

If the duck had a human mind, it would keep the fight alive by thinking, by story making. This would probably be the duck's story: "I don't believe what he just did. He came to within five inches of me. He thinks he owns this pond. He has no consideration for my private space. I'll never trust him again. Next time he'll try something else just to annoy me. I'm sure he's plotting something already. But I'm not going to stand for this. I'll teach him a lesson he won't forget." And on and on the mind spins its tales, still thinking and talking about it days, months, or years later. As far as the body is concerned, the fight is still continuing, and the energy it generates in response to all those thoughts is emotion, which in turn generates more thinking. This becomes the emotional thinking of the ego. You can see how problematic the duck's life would become if it had a human mind. But this is how most humans live all the time. No situation or event is ever really finished. The mind and the mind-made "me and my story" keep going.

We are species that has lost its way. Everything natural, every flower or tree, and every animal have important lessons to teach us if we would only stop, look and listen. Our duck's lesson is this: Flap your wings—which translates as "let go of the story"—and return to the only place of power: the present moment.

CARRYING THE PAST - The inability or rather unwillingness of the human mind to let go of the past is beautifully illustrated in the story of two Zen monks. Tanzan and Ekido, who were walking along a country road that had become extremely muddy after heavy rains. Near a village, they came upon a young woman who was trying to cross the road, but the mud was so deep it would have ruined the silk kimono she was wearing. Tanzan at once picked her up and carried her to the other side.

The monks walked on in silence. Five hours later, as they were approaching the lodging temple, Ekido couldn't restrain himself any longer. "Why did you carry that girl across the road?" he asked.
"We monks are not supposed to do things like that."

"I put the girl down hours ago," said Tanzan. "Are you still carrying her?"

Now imagine what life would be like for someone who lived like Ekido all the time, unable or unwilling to let go internally of situations, accumulating more and more "stuff" inside, and you get a sense of what life is like for the majority of people on our planet. What a heavy burden of past they carry around with them in their minds.

The past lives in you as memories, but memories are not a problem. In fact, it is through memory that we learn from the past and from past mistakes. It is only when memories, that is to say, thoughts about the past, take you over completely that they turn into a burden, turn problematic, and become part of your sense of self. Your personality, which is conditioned by the past, then becomes your prison. Your memories are invested with a sense of self, and your story becomes who you perceive yourself to be. The "little me" is an illusion that obscures your true identify as timeless and formless Presence.

Your story, however, consists not only of mental, but also of emotional memory—old emotion that is being revived continuously. As in the case of the monk who carried the burden of his resentment for five hours by feeding it with his thoughts, most people carry a large amount of unnecessary baggage, both mental and emotional, throughout their lives. They limit themselves through grievances, regret, hostility, guilt. Their emotional thinking has become their self, and so they hang on to the old emotion because it strengthens their identity.

Because of the human tendency to perpetuate old emotions, almost everyone carries in his or her energy field an accumulation of old emotional pain, which I call the "pain-body."

We can, however, stop adding to the pain-body that we already have. We can learn to break the habit of accumulating and perpetuating the old emotions by flapping our wings, metaphorically speaking, and refrain from mentally dwelling on the past, regardless of whether something happened yesterday or thirty years ago. We can learn not to keep situations or events alive in our minds, but to return our attention continuously to the pristine, timeless present moment rather than be caught up in mental movie-making. Our very Presence then becomes our identity, rather than our thoughts and emotions.

Nothing ever happened in the past that can prevent you from being present now: and if the past cannot prevent you from being present now, what power does it have?

INDIVIDUAL AND COLLECTIVE – Any negative emotions that is not fully faced and seen for what it is in the moment it arises does not completely dissolve. It leaves behind a remnant of pain.

Children in particular find strong negative emotions too overwhelming to cope with and tend to try not to feel them. In the absence of a fully conscious adult who guides them with love

and compassionate understanding into facing the emotion directly, choosing not to feel it is indeed the only option for the child at that time. Unfortunately, that early defense mechanism usually remains in place when the child becomes an adult. The emotion still lives in him or her unrecognized and manifests indirectly, for example, as anxiety, anger, outbursts of violence, a mood, or even as a physical illness. In some
cases, it interferes with or sabotages every intimate relationship. Most psychotherapists have met patients who claimed initially to have had a totally happy childhood, and later the opposite turned out to be the case. Those may be the more extreme cases, but nobody can go through childhood without suffering emotional pain. Even if both of your parents were enlightened, you would still find yourself growing up in a largely unconscious world.

This energy field of old but still very-much-alive emotion that lives in almost every human being is the pain-body.

The pain body, however, is not just individual in nature. It also partakes of the pain suffered by countless humans throughout the history of humanity, which is a history of continuous tribal warfare, of enslavement, pillage, rape, torture, and other forms of violence. This pain still lives in the collective psyche of humanity and is being added to on a daily basis, as you can verify when you watch the news tonight or look at the drama in people's relationships. The collective pain-body is probably encoded within every human's DNA, although we haven't discovered it there yet.

Every newborn who comes into the world already carries an emotional pain-body. In some it is heavier, denser than in others. Some babies are quite happy most of the time. Others seem to carry an enormous amount of unhappiness with them. It is true that some babies cry a great deal because they are not given enough love and attention, but others cry for no apparent reason, almost as if they were trying to make everyone around them as unhappy as they are —and often they succeed. They have come into this world with a heavy share of human pain. Other babies may cry frequently because they can sense the emanation of their mother's and father's negative emotion, and it causes them pain and also causes their pain-body to grow already by absorbing energy from the parents' pain-bodies. Whatever the case may be, as the baby's physical body grows, so does the pain-body.

An infant with only a light pain-body is not necessarily going to be a spiritually "more advanced" man or woman than somebody with a dense one. In fact, the opposite is often the case. People with heavy pain-bodies usually have a better chance to awaken spiritually than those with a relatively light one. Whereas some of them do remain trapped in their heavy pain-bodies, many others reach a point where they cannot live with their unhappiness any longer, and so their motivation to awaken becomes strong.

Why is the suffering body of Christ, his face distorted in agony and his body bleeding from countless wounds, such a significant image in the collective consciousness of humanity? Millions of people, particularly in medieval times, would not have related to it as deeply as they did if something within themselves had not resonated with it, if they had not unconsciously recognized it as an outer representation of their own inner reality—the pain body. They were not yet conscious enough to recognize it directly with themselves, but it was the beginning of their becoming aware of it. Christ can be seen as the archetypal human, embodying both the pain and possibility of transcendence.

HOW THE PAIN-BODY RENEWS ITSELF – The pain-body is a semiautonomous energy-form that lives within most human beings, an entity made up of emotion. It has its own primitive intelligence, not unlike a cunning animal, and its intelligence is directed primarily at survival. Like all life-forms, it periodically needs to feed—to take in new energy—and the food it requires to replenish itself consists of energy that vibrates at a similar frequency. Any emotionally painful experience can be used as food by the pain-body. That's why it thrives on negative thinking as well as drama in relationships. The pain-body is an addiction to unhappiness.

It may be shocking when you realize for the first time that there is something within you that periodically seeks emotional negativity, seeks unhappiness. You need even more awareness to see it in yourself than to recognize it in another person. Once the unhappiness has taken you over, not only do you not want an end to it, but you want to make others just as miserable as you are in order to feed on their negative emotional reactions.

In most people, the pain body has a dormant and an active stage. When it is dormant, you can easily forget that you carry a heavy dark cloud or a dormant volcano inside you, depending on the energy field of your particular pain-body. How long it remains dormant varies from person to person: A few weeks is the most common, but it can be a few days or months. In rare cases the pain-body can lie in hibernation for years before it gets triggered by some event.

HOW THE PAIN-BODY FEEDS ON YOUR THOUGHTS – The pain-body awakens from its dormancy when it gets hungry, when it is time to replenish itself. Alternatively, it may get triggered by any event at any time. The pain-body that is ready to feed can use the most insignificant event as a trigger, something somebody says or does, or even a thought. If you live alone or there is nobody around at the time, the pain-body will feed on your thoughts. Suddenly, your thinking becomes deeply negative. You were most likely unaware that just prior to the influx of negative thinking a wave of emotion invaded your mind—as a dark and heavy mood, as anxiety or fiery anger. All thought is energy and the pain-body is now feeding on the energy of your thoughts. But it cannot feed on any thought. You don't need to be particularly sensitive to notice that a positive thought has a totally different feeling-tone than a negative one. It is the same energy, but it vibrates at a different frequency. A happy, positive thought is indigestible to the pain-body. I can only feed on negative thoughts because only those thoughts are compatible with its own energy field.

All things are vibrating energy fields in ceaseless motion. The chair you sit on, the book you are holding in your hands appear solid and motionless only because that is how your senses perceive their vibration frequency, that is to say, the incessant movement of the molecules, atoms, electrons, and subatomic particles that together create what you perceive as a chair, a book, a tree, or a body. What we perceive as physical matter is energy vibrating (moving) at a particular range of frequencies. Thoughts consist of the same energy vibrating at a higher frequency than matter, which is why they cannot be seen or touched. Thoughts have their own range of frequencies, with negative thoughts at the lower end of the scale and positive thoughts at the higher. The vibrational frequency of the pain-body resonates with that of negative thoughts, which is why only those thoughts can feed the pain-body.

The usual pattern of thought creating emotion is reversed in the case of the pain-body, at least initially. Emotion from the pain-body quickly gains control of your thinking, and once your mind has been taken over by the pain-body, your thinking becomes negative. The voice in your head will be telling sad, anxious, or angry stories about yourself or your life, about other people, about past, future, or imaginary events. The voice will be blaming, accusing, complaining, imagining. And you are totally identified with whatever the voice says, believe all its distorted thoughts. At that point, the addiction to unhappiness has set in.

It is not so much that you cannot stop your train of negative thoughts, but that you don't want to. This is because the pain-body at that time is living through you, pretending to be you. And to the pain-body, pain is pleasure. It eagerly devours every negative thought. In fact, the usual voice in your head has now become the voice of the pain-body. It has taken over the internal dialogue. A vicious circle becomes established between the pain-body and your thinking. Every thought feeds the pain-body and in turn the pain-body generates more thoughts. At some point, after a few hours or even a few days, it has replenished itself and returns to its dormant stage, leaving behind a depleted organism and a body that is much more susceptible to illness. If that sounds to you like a psychic parasite, you are right. That's exactly what it is.

HOW THE PAIN-BODY FEEDS ON DRAMA – If there are other people around, preferably your partner or a close family member, the pain-body will attempt to provoke them—push their buttons, as the expression goes—so it can feed on the ensuing drama. Pain-bodies love intimate relationships and families because that is where they get most of their food. It is hard to resist another person's pain-body that is determined to draw you into a reaction. Instinctively it knows your weakest, most vulnerable points. If it doesn't succeed the first time, it will try again and again. It is raw emotions looking for more emotion. The other person's pain-body wants to awaken yours so that both pain-bodies can mutually energize each other.

Many relationships go through violent and destructive pain-body episodes at regular intervals. It is almost unbearably painful for a young child to have to witness the emotional violence for their parent' pain-bodies, and yet that is the fate of millions of children all over the world, the nightmare of their daily existence. That is also one of the main ways in which the human pain-body is passed on from generation to generation. After each episode, the partners make up, and there is an interval of relative peace, to the limited extent that the ego allows it. Excessive consumption of alcohol will often activate the pain-body, particularly in men, but also in some women. When a person becomes drunk, he goes through a complete personality change as the pain-body takes him over. A deeply unconscious person whose pain-body habitually replenishes itself through physical violence often directs it toward his spouse or children. When he becomes sober, he is truly sorry and may say he will never do this again, and he means it. The person who is talking and making promises, however, is not the entity that commits the violence, and so you can be sure that it will happen again and again unless he becomes present, recognizes the pain-body within himself, and thus disidentifies from it. In some cases, counseling can help him do that.

Most pain-bodies want to both inflict and suffer pain, but some are predominately either perpetrators or victims. In either case, they feed on violence, whether emotional or physical. Some couples who may think they have "fallen in love" are actually feeling drawn to each other because their respective pain-bodies complement each other. Sometimes the roles of perpetrator and victim are already clearly prescribed the first time they meet. Some marriages that are thought to be made in heaven are actually made in hell.

If you have ever lived with a cat, you will know that even when the cat seems to be asleep, it still knows what is going on, because at the slightest unusual noise, its ears will move forward toward it, and its eyes may open slightly. Dormant pain-bodies are the same. On some level, they are still awake, ready to jump into action when an appropriate trigger presents itself.

In intimate relationships, pain-bodies are often clever enough to lie low until you start living together and preferably have signed a contract committing yourself to be with this person for the rest of your life. You don't just marry your wife or husband, you also marry her or his pain-body—and your spouse marries yours. It can be quite a shock when, perhaps not long after moving in together or after the honeymoon, you find suddenly one day there is a complete personality change in your partner. Her voice becomes harsh or shrill as she accuses you, blames you, or shouts at you, most likely over a relatively trivial matter. Or she becomes totally withdrawn. "What's wrong?" you ask. "Nothing is wrong," she answers." But the intensely hostile energy she emanates is saying, "Everything is wrong." When you look into her eyes, there is no light in them anymore; it is as if a heavy veil has descended, and the being you know and love which before was able to shine through her ego, is now totally obscured. A complete stranger seems to be looking back at you, and in her eyes there is hatred, hostility, bitterness, or anger. When she speaks to you, it is not your spouse or partner who is speaking but the pain-body speaking through them. Whatever she is saying is the pain-body's version of reality, a reality completely distorted by fear, hostility, anger, and a desire to inflict and receive more pain.

At this point you may wonder whether this is your partner's real face that you had never seen before and whether you made a dreadful mistake in choosing this person. It is of course, not the real face, just the pain-body that temporarily has taken possession. It would be hard to find a partner who does not carry a pain-body, but it would perhaps be wise to choose someone whose pain-body is not excessively dense.

DENSE PAIN-BODIES - Some people carry dense pain-bodies that are never completely dormant. They may be smiling and making polite conversation, but you do not need to be psychic to sense that seething ball of unhappy emotion in them just underneath the surface, waiting for the next event to react to, the next person to blame or confront, the next thing to be unhappy about. Their pain-bodies can never get enough, are always hungry. They magnify the ego's need for enemies.

Through their reactivity, relatively insignificant matters are blown up out of all proportion as they try to pull other people into their drama by getting them to react. Some get involved in protracted and ultimately pointless battles or court cases with organizations or individuals. Others are consumed by obsessive hatred toward an ex-spouse or partner. Unaware of the pain they carry inside, by their reaction, they project the pain into events and situations. Due to a complete lack of self-awareness, they cannot tell the difference between an event and their reaction to the event. To them, the unhappiness and even the pain itself is out there in the event or situation. Being unconscious of their inner state, they don't even know that they are deeply unhappy, that they are suffering.

Sometimes people with such dense pain-bodies become activists fighting for a cause. The cause may indeed be worthy, and they are sometime successful at first in getting things done; however, the negative energy that flows into what they say and do and their unconscious need for enemies and conflict tend to generate increasing opposition to their cause. Usually they also end up creating enemies within their own organization, because wherever they go, they find reasons for feeling bad, and so their pain-body continues to find exactly what it is looking for...

APPENDIX K

Power by limiting the Ego by Dr. David R. Hawkins, Ph. D. (excerpt from <u>Power vs. Force - The Hidden Determinants of Human Behavior)</u>

"...Back in the 1930's. alcoholism was accepted, as it had been over the centuries as a hopeless, progressive disease that had baffled medical science and religion as well. (In fact, the prevalence of alcoholism among the clergy itself was alarmingly high.) All forms of the drug addiction were thought to be incurable, and when they reached a certain stage, victims were simply "put away."

In the early 1930s, a prominent American businessman (known to us a Rowland H.), had sought every cure for his alcoholism, without avail. He then went to see the famous Swiss psychoanalyst Carl Jung for treatment. Jung treated, Rowland H. for approximately a year, by which time he'd achieved some degree of sobriety. Rowland returned" home " full of hope...only to fall ill again with active alcoholism.

Rowland went back to Switzerland to see Jung again and ask for further treatment. Jung humbly told him that neiter his science nor art could help him further, but throughout man's history--rarely, but from time to time--some who had abandoned themselves completely ato some spiritual organization and surrendered to God (HOLY SPIRIT) for help had recovered.

Rowland returned" home " dejected, but he followed Jung's advice and sought out an organization of that time called the Oxford Groups. These were groups of individuals who met regularly to discuss living life according to spiritual principles, very much like those later adopted by AA. Through these means, Rowland in fact recovered, and his recovery was a source of astonishment to another concerned part named Edwin T., or "Ebby," who was also a desperate alcoholic beyond all help. When Rowland told Ebby of how he had recovered, Ebby followed suit and also got sober. The pattern then extended form Ebby to his friend Bill W., who had been hospitalized frequently for hopeless, incurable alcoholism and whose condition was medically grave. Ebby told Bill that his recovery was based on service to others, moral housecleaning, anonymity, humility, and surrendering to a power greater than himself.

Bill W. was an atheist, and found the idea of surrendering to a higher power unappealing, to say the least. The whole idea of surrender was abhorrent to Bill's pride; consequesntly, he sank into an absolute, black despair. He had a mental obsession with, and physical allergy to, alcohol-which condemned him to sickness, insanity, and death, a prognosis that had been clearly spelled out to him and his wife, Lois. Ultimately, Bill gave up completely; at this point he had the profound experience of an infinite light, he was finally able to sleep, and when he awoke the next day, he felt as though he'd been transformed in some indescribable way.

The efficacy of Bill's experience was confirmed by Dr.Wiilliam D. Silkworth, his physician at what was then Town's Hospital, on the west side of New York City. Silkworth had treated more than 10,000 alcoholics and, in the process, had acquired enough wisdom to rocognize the profound importance of Bill's experience. It was he who later introduced Bill to the great psychologist Willima James's classic book, <u>The Varieties of Religious Experience.</u>

Bill wanted to pass his gift on to others, an as he himself said, "I spent the next few months trying to sober up drunks, but without success." Eventually, he discovered that it was necessary to convince the subject of the hopelessness of his conditions--in modern psychological terms, to overcome his denial. Bill's first success was Dr. Bob, a surgeon from Akron, Ohio, who turned out to have a great aptitude for the spiritual--he later became a cofounder of AA. Until his death in 1956, Dr. Bob never took another drink (neither did Bill W., who died in 1971.)

The enormous power that was realized through Bill W.'s experience has manifested itself externally in the millions of lives that have been transformed because of it. ...According to its preamble, AA is "not allied with any sect, denomination, politics, or organization." It's neither for nor against any other approach to the problem of alcoholism. ...Not only are all the members equal, but all AA groups are self supporting and autonomous. Even the 12 basic steps by which members recover are specified as only "suggestions." The use of coercion of any kind is avoided and is emphasized by slogans such as "One day at a time," "Easy does it," "First things first," and, most important, "Live and let live." AA repects freedom, in that it leave choice up to the individual. Its indentifiable power patterns are those of honesty, responsibilitiy, humility, service, and the practice of tolerance, goodwill, and brotherhood. AA doesn't subscribe to any particular ethic, has no code or right and wrong or good and bad, and avoids moral judgments. AA doesn't try to control anyone, including its own members. What it does instead is chart a path. It merely says to its members, "If you practice these principles in all of your affairs, you'll recover from this grave and progressive fatal illness, and regain your health and self-respect, and the capacity to live a fruitful and fulfilling life for yourself and others. AA is the original example of the power of these principles to cure hopeless disease and change the destructive personality patterns of members.

...In AA, its said that there can be no recovery until the subject experiences an essential change of personality. This is the basic change first manifested by AA founder, Bill W.--a profound transformation in his total belief system, followed by a sudden leap in consciousness. Such a major metamorphosis in attitude was first formally studied by American psychiatrist Harry Tiebout, who treated a hopeless alcoholic who was the first woman in AA. She underwent a profound change of personality to a degree unaccountable through any known therapeutic method. In the first of a series of papers on this observation, Tiebout documented that she was transformed from an angry, self-pitying, intolerant, and egocentric creature to a kind, gentle, forgiving, and loving person. This example is important because it clearly demonstrates how key this element of transformation is in the recovery from any progressive or hopeless disease.

In every studied case of recovery from hopeless and untreatable disease, there has been this major shift in consciousness so that the attractor patterns that resulted in the pathologic process no longer dominated. The steps necessary for recovery from such grave illness were formalized by the by the first" ..."alcoholics who recovered from their disease; these became the well-known 12 steps suggested by AA and all of the 12-step recovery groups has resulted in the recovery of millions of people suggests that this experience may have a universal applicability to all disease processes. The advice Carl Jung gave Rowland H--"Throw yourself wholeheartedly into any spiritual group that appeals to you, whether you believe in it or not, hope tha in your case a miracle may occur"--may hold true for anyone who wishes to recover from a progressive disease

APPENDIX L

Origin of the 12 Steps by Bill W. (excerpt from The Language of the Heart - Bill W.'s Grapevine Writings)

"...So far as people were concerned, the main channels of inspiration for our Steps were three in number -- the Oxford Groups, Dr. William D. Silkworth of Towns Hospital, and the famed psychologist William James, called by some the father of modern psychology. The story of how these streams of infuence were brought together and how they led to the writing of our Twelve Steps is exciting and in spots downright incredible.

Many of us will remember the Oxford Groups as a modern evangelical movement which flourished in the 1920's and early 30's, led by a onetime Lutheran minister, Dr. Frank Buchanan. The Oxford Groups of that day threw heavy emphasis on personal work, one member with another. AA's Twelfth Step had its origin in that vital process. The moral backbone of the "O.G." was absolute honesty, absolute purity, absolute undelfishness, and absolute love. They also practiced a type of confession, which they called "sharing"; the making of amends for harms done they called "restitution." They believed deeply in their "quiet time," a meditation practiced by groups and individuals alike, in which the guidance of God was sought for every detail of living, great or small.

These basic ideas were not new; they could have been found elsewhere. But the saving thing for us first alcoholics who contacted the Oxford Groupers was that they laid great stress on these particular priniciples. And fortunate for us was the fact that the Groupers took special pains not to interfere with one's personal religious views. Their society, like ours later on, saw the need to be strictly nondenominational.

In the late summer of 1934, my well-loved alcoholic friend and schoolmate, Ebbie, had fallen in with these good folks and had promptly sobered up. Being alcoholic, and rather on the obstinate side, he hadn't been able to "buy" all the Oxfrord Group ideas and attitudes. Nevertheless, he was moved by their deep sincerity and felt mighty grateful for the fact that their ministrations had, for the time being, lifted his obsession to drink.

When he arrived in New York in the late fall of 1934, Ebbie thought at once of me. On a bleak November day he rang up. Soon he was looking at me across our kitchen table at 182 Clinton Street, Brooklyn, New York. As I remember the converstation, he constantly used phrases like these: "I found that I couldn't run my own life"; "I had to get honest with myself and somebody else"; "I had to make restitution for the damage I had done"; "I had to pray to God for guidance and strength, even though I wasn't sure there was any God"; "And after I'd tried hard to do these things I found that my craving for alcohol left." Then, over and over, Ebbie would say something like this: "Bill, it isn't a bit like being on the water-wagon. You don't fight the desire to drink -- you get released from it. I never had such a feeling before."

Two or three weeks later, December 11th to be exact, I staggered into the Charles B. Towns Hospital, that famous drying-out emporium on Central Park West, New York City. I'd been there before, so I knew and already loved the doctor in charge -- Dr. Silkworth. It was he who was soon to contribute a very great idea without which AA could never have succeeded. For years he had been proclaiming alcoholism an illness, an obsession of the mind coupled with an allergy of the body. By now I knew this meant me. I also understood what a fatal combination these twin ogres could be. Of course, I'd once hoped to be among the small percentage of victims who now and then escape their vengeance. But this outside hope was now gone. I was about to hit bottom. That verdict of science -- the obsession that condemned me to drink and the allergy that condemned me to die -- was about to do the trick. That's where medical science, personified by this benign little doctor began to fit in. Held in the hands of one alcoholic talking to the next, this double-edged truth was a sledgehammer which could shatter the tough alcoholic's ego at depth and lay him wide open to the grace of God.

In my case it was of course Dr. Silkworth who swung the sledge while my friend Ebbie carried to me the spiritual principles and the grace which brought on my sudden spiritual awakening at the hospital three days later. I immediately knew that I was a free man. And with this astonishing experience came a felling of wonderful certainty that great numbers of alcoholics might one day enjoy the priceless gift which had been bestowed upon me.

At this point a third stream of influence entered my life through the pages of William James's book, Varieties of Religious Ex[perience. Somebody had brought it to my hospital room. Following my sudden experience, Dr. Silkworth had taken great pains to convince me that I was not hallucinating. But Willliam James did even more. Not only, he said, could spiritual experiences make people saner, they could transform men and women so that they could do, feel, and believe what had hitherto been impossible to them. It matters little whether these awakening were sudden or gradual; their variety could be almost infinite. But the biggest payoff of that noted book was this: In most of the cases described, those who had been transformed were hopeless people. In some controlling area of their lives they had met absolute defeat. Well, that was me all right. In complete defeat, with no hope or faith whatever, I had made an appeal to a Higher Power. I had taken Step One of today's AA program -- "Admitted we were powerless over alcohol, that our lives had become unmanageable." I'd also taken Step Three -- "Made a decdision to turn our will and our lives over to the care of God as we understood him." Thus was I set free. It was just as simple, yet as mysterious, as that.

These realizations were so exciting that I instantly joined up with the Oxford Groups. But to their consternation I insisted on devoting myself exclusively to drunks. This was disturbing to the O.G.'s on two counts. Firstly, they wanted to help save the whole world. Secondly, their luck with drunks had been poor. Just as I joined they had been working over a batch of alcoholics who had proved disappointing indeed. One of them, it was rumored, had flippantly cast his shoe through a valuable stained glass window of an Episcopal church across the alley from O.G. headquarters. Neither did they take kindly to my repeated declaration that it shouldn't take long to sober all the drunks in the world. They rightly declared that my coneit was still immense.

After some six months of violent exertion with scores of alcoholics which I found at a nearby mission and Towns Hospital, it began to look like the Groupers were right. I hadn't sobered up anybody. In Brooklyn we always had a houseful of drinkers living with us, sometimes as many as five. My valiant wife, Lois, once arrived home from work to find three of them fairly tight. The remaining two were worse. They were whaling each other with two-by fours. Though events like these slowed me down somewhat, the persistent coviction that a way to sobriety could be found never seemed to leave me. There was, though, on bright spot. My sponsor, Ebbie, still clung precariously to his newfound sobriety.

What was the reason for all these fiascos? If Ebbie and I could achieve sobriety, why couldn't all the rest find it too? Some of those we'd worked on certainly wanted to get well. We speculated day and night why nothing much had happened to them. Maybe they couldn't stand the spiritual pace of the Oxford Group's four absolutes of honesty, purity, unselfishness, and love. In fact some of the alcoholics declared that this was the trouble. The agressive pressure upon them to get good overnight would make them fly high as geese for a few weeks and then fl op dismally. They complained, too, about another form of coercion -- something the Oxford Groupers called "guidance for others." A "team" composed of nonalcoholic Groupers would sit down with an alcoholic and after a "quiet time" would come up with precise instructions as to how the alcoholic should run his own life. As grateful as we were to our O.G. friends, this was sometimes tough to take. It obviously had something to do with the wholesale skidding that went on.

But this wasn't the entire reason for failure. After months I saw the trouble was mainly in me. I had become very aggressive, very cocksure. I talked a lot about my sudden spiritual experience, as though it was something very special. I had been playing the double role of teacher and preacher. In my exhortations I'd forgotten all about the medical side of our malady, and the need for deflation at depth so emphasized by William James had been neglected. We weren't using that medical sledgehammer that Dr. Silkworth had so providentially given us.

Finally, one day, Dr. Silkworth took me back down to my right size. Said he, "Bill, why don't you quit talking so much about that bright light experience of yours; it sounds crazy. Though I'm convinced that nothing but better morals will make alcoholics really well, I do think you have the cart before the horse. The point is that alcoholics won't buy all this moral exhortation until they convince themselves that they must. If I were you I'd fo after them on the medical basis first. While it has never done any good for me to tell them how fatal their malady is, it might be a very different story if you, a formerly hopeless alcoholic, gave them the bad news. Because of the indentifi cation you naturally have with alcoholics, you might be abe to penetrate where I can't. Give them the medical business first, and give it to them hard. This might soften them up so they will accept the principles that will really get them well.

Shortly after this history making conversation, I found myself in Akron, Ohio, on a business venture which promptly collapsed. Alone in the town, I was scared to death of getting drunk. I was no longer a teacher or a preacher, I was an alcoholic who knew that he needed another alcoholic as much as that one could possibly need me. Driven by that urge, I was soon face to face with Dr. Bob. It was at once evident that Dr. Bob knew more of spiritual things than I did. He also had been in touch with the Oxfrord Groupers at Akron. But somehow he simply couldn't get sober. Following Dr. Silkworth's advice, I used the medical sledgehammer. I told him what alcoholism was and just how fatal it could be. Apparently this did something to Dr. Bob. On June 10, 1935, he sobered up, never to drink again When, in 1939, Dr. Bob's story first appeared in the book Alcoholics Anonymous, he put one paragraph of it italics. Speaking of me, he said: "Of far more importance was the fact that he was the first living human with whom I had ever talked, who knew what he was talking about in regard to alcoholism from actual experience."

Dr. Silkworth had indeed supplied us the missing link without which the chain of principles now forged into our Twelve Steps could never have been complete. Then and there, the spark that was to become Alcoholics Anonymous was struck.

During the next three years after Dr. Bob's recovery, our growing groups at Akron, New York and Cleveland evolved the so-called word-of-mouth program of our pioneering time. As we commenced to form a Society separate from the Oxford Group, we began to state our principles something like this:

1   We admitted we were powerless over alcohol.
2   We got honest with ourselves.
3   We got honest with another person, in confidence.
4   We made amends for harms done others.
5   We worked with other alcoholics without demand for prestige or money.
6   We prayed to God to help us to do these things as best we could.

Though these principles were advocated according to the whim or liking or each of us, and though in Akron and Cleveland they still stuck by the O.G. absolutes of honesty, purity, unselfishness, and love, this was the gist of our message to incomeing alcoholics up to 1939, when our present Twelve Steps were put to paper.

I well remember the evening on which the Twelve Steps were written. I was lying in bed quite dejected and suffering from one of my imaginary ulcer attacks. Four chapters of the book, Alcoholics Anonymous, had been roughed out and read in meetings at Akron and New York. We quickly found that everyone wanted to be an author. The hassles as to what should go into our new book were terrific. For example, some wanted a purely psychological book which would draw in alcoholics without scaring them. We could tell them about the "God business" afterward. A few, led by our wonderful southern friend, Fitz M., wanted a fairly religious book infused with some of the dogma we had picked up from the churches and missions which had tried to help us. The louder these arguments, the more I felt in the middle. It appeared that I wasn't going to be the author at all. I was only going to be an umpire who would decide the contents of the book. This didn't mean, though, that there wasn't terrific enthusiasm for the undertaking. Every one of us was wildly excited at the possibility of getting our message before all those countless alcoholics who still didn't know.

Having arrived at Chapter Five, it seemed high time to state what our program really was. I remember running over in my mind the word-of-mouth phrases then in current use. Jotting these down, they added up to the six named above. Then came the idea that our program ought ot be more accurately and clearly stated. Distant readers would have to have a precise set of principles. Knowing the alcoholic's ability to rationalize, something airtight would have to be written. We couldn't let the reader wiggle out anywhere. Besides, a more complete statement would help in the chapters to come where we would need to show exactly how the recovery program ought to be worked.

At length I began to write on a cheap yellow tablet. I split the word-of-mouth program up into smaller pieces, meanwhile enlarging its scope considerably. Uninspired as I felt, I was surprised that in a short time, perhaps half and hour, I had set down certain principles which, on being counted, turned out to be twelve in number. And for some unaccountable reason, I had moved

STEVE H.

the idea of God into the second step, right up front. I named God very liberally throughout the other Steps. In one of the Steps I had even suggested that the newcomer get down on his knees.

When this document was shown to our New York meeting, the protests were many and loud. Our agnostic friends didn't go at all for the idea of kneeling. Others said we were talking altogether too much about God. And anyhow, why, should there be Twelve Steps when we done fine with five or six? Let's keep it simple, they said.

This sort of heated discussion went on for days and nights. But out of it all there came a ten-strike for Alcoholics Anonymous. Our agnostic contingent, speared by Hank P. and Jim B., finally convinced us that we must make it easier for people like themselves by using such terms as "a Higher Power" or "God, as we understand him." Those expression, as we so well know today, have proved lifesavers for many an alcoholic. They have enabled thousands of us to make a beginning where none could have been made had we left the Steps just as I originally wrote them. Happily for us there were no other changes in the original draft and the number of Steps still stood at twelve. Little did we then guess that our Twelve Steps would be widely approved by clergy of all denominations and even by our later-day friends, the psychiatrists. This little fragment of history ought to convince the most skeptical that nobody invented Alcoholics Anonymous. It just grew -- by the grace of God.

BIBLIOGRAPHY:
List of works which were extensively quoted to produce this document
AA Questions and Answers on Sponsorship, Anonymous. New York
A Course in Miracles, Anonymous. New York
Alcoholics Anonymous, Anonymous. New York
Alcoholics Anonymous Comes of Age: A Brief History, Anonymous. New York
A New Earth : Awakening to Your Life's Purpose, Eckhart Tolle. New York
Ask and It Is Given, Esther and Jerry Hicks, Hayhouse.
Being A Christ, Ann & Peter Meyer. SD, CA
The AA Service Manual with Twelve Concepts for World Service, Bill W. New York
The Bhagavad Gita, Paramahansa Yogananda. LA, CA
The Disappearance of the Universe, Gary Renard. Hayhouse
The Language of the Heart, by Bill Wilson, The Grapevine Inc., New York
The Science of Mind, Enerst Holmes, New York
The Twelve Concepts for World Service, illustrated, Anonymous. New York
To Love Or To Be Loved, Tom Johnson. Redondo Beach, CA
Power vs. Force, by Dr. David R. Hawkins, Ph. D., Hayhouse
Twelve Steps and Twelve Traditions, Anonymous. New York
What Love Is Not (E-Article), Robert Perry. Sedona, Az

References

AA REFERENCES:

(available at any AA central office - located by calling Alcoholic Anonymous from the number in any phone book)

1. "Alcoholic Anonymous".
2. "AA Twelve Steps & Twelve Traditions" (AKA 12 & 12)
3. "AA Comes of Age"
4. "The Language of the Heart"
5. "Pass It On" *

* "Dr. Bob and the Good Old-timers" is not used as part of this work only because it established a hierarchical, paternal organizational system in AA that the editor of this proposal is not in favor. The editor feels that it creates conflict with other organizational ideas from Bill Wilson's style. (Bill Wilson and Dr. Bob Smith had different management styles; and the early Cleveland groups had a very conservative influence on how things were to be done in the Midwest.) It is however an excellent book discussing the history of AA and has some very effective spiritual enlightenment techniques.

1. "The AA Service Manual combined with Twelve Concepts for World Service,"
2. "The Twelve Concepts for World Service", AA pamphlet
3. "The AA Group", AA pamphlet
4. "Circles of Love and Service", AA pamphlet
5. "AA Questions & Answers on Sponsorship", AA pamphlet
6. " G.S. R. - General Service Representative", AA pamlet
7. Alcoholics Anonymous – World Service Office www.aa.org Other references:

1. "A Course in Miracles" – Foundation for Inner Peace
2. "Jesus' Course in Miracles - The complete Hugh Lyn Cayce version", Course in Miracles Society
3. "The Disappearance of the Universe" by Gary Renard
4. "The Bhagavad Gita - Translation and Commentary" by Paramahansa Yogananda
5. "Power vs. Force - Determinants of Human Behavior by Dr. David R. Hawkins, Hayhouse
6. "Science of Mind" by Ernest Holmes
7. "To Love or Be Loved" by Tom Johnson
8. "Ask and It is Given" by Jerry and Ester Hicks
9. "Being a Christ" by Ann P. Meyer and Peter V. Meyer
10. "Journey Without Distance" by Robert Skutch
11. "Inside AA" by Nan Robertson
12. "A New Earth" by Eckhart Tolle
13. "On Becoming A Person" by Carl Rogers
14. "Ye are Gods" by Analee Skarin
15. "Success Through a Positive Mental Attitude" by Napoleon Hill and Clement Jones
16. "The Way of the Peaceful Warrior" by Dan Milman
17. "A Case for Christ" by Lee Stroebel
18. "Beyond Belief" by Elaine Pagels
19. "The Aquarian Gospel of Jesus Christ" by Levi
20. "The New Testament - The Book of Revelation" by the Apostle, John

21	Circle of Atonement - Robert Perry [robert@circleofa.org]
22	Miracles (publication) by Jon Mundy
23	The Monroe Institute www.monroeinstitute.com
24	The Self Realization Fellowship http://www.yogananda-srf.org/
25	The Teaching of the Inner Christ www.teachingoftheinnerchrist.com
26	A Course In Miracles (ACIM) www.acim.org

"A Course in Miracles is anonymous." Tara Singh 1919- 2006

How To Find An A.A. Meeting

Alcoholics Anonymous is worldwide with A.A. meetings in almost every community. You can fi nd times and places of local A.A. meetings or events by contacting a nearby central office, intergroup or answer-ing service of U.S. and Canada. The General Service Office does not maintain local meeting information.

A.A. members traveling within the U.S. and Canada may also obtain the regional A.A. directories, which pro-vide confidential A.A. contact information within the U.S. and Canada. These directories can be obtained from local intergroup/Central Offices or by contacting the General Service Office. These directories are for A.A. members only. General Service Conference Area Web sites provide information about General Service activi-ties in their local Area and, in some cases, may include local meeting information. To access the list of General Service Conference Area Web sites please call or access web page. Outside the U.S. and Canada you can find times and places of local A.A. meetings or events by contacting a nearby office from the list of General Ser-vice offices, Central Offices, Intergroups and Answering Services Overseas. Please download PDF from Web page. For information on how to contact the International General Service Office nearest you, go to aa.org.

A.A. members traveling abroad may also obtain the International A.A. Directory, which provides con-fidential A.A. contact information overseas. This directory can be obtained from local intergroups/Cen-tral Offices or by contacting the General Service Office. This directory is for A.A. members only.

One of the ways A.A. members stay sober is by helping others to recover from alcoholism. We encour-age you to contact the nearest A.A. office, where local A.A. members will provide information to anyone.

Made in the USA
Columbia, SC
26 June 2024

4c3472ea-18c9-42d6-99b7-793f325001eeR01